Who Cares for the Baby?

Who Cares for the Baby?

Choices in Child Care

Beatrice Marden Glickman
& Nesha Bass Springer

SCHOCKEN BOOKS • NEW YORK

First published by SCHOCKEN BOOKS 1978
10 9 8 7 6 5 4 3 79 80 81

Copyright © 1978 by Schocken Books Inc.

Library of Congress Cataloging in Publication Data

Glickman, Beatrice.
  Who cares for the baby?

  Bibliography: p. 239
  Includes index.
  1. Day care centers—United States. 2. Child development. 3. Infants—Care and hygiene. 4. Mother and child. 5. Baby sitters. 6. Day care centers—Information services—United States. I. Springer, Nesha, joint author. II. Title.

HV854.G56   362.7'1   77-75293

Manufactured in the United States of America

To our children:
 Carrie, Mark, and Stephen Springer
 Nancy Springer Westendorf
 Lizbeth Glickman

CONTENTS

	PREFACE	xi
	INTRODUCTION	1
1.	The Pressure Cooker	9
2.	Answers—Plural	38
3.	Day-Care Centers	74
4.	Primate Time	93
5.	One Person—One Very Special Person	109
6.	Group Care in Other Societies	129
7.	The Doctors Speak Out	162
8.	Choosing	195
	EPILOGUE	236
	REFERENCES	239
	INDEX	247

ACKNOWLEDGMENTS

For detailed and informative personal interviews, we thank Doctors T. Berry Brazelton, Jerome Kagan, Marion Kagan, Freda Rebelsky and Edward Tronic. The ideas we tested with them became important in our book.

Our communications with Doctors John Bowlby, Robert Coles, Humberto Nagera, Mary Rowe, Bettye Caldwell, and Mary Elizabeth Keister were invaluable. They were generous with their time and effort, and sent us material which broadened our understanding.

The many months and years that we spent investigating day-care centers and parent-child centers were made possible by Priscilla Cobb, Luise Flaven, Miriam Kertzman, Alma McKinnon, Fran Perkins, June Randolph, Emily Robertson, George Saia, Ruth Sharpe, Heidi Urick, and Mary Jane Yurchak.

We owe a special thanks to Betty Powell and Nacie Graves and the mothers at the Crispus Attucks Day Care Center, who spoke for mothers everywhere who put their children first but work for an independent, satisfying life of their own.

If there is a special warmth in the chapter *One Person—One Very Special Person*, it derives from Carol Otto, mother of two babies, who shared her joys and frustrations with us and kept us honest in our writing on a subject that could be neither saccharine nor academic.

ACKNOWLEDGMENTS

We thank Schocken Editor Eva Glaser for her understanding of what we were saying and what needed to be said.

And finally, we thank Harold Glickman and Robert Springer, whose love and concern for children is reflected in this book.

PREFACE

We were mothers of small children when mothers stayed home with small children, and if it wasn't always fun, it was often fun. We weren't lonely or isolated or bored, and if honored is too strong a word to describe the world's evaluation of us, respected is certainly apt.

Our professional training and experience taught us the importance of what we had done after we had stopped doing it. One way or another, children have always been the focus of our lives.

So when we realized that the day-care center was rapidly supplanting the mother in the home, we set out to write a book that would destroy day-care centers, and bring the babies back home.

We learned a lot over the next few years. We interviewed mothers and babies who were together, and were wonderful together. We met mothers and babies that would have been better off apart a good deal of the time. We saw day-care centers that appalled us, and we saw day-care centers that glowed with love and warmth.

We became familiar with the wide range of choices that lie between day care and full-time mothers at home. And once again, we saw that any single option was sometimes good for mother and baby, and sometimes not.

Most of all, we became convinced that choice is the key word. Our world is too complex and difficult today to lay out any one pattern for parents to follow.

But we must offer good choices, and make it possible for parents to freely choose. What is necessary for good choices and how we can enable parents to freely choose, is the subject of the book we have finally written.

Who Cares for the Baby?

INTRODUCTION

Children have always been a burden; when that burden has become insupportable, men and women have found ways to lighten it. The glory that was Greece and the grandeur that was Rome permitted infanticide as a means of population control. Wealthy fathers who wished to leave large estates unfragmented killed off excess children with the approval of society. With the sanction of the state they disposed of those infants who were weak, or deformed, or female, or of uncertain parentage.

Centuries later, foundling hospitals were established for the children of women who had borne them secretly and left them at church doors. Charlemagne decreed that those who rescued and reared exposed children could legitimately claim them as slaves.

The infamous baby farms of Victorian England have long been a blot on British history, and Charles Dickens, in *Oliver Twist*, gives us a chilling example of the indifferent care given those unlucky enough to find themselves without home and family.

Historian Will Durant, with exquisite sarcasm, tells us, "The abandonment of unwanted babies . . . is a custom to be found in all but the most uncivilized societies."[1]

In this century, one of the proudest boasts of the Communist regime in China has been that famine and poverty no longer force Chinese families to sell off young daughters to prostitution or concubinage.

And in the United States today, with its acute shortage of adoptable babies, mothers who cannot keep their own children can and sometimes do sell them on the black market to the highest bidder like so many sides of beef or pounds of butter.

History teaches us that even when "solutions" have been found to problems caused by the care of children—whether those problems were economic, social, or cultural in nature—there has been no guarantee that these "solutions" were good for either children or parents.

Today, as always, young children, particularly in the most vulnerable years between birth and three, are a burden. Some parents are beset by the age-old problems of hunger, poverty, deprivation, illness. Some struggle with new problems peculiar to today's civilization. A principal problem is the liberation of women with its attendant job opportunities, chances for higher education, and enhanced expectations of what life should offer. In turn, these advances encourage dissatisfaction with old life styles and intensification of economic striving. Another serious modern problem is the growing number of single-parent families.

The feelings of women today can be exemplified by some of the things they say: "I need a job because the cost of living is so high that my family can't live on one salary." "I need a job because I'm the sole support of myself and my children." "I need a job because I love my work and I don't want to have to give it up." "I need a job because I can't stand being locked up with the baby all day and no adult companionship." "I need a job to prepare myself for a full life after the children are in school. What will I be able to do and who will hire me if I've spent the last ten years at home?"

These needs are real, but they do not address themselves to the largely unspoken needs of infants and toddlers who remain stubbornly inarticulate, despite the protective, interpretive role played by the child advocates. Many of the people who purport to speak for them—doctors, psychiatrists, and behavior specialists—speak from a world in which emotions and feelings are described as "affect," school learning is "cognition," and the results of research are stated in null hypotheses to the nearest tenth of a point. This professional jargon insures that there is going to be some fuzzy communication with the rest of us.

But there is another reason why the child professionals make unsatisfactory spokesmen for children. They disagree with each other. Some believe infants and mothers belong together. Others believe that some kind of infant day care can work, but their beliefs are based on research that has barely begun.

Not only do they disagree with each other, occasionally they disagree with themselves. When we asked Jerome Kagan of Harvard in early 1973 to comment on several statements he had made in his book on infancy, published in 1971, he told us he no longer believed what he had written. This openness and flexibility is necessary and admirable in a researcher but causes difficulties for parents who must make decisions today about what is best for their children.

So we are faced with a strong articulate push from women to be relieved of the full-time burden of raising young children, confusing, conflicting advice from the child researchers whose studies may not yet have been completed, quantified, or translated into normal speech, and many solutions handcrafted to meet individual needs. It is a tribute to the determination and ingenuity of parents today that virtually without any help they have found, created, or pressured the public and private sectors of our society to create a number of different answers for substitute care for their infants and toddlers. Children are being cared for by grandmothers or other family members; baby-sitters; family day-care homes in which a mother with one or two children of her own bolsters her income by caring for the children of other parents; cooperative arrangements with other parents; parents, each of whom work part time and share child care; fathers who assume the child rearing and home responsibilities as their full-time job while their wives work full time; and full-time group care in day-care centers that can be state or federally sponsored, cooperative, or run privately for profit.

All of these answers born of necessity vary widely in the quality of care given, and are perceived by the parents themselves as sometimes being perfectly satisfactory and at other times inadequate, even disastrous. Our interviews with parents indicate that quality care is uppermost in their minds, and that within the limitations of what is available to them and what they can afford they will try a variety of alternatives.

As society as a whole looks at other-than-mother care for children, it is clear that more thoughtful evaluation is called for. To say that two incomes are needed to support a family decently—more and more often a true statement—does not prove that babies are brought up as well by caretakers as by mothers. To say that women are as bright, competent, and ambitious as men, and that all careers should be open to them—which is absolutely incontestable—does not say that an infant does not need one human being in fairly constant, loving attendance on him for the first few years of his life. To say that babies are raised successfully in authoritarian or collective societies in Russia, China, Israeli kibbutzim, and Socialist Sweden is not particularly pertinent to an independent, pluralistic society like the United States. In fact, to say that babies are raised successfully even in these countries demands an agreement by society on the fundamental question of what they are being raised for. Finally, to say that babies reared in day care are bright, cheerful, healthy, and adapted to group living does not answer the critical question: What kind of adults will these babies become?

In short, the agreement that women's lives—especially if prompted by economic need—should be changed in fairly drastic ways does not necessarily justify the fairly drastic proposition that full-time group care is qualified to take over the job of rearing our young. Any proof that such a proposition actually works will need several generations of proof. When you make a fundamental change in the method of rearing children, it is not enough to see what kind of one-year-olds or two-year-olds they become. We will want to know what kind of adults they become and what kind of parents they become.

Further complicating a reasonable evaluation of how we are to care for our children outside the home is the difficulty of finding evaluators who are able to be objective, for this is a field in which we all have an ax to grind. In the first place, we were all babies and young children. We were raised in a way that to some extent has either made us defensive of that method as the only good one or antagonistic toward it and willing to consider almost any alternative that will not hurt our young as we were hurt. Beyond that, many of us have children, and there is a great deal of natural self-justification involved in our attitudes toward child care.

Women who have worked since their babies were born almost always feel that the arrangements they made for their children's care were at least as adequate as and often superior to what they could have provided had they stayed at home. On the other hand, mothers who spent 20 years at home raising a family are understandably sensitive to the suggestion that they have thrown away 20 years of a life better lived otherwise.

And even the people who should have the best information and opinion on alternative child care—those who are engaged with it as researchers, workers, or writers—are influenced by the inescapable fact that they are earning their living, their prestige, or their grants this way, and it is only human and healthy to believe in what one is doing.

So this is a subject that must be approached with great caution and a certain amount of skepticism, not only toward those who are giving us the information but toward ourselves and the way we are receiving it.

Society as a whole must be concerned, including local,

state, and national government. Alternative child care is not and cannot be a matter simply between individual mothers and individual care givers or day-care centers. If increasing numbers of women are going to opt out of full-time mothering, for whatever reason, we are all going to pay for it, certainly in monetary terms and possibly in ultimate changes in the structure of our society. At the very least, some changes will have to be made by all of us to evolve a social structure that will be sufficiently flexible to meet women's needs, provide them with wide life opportunities, and still give our babies the best possible start in life.

The decisions that we as a society make about care outside the home will inevitably have an effect on those mothers who choose to stay home with their children. A balance must be struck that allows responsible freedom of choice in mothering roles without inflicting heavy burdens of guilt. As we move away from a society that castigated working mothers for neglecting their children, we must not move toward a society that makes mothers at home feel that their chosen role is unworthy of respect and support. For to the degree that full-time motherhood is undervalued and ill-esteemed, to that degree will it be poorly done. And that will lead us to a situation in which caring for children outside the home will unquestionably become the best method available for raising children. It is much too soon to make that kind of far-reaching, possibly irreversible decision.

Two important points must be made for the rest of the book to be clear. By "mother" we do not necessarily mean the biological mother but the parent in fact, that person who, for a prolonged period of time extending over years, is securely *there* to protect, provide for, interact with, love, and enjoy the baby. Under this definition, whether that person is the father, the grandmother, or the hired nanny, he or she is what Anna Freud calls the psychological parent, and for all practical purposes that is whom we shall be talking about when we say "mother."

The second point is that "day care" refers to all of the alternatives for caring for children during the day in the mother's absence, whereas "day-care center" refers to an institution staffed by teachers or paraprofessional caretakers that cares for groups of children, usually on a full-day basis.

In chapter 1, "The Pressure Cooker," we shall discuss the many pressures—economic, emotional, and social—that weigh on young mothers today. These pressures largely determine the decisions that people make about how to raise their children.

In chapter 2, "Answers—Plural," we shall describe family responses to these pressures and explore many of the various solutions currently in use. Much of the material comes from interviews with young parents from all walks of life. Options discussed will include family planning, parent cooperatives, communes, part-time work programs and part-time study programs, shared parenting, full-time father care, community-based support programs, and family day-care programs.

Chapter 3, "Day-Care Centers," will report on a number of different kinds of centers that parents are using—publicly sponsored centers, run-for-profit private centers, parent cooperative centers, and industry- and business-based centers.

In chapters 4 and 5 we turn to the study of infants. In chapter 4, "Primate Time," we look to the large body of animal research on mothers and infants, and particularly to the outstanding primate studies of Harry Harlow in which he manipulates infant environments and arrives at some conclusions that are relevant to our concerns about alternative child care.

"One Person—One Very Special Person," chapter 5, brings together the best of current thinking about human mothers and babies. We focus on symbiosis (a relationship in which two organisms live as one), reciprocal learning, trust, and attachment as those processes that may be most vulnerable to mother-infant separations.

Obviously other societies are raising children in groups,

apart from their mothers, and if they can do it, we can do it. But can we? And do we really want to? We look at this whole problem in chapter 6, "Group Care in Other Societies."

In chapter 7, "The Doctors Speak Out," we interview two eminent social scientists, Jerome Kagan, professor of developmental psychology at Harvard, and T. Berry Brazelton, pediatrician, author, and chief of the Child Development Center at Boston's Children's Medical Center, and ask them the questions that have been raised in the preceding pages. Their views are provocative, stimulating, and helpful to everyone concerned with children.

Then in chapter 8, "Choosing," we offer some guidelines on the way to select care for children based on individual need. There are also recommendations of ways in which education, government, and industry can improve life for American families.

Chapter 9, "Epilogue," reviews our findings and concerns, and offers our conclusions as to how young parents can best resolve the problems of child care.

NOTES

[1] Will Durant, *Caesar and Christ* (New York: Simon and Schuster, 1944) p. 364.

1

THE PRESSURE COOKER

On July 30, 1973, *Newsweek* ran an advertisement inserted by the American Red Cross. In bold, black type in the top quarter of the page was the single word "Batman." Beneath this title was not the dashing caped and masked crime fighter but a ten-year-old black boy in T-shirt and shorts, gazing levelly into the camera.

The copy ran as follows:

> Kent Hansen lives in Minneapolis. And like many another fifth grader there, Ken goes to BAT (Basic Aid Training) classes given by Red Cross Volunteers. Other cities may have other names for their Red Cross first aid programs. But by any name—Red Cross Basic First Aid is a life saver.
>
> There are special training programs for young kids who are left home in charge of even younger kids—in homes where the parents are out working. Or looking for work.
>
> What do the kids learn? Things like how to stop bleeding. Mouth-to-mouth resuscitation. How to care for a burn. What to do if there's a fire. Or some other emergency. Things that could save a life. Prevent an injury. And things that make life just a little more bearable.

In another city, in another part of the country, one woman had to face economic facts:

Working was an economic necessity at our house. We had five children, over $5,000 in uninsured medical bills (our three youngest boys seemed to feel that oxygen tents and pneumonia were the way every little kid grew up), periodic unemployment, a house fire—in other words, all the choice little problems you live through in a state of shock, telling yourself that this stuff really doesn't happen, it's fodder for the soaps on Channel 4 at 2:30. Our youngest was three; we were not only flat broke but deeply in debt. Going to work seemed the only way out.[1]

Turning back to the same issue of *Newsweek* that gave us "Batman," readers were confronted by an advertisement inserted by the NOW Legal Defense and Education Fund. The picture is a rear view of a sturdy two-year-old baby girl in ruffled panties, and the copy read, "This healthy, normal baby has a handicap. She was born female."

Perhaps it was an effort to deny this alleged handicap that gave rise to the dinner-party conversation overheard in bemusement by a middle-aged hostess recently. Present as guests were four young couples, all parents of children, the oldest of whom was five. When the women gathered for conversation after dinner the topic was, "What do you do?" One worked full time, one was taking courses toward her master's degree, one had a part-time job (but at a college—very prestigious!), and one was noticeably silent, having shot her conversational bolt when she admitted she stayed home with the baby. The hostess was silent, too, the contrast between generations hitting home hard and personally. Who had asked 20 years ago what *she* did? She and all her contemporaries were bringing up their children, and though the conversation then might have run to "how do you do" or "why do you do," the "what do you do" was pretty much known.

The contrast between generations was underlined even more strongly when an early childhood education consultant of our acquaintance was approached by a single mother with a new baby who was looking for full-time care. Judy, an involved, outgoing, self-sufficient young woman in her late 20s, had bounced around for years in a series of dead-end jobs. Direction had finally come to her life and she had just started night school, working toward a degree in business administration, an achievement that she felt sure would lead to a satisfying career.

But a chance meeting with an old, dear friend, whom she had long ago decided was not a man she ever wanted to marry, had led to a sexual encounter, and Judy found herself pregnant. Unwilling to consider abortion, appalled by the thought of giving up her baby for adoption, unable even to discuss the matter with her parents, who lived thousands of miles away, Judy decided she wanted to do it all herself—her daytime job, night school, *and* her baby.

Anecdotal bits and pieces? Of course. But pieces of a puzzle that fit together to build a picture of the forces that are driving us on a national scale toward day care for children from birth to three. Brick by brick we are building an American society in which large numbers of infants and children will be raised in day-care centers. The consequences of this daily family exodus in which *everyone* leaves home are as yet unknown.

COST OF LIVING

Basic to the entire issue of day care are the some 38.6 million women currently in the labor force. Forty percent of over 25 million American mothers with children under 18 now work full or part time away from home. These women leave behind 6.1 million children below regular school age who need some kind of care in their mothers' absence. Of the 6.1 million, 5.1 million are children of working mothers whose fathers are also present and working, 913,000 have mothers who are the heads of their families, and 96,000 live in families with a male family head other than the father. *The fastest-growing group of mothers coming into the labor force are those 35 years old or younger, with children under the age of three.*[2] The majority of these working mothers, 69 percent, work full time, according to the *Monthly Labor Review* of January 1975.[3] More than half of all working mothers cite economic necessity as the main reason for working away from home.

Let us look at the family expenditure figures published by the U.S. Department of Labor for three different income groups so that we can see the financial pressures that lead women to work and thus force them to find care for their children.

U.S. Bureau of Labor statistics for the fall of 1976 divide most of the population into three hypothetical standards of living—low, intermediate, and higher—each computed for an urban family of four.[4] Families in the low bracket must expend $10,041, families in the intermediate group must expend $16,236, and families in the higher bracket must expend $23,759.

When we turn back to the *Monthly Labor Review*,[5] we see that there are 63.5 million white and black children under 18 in the United States. These children live in families with a median income of $12,500. Of this total, 26.5 million live in families with working mothers and annual incomes of $13,500. Even with two parents working, this is still $1,818 less than the amount needed to maintain an intermediate standard of living, according to the Department of Labor.

If we look only at white families in which both fathers and mothers are present and working, the total family income in 1974 was just above $15,000, just about enough money to maintain an intermediate standard of living. In families in which the mother was not working, the total family income was $13,428.[6]

This does not imply that the white working mothers earned only $1,600 a year. The report gives no figures on the income of the father separate from that of the mother, but it is reasonable to conclude that the families in which the father earned perhaps $8,000 or $9,000 a year found that they couldn't get along without a second full-time wage earner, the wife and mother, who then perhaps brought in another $6,000.

Black mothers apparently make an even greater contribution to their families' total earnings. The median income of the black family with both parents employed was $12,667. But where the mother did not work it fell to $8,135, $1,435 less than the low standard of living budget projected by the Labor Department.

Inflation has contributed to the importance of the role of the working mother. In families in which both husband and wife worked, the purchasing power of the family declined 1.3 percent during the inflation of 1973-1974. In families in which only the husband worked, purchasing power declined 3.1 percent.

We have been looking at families in which a husband and wife are both present and in which, in all cases, at least the father is working. But in March 1974 over 12 million children, black and white, lived in families in which the father was either absent (8.6 million), unemployed (1.5 million), or not in the labor force (2.0 million). In this group income falls sharply. Where the father is unemployed, income ranges from $9,100 to $11,100. The higher figure, of course, applies to families with working mothers. Unemployment benefits undoubtedly contribute to holding up this income level.

In families in which the father is not in the labor force at all, income drops to $6,000, apparently mostly from welfare, when the mother is not working, and to $9,000 when she is working. And at the low end of the scale we find no less than 8.5 million children living in families in which the father is not present and the mother is the family head. In these families the median income falls to $6,195 for families with working mothers, $3,678 for families with unemployed mothers, and $3,758 for families in which the mother is not in the labor force at all. These incomes range from $3,393 to $6,910 *below* the lowest standard of living budget set by the Labor Department.

Families headed by women include those in which the woman is divorced, separated, widowed, or a single parent. One American child in six is now being raised by a single parent.[7]

In a country in which the divorce rate is high and climbing (800,000 divorces annually, affecting one million children),[8] the National Commission on the Observance of International Women's Year has reported that of divorced women only 14 percent were awarded alimony, and of that 14 percent only 46 percent were receiving it regularly. To simplify, only 6.4 percent of divorced women actually receive regular alimony payments. Of divorced mothers, 44 percent were awarded child support. But only 21 percent of that 44 percent, or 13 percent of all divorced mothers, receive regular child support.[8]

Further, the National Commission charged that many judges assume that the wife and her children should automatically lower their standard of living when the husband leaves but that *his* standard of living should be maintained at a relatively high rate. If this charge is true, and there are many divorced men who would dispute it, then one must recognize that even the tiny percentage of children whose mothers are receiving support are not receiving as much as they might legitimately have expected or need. These women must go out to work or accept welfare.

CHANGING LIFE STYLES

Other factors contribute to the numbers of women who work. While none is as important as financial need, each—like the millions of tiny dots that make up a printed photograph—helps to comprise the total picture. First we have the facts of long life and good health. The life expectancy of women has increased by 20 to 35 years in most industrialized countries in this century. Additionally, we have smaller families, with only the occasional young woman planning to have more than two children, if indeed she is planning to have any at all.*

These facts of long life, good health, and small families are among those that led sociologist Jeanne Binstock to jump into print with an article entitled "Motherhood: An Occupation Facing Decline." This is a fascinating dissertation in which Dr. Binstock concludes that, lest we be throttled by an overproduction of babies, we must "demand that the ancient and honorable occupation of motherhood fall into disrepute." This ancient and honorable occupation will do so because of what it has already become, continues Dr. Binstock:

> Today the American woman has two or three children, instead of six or eight; childbirth for her is not a battle for survival; she is rarely up at night with a sick child; she has plenty of household appliances, processed foods and other technological innovations that function as para-mothers. In addition specialized agencies such as schools, clubs and television share her burdens. She has succumbed, half willingly and half reluctantly, as her job has been effectively reduced from an important, 18 hours a day occupation, crucial to society's survival, to a marginal, three-hours-per-day activity, almost as easily done by someone else.[10]

It would be interesting to know where Dr. Binstock gets her figures about hours per day that the average mother works in the home—and her conclusions. Are we to believe that mothering is no longer important because housework takes less time, that mothering no longer takes 18 hours a day, that mothering is not crucial to society, and that it can be done in 3 hours by anyone at all? If we're talking about twelve-year-olds, some of it is true; if we're talking about eight-month-olds, none of it is true.

But we were discussing the pressures that are pushing our

---

*There are indications that women may be planning larger families again. The Gerber Co., whose business is babies, has done market research that shows that the current intent is to have more than two children.[9]

society toward an acceptance of infant day care and, right or wrong, Dr. Binstock illustrates these pressures well. A young woman who knows that she may expect to live out a long and vigorous life during which she will have only one or two children to raise, and who further understands that society will regard the mothering of those children as an acceptable contribution only in small part, needs to look around for a career in exactly the same way that a man does. And having found that career and invested a large part of herself in it, she will find that neither inside nor outside forces will look kindly upon her for taking a five-to-ten-year absence from it. If, then, she wants to have children, she will be looking for an acceptable way of combining the raising of children with her career.

INFLUENCE OF HIGHER EDUCATION

The increasing number of well-educated young women plays directly into this schema in two ways. First, of course, the range of careers open to the well educated is so much wider and more attractive than the possibilities open to the less educated. Take two extreme examples. To the woman who works eight hours a day on an assembly line, homemaking and child rearing can offer unlimited freedom and scope for creativity, excitement, and a sense of worthwhile contribution. To the woman who works, say, as a business consultant—a job involving expertise, decision making, flexibility, responsibility, travel, high salary, and recognition—homemaking and child rearing may present a much less attractive prospect. This aspect of the influence of education is well understood and needs no further belaboring.

But higher education can exert pressures on young women to stay out of the home far beyond the mere ability it gives them to command interesting employment. During these extremely vulnerable years they are subject to the precept and example of the women who are in many cases their teachers. As only one example we could cite Dr. Freda Rebelsky of Boston University, winner of two awards for teaching excellence.

Dr. Rebelsky has it all—academic honors, position, salary, prestige, home, husband, family. She stands before her classes as a woman who has made it, and on her own terms. As such, she presents a powerful incentive to her students to go and do likewise. Dr. Rebelsky believes that taking care of young children full time makes women childish. Not childlike, which has a sort of endearing quality, but childish, which none of us wants to be. She puts it strongly: "I think it's devastating to women as adults to remain alone with children for many hours of the day."[11] She cites a two-year study that her students have done in Boston-area supermarkets in which they report a high incidence of yelling, child hitting, and tantrums on the part of mothers. "You just have to walk into a supermarket to see middle-class women behaving like animals."[12]

Now here is this attractive, personable young professor, exceedingly articulate, likeable, even spellbinding, and she tells you that life at home with your young children is a sure step on the road to degradation. Such an evaluation must certainly influence young women who are thinking about their future life styles.

Unfortunately, teachers, who have the most direct face-to-face contact with young people, and writers and other media people, who are also very influential, often don't work the same week as most workers. While they speak honestly, from their own experiences, their job flexibility simply is not comparable to the nine-hour day away from home that most employed women are locked into.

There is also another problem to be considered—the human desire of the professors to be responsive to their students' expressed needs. In education as in business, market demand in large part determines the shape of the product. This phenomenon is dramatically illustrated in the courses that have been offered during the 1970s on marriage and family life. The overall thesis of these courses is that the old family model is outdated, and alternative ways of living that include group marriage, homosexual marriage, communal families, polygamy, and sex outside marriage must all be considered as possibilities. Women and their futures are of primary concern. Staying home and raising children is old. Raising children without staying home is new. So the students line up for the courses that tell them it can be done.

CHANGING FAMILY PATTERNS

The isolation of young mothers is another pressure that impels them to look for alternatives for their children's care. We are extremely transient people, and this continual moving around has contributed to an isolation that is often unbearable:

> In a single year . . . 36,000,000 Americans (not counting children less than one year old) changed their place of residence. This is more than the total population of Cambodia, Ghana, Guatemala, Honduras, Iraq, Israel, Mongolia, Nicaragua, and Tunisia combined. . . . And movement on this massive scale occurs every year in the United States. . . . The age-old ties between man and place are being shattered.[13]

Anne Adams and her husband Brooks lived in five houses and two apartments in six different cities in nine years; Mary Bralove, writing in the *Wall Street Journal*, described the Adams's life as typical of that of "executive nomads,"[14] men and women who follow the husband's career wherever it leads. The consensus seems to be that this kind of constant moving, while good for employers, careers, moving companies, and realtors, is bad for the people being moved. The mother is deprived of the traditional supportive network of family, friends, and community at just the moment when she is experiencing the trauma of moving, which some psychiatrists consider as severe as that of divorce. For the husband this relocation trauma is mitigated by the fact that he leaves one office and plugs into another, carrying an occupational identity with him and providing him with an instant circle of acquaintances. For the wife the trauma is maximized by the fact that, beyond the front door of her new home, she has lost all identity. There is no one to recognize her as Mark's mother, or the past president of the PTA, or the best gardener on the block. That kind of life fabric takes a long time to weave. But if she's a skilled operating-room nurse or a full-charge bookkeeper and goes back to work immediately, she, too, will be provided with a familiar environment, a circle of acquaintances, and an acknowledged worth. In a life of constant moving, an occupational identity is a strong anchor. There's just that question of who is going to take care of little Janey.

If you accept the fact that life in the future is going to require more and more of us to move, that, as *Future Shock* has it, we will become increasingly a nation of transients, of people with wide, shallow relationships rather than narrow deep ones, that we are going to have to acquire the skills that enable us to make new friends fast and often and leave old friends fast and painlessly, that we will have to be more and more dependent on ourselves and less and less on each other, then you will also be likely to think differently about the proper preparation for life for your children. Toffler puts it this way:

> Until the rate of human turnover is substantially slowed, education must help people to accept the absence of deep friendships, to accept loneliness and mistrust—or it must find new ways to accelerate friendship formation.[15]

Care by others can then be seen both as enabling the mother to continue with her work without interruption and as a positive means of socializing the baby for the life that lies ahead of him.

The explosion of small, inexpensive housing that erupted after World War II shaped our lives in ways more fundamental than those of us who are not architects usually admit. Before 1945 lots of people, loosely and not so loosely related, lived together. Farm families, because it took a lot of hands to run a farm, spread out in homes that sprang additions from every corner to house married sons and daughters-in-law. Immigrant families, because they were impoverished, were jammed into tiny tenements—a situation still existing today. Middle-class families, because houses tended to be large and roomy, found no difficulty in accommodating spinster aunts, unmarried brothers, and aging parents. During the Depression most of us were happy to have any roof at all over our heads, and during the war home building was at a standstill. And then, in a flood, came the minimum type of housing for which the market was crying—tiny two- or three-bedroom houses with kitchen, bath, and living-dining room combination, often set on a concrete slab and boasting only an illusory crawl space for an attic. They weren't much, those little houses. But to the returning veteran, fresh from barracks life, and to his wife, who had either been camp-following in rented rooms or living at home with her parents, those little houses looked awfully good. And the fact that there was only room for husband, wife, and a few babies was not a liability but the answer to a dream.

But there was no third-floor bedroom and bath where grandparents could stay, or a basement that could be converted into an apartment, or even a lot large enough to accommodate expansion. A third adult in those tiny quarters had a bad time of it. So, with our human genius of making a virtue out of a necessity, we decided that the family of husband, wife, and young children was the ideal. This decision affected more people than those who lived in the little houses. We came as a society to a general agreement that no two women could reasonably be expected to share a kitchen; that old people are much happier with other old people; that it is perfectly moral and permissible for unmarried women to live alone; and that absence, since it makes the heart grow fonder, is practically a filial duty.

When you combine our transient population with our small, discrete housing units, you come up with a lot of isolated women. A young mother who moves halfway across the country and buys a small house in the suburbs is sooner or later in for a long hard winter. Even if there is a disposition on her part and on the part of her neighbors to be friendly, the chances are good that most of her new neighbors will be working during the day. But often there is no such disposition. Anne Adams, whose nine-year safari from coast to coast we detailed earlier, said, "Middletown is filled with people who say hello, but don't bother to make friends because they know they won't be here long. I'm the same way."[16]

It can be very hard to make friends. Neighborhood shopping centers are too large and impersonal to function as community centers. Neighborhood parks are a thing of the past in suburbs where every house has its own quarter acre. The church or temple used to function as an extended family to newcomers in a community. Some still do, but church affiliations are not as much a part of our national life as they used to be.

The chances are good that our young mother, recently arrived in her new home, far distant from family and friends, laboring under the restrictions imposed by small children and a smaller budget, is going to find herself one early evening with her nose pressed against the windowpane, awaiting her husband's return and clinging to the tattered shreds of her sanity. And the chances are excellent that after a few weeks of *this* she'll begin to think seriously about going back to work.

The abrasive effect of this kind of physical and social isolation is well documented. Philip Slater speaks for many writers on the contemporary scene:

> One has only to see a village community in which women work and socialize in groups with children playing nearby, also in

groups, supervised by the older ones, or by some of the mothers on a haphazardly shared basis, to realize what is awkward about the domestic role in America. Because the American mother is isolated, she can engage in only one of these three activities at a time—with effort, two. Even taken together they hardly constitute a satisfying occupation for a civilized woman. . . . The idea of imprisoning each woman alone in a small, self-contained and architecturally isolating dwelling is a modern invention.[17]

FREEDOM, LIBERTY, AND INDEPENDENCE

Our national bias toward independence keeps us from recognizing the suffering that isolation inflicts. This bias is in large part probably a matter of natural selection. It was, after all, only the independent man and woman who got here in the first place, who left home and family and familiar environment to cross the oceans and settle in these United States. And it was only the most independent of these who left clinging coastal communities and pushed inland.

It takes a wrenching effort to entertain the possibility that independence might be a problem rather than an absolute good. Lawrence Fuchs calls our preoccupation with personal independence an American cultural phenomenon at sharp variance with the "condition of dependency and inequality which mark human families and societies." In his view, the independence that is expected and demanded from children, wives, husbands, mothers, fathers, brothers, sisters, and grandparents "turns upside down five to six thousand years of social history in the Western world, and . . . challenges the evolutionary bases of human families as we know them"[18] From the beginning of our country he finds our family system to be noted for its dispersive, competitive characteristics, and he contrasts this with the fact that "For thousands of years men, women and children in families understood to the depths of their being how totally dependent they were on each other."[19]

Elizabeth Hardwick, in a moving article entitled "Suicide," also examines the drive toward independence and its untoward results:

> Dependence is scorned and it is natural to seek happiness by going away from the family. All of the arrangements and values of society move in that direction—our own desires lead us there, also. For young women this may be an imprudent risk and the luckiest are those who manage to keep some lifeline to the past, to their dependent days. No one to turn to, adrift, always having to earn the consideration of friends, lovers, fellow workers. Robert Frost said "Home is where they have to take you in." Very few runaways complain of having fled too much love. Parents complain of their children's waywardness and yet many things suggest that the parents do not wish to prolong connections that require effort, compassion, sacrifice. So, when things go badly for the young there isn't much strength to draw from. The suicide is a dependent with no one to depend on.[20]

At this point, however, as we explore pressures in our society that will lead us to raising large numbers of infants in groups outside the home, we are more interested in our national impetus toward independence than in the problems arising from it. The evidence floods in from all sides. We are a people who have increasingly brooked no interference with this personal independence. Step by step we have divested ourselves of those who might be dependent upon us by finding institutions that relieve us of our burdens. Birth, death, illness, old age, incompetence, whether physical, mental, or emotional, and secular or religious education are all relegated to institutions. We are more and more a nation of individuals who want to be free to pursue our own interests, and dependence interferes with this freedom. Increasingly, often covertly, we relieve our need for intimacy, dependence, and support by turning to psychiatrists, social workers, psychologists, and encounter groups.

The most dependent group of all, however, our infants, have remained dependent. This dependency worries a certain group of psychologists and pediatricians who want to discourage the intimate one-to-one mother-child relationship early in life. As far back as 1928 social theorist John B. Watson described the kind of child he felt would be best adapted to the changing American scene:

> We have tried to sketch in the foregoing chapters a child as free as possible of sensitivities to people and one who, almost from birth, is relatively independent of the family situation. . . .[21]

From this it is not a far jump to Graham Blaine, Jr., M.D., who in 1973 recommended that children from three months to age seventeen be placed in extended-care schools from eight in the morning until six in the evening, six days a week, eleven months of the year.[22] Carrying the theory to its ultimate conclusion, Alvin Toffler simply does away with children altogether, pointing out that two people constitute a streamlined unit that can cope with life much more efficiently than what he describes as "the ordinary child-cluttered family."[23]

Margaret Mead foresees a smaller number of families whose principal function would be childbearing, leaving the rest of the population "free to function—for the first time in history—as individuals."[24] On the pop level there is outspoken author Ellen Peck: "Usually there is a choice to be made. Take your pick. One or the other. Housework and children—or the glamour, involvement and excitement of a free life."[25] Ms. Peck vies with author Shirley Radl, mother of two, in glorifying the childless life, and there is no question that their siren song has pull. Says Radl:

> During those eight years (before my children were born) I had a career that was enjoyable and enriching, and a home life that

made the end of a rewarding workday one more experience to anticipate with pleasure. Each night we would both race home from work, have cocktails, watch the evening news, and relate the gossip while I tried my hand at a new gourmet recipe. We had lots of friends, entertained often, and (as much as we enjoyed our home) traveled when we felt like it. We went to Mexico, to distant cities to visit friends, and periodically, just for the hell of it, we spent weekends in San Francisco, only thirty-five miles away.[26]

Over and over the point is made: Children = Dependency = Slavery. Lucy Komisar speaks for the feminists: "Today's feminists declare that women cannot be equal to men until everyone shares tasks of housekeeping and child care. Why, they ask, should children be allowed to interrupt a mother's career but not a father's?"[27]

If it occurs to you at this point that doctors, nurses, hairdressers, waiters, and sundry others also devote their lives to taking care of others and do not find that role to be overly onerous, it is because you are forgetting a crucial distinction. Taking care of others is all right if you're paid for it, and the more you are paid for it the righter it is. It's only demeaning work when you do it for love.

Freedom, liberty, and independence are ideas that are looming large and personally in the lives of young women today, and if they loom large enough we will have no problem about day care. We'll simply have no children. But if, as is much more likely, they only half-loom, and women decide to have their freedom and their babies, too, then day care is going to be big and we'd better be on speaking terms with it.

HOW WE VALUE WORK

The federal government plays an important role in accelerating the trend toward day care. Nathan B. Talbot, M.D.,

Harvard's chief of pediatrics at Massachusetts General Hospital, underscores the problem:

> Despite much lip service paid to the importance of caring for children, the role of being a parent, a parent's aide, or child caretaker is still given very low priority by our national government. Mothers are not even considered to be working unless they are performing tasks outside of the home for pay. Moreover, mothers' helpers and child workers are placed below fishermen, lumbermen, garbage collectors, and a host of other occupations in a list of vocations according to pay scale in the national census.[28]

When Dr. Talbot refers to "tasks outside of the home for pay," he is touching on two separate problems. The concept of a job being worth what someone is willing to pay for having it done is understandable to most of us, although we may object to it. The inside-outside aspect of valuing may need a little clarification.

Over the course of time a territorial division grew up between the sexes. The woman's territory was inside the home, the man's outside. This division became a moral one, with the home reserved for the good woman, the street for the bad one. Roles were strictly defined. Those activities that took place inside the home—cooking, cleaning, sewing, child care—were described as feminine; those that took place outside the home—business, politics, war—were defined as masculine. This polarity of inside-outside, interior-exterior, became a distinction between inferiority and superiority. Activities that took place inside were considered inferior to those that took place outside. It is to the everlasting shame of those who style themselves feminists that they have swallowed this age-old masculine put-down without choking on it, and agreed to a woman to meet men on grounds of men's choosing rather than question the grounds.

The theory is simple. Outside is good, inside is bad. But in an attempt to justify it people get pretty abstruse. Listen to the social scientists as they deprecate women's traditional activities: "The best known and most influential [theory] is the instrumental expressive one. It states that there is a difference between the roles of the sexes: Men have 'instrumental' (task-oriented) roles and women have 'socio-emotional' ones."[29] Therefore a man whose work consists essentially of paper-shuffling is said to be performing an instrumental role. His wife, whose day may include cleaning, marketing, speaking for the family at the PTA, bringing the children to the pediatrician, and fulfilling civic obligations, is not credited by the theorists with task-oriented, hard labor. The real difference between their jobs is not a matter of "instrumental" versus "socio-emotional" tasks but of higher-status versus lower-status or more valued versus less valued jobs.

If in the above analysis you get echoes of strong sexual overtones, you are not alone. It is not necessary to line up the Freudians against the Behaviorists on this one. We will simply note the interesting coincidences that seem apparent. Male sexual organs are outside, visible, instrumental. Their use involves activity and aggression, and a male-dominated world values that which takes place outside and gives it prestige and monetary rewards. Female sexual organs are inside, hidden, unseen. Passivity is no hindrance to their use, and a male-dominated world values that which takes place inside on a lower scale and accords it no prestige or monetary reward.

The game is being played with men's rules, and unless and until the rules are changed a woman knows that if she wants her share of kudos in this world, she's going to have to find them outside. Over 25 years ago Margaret Mead wrote:

> Half of our population, the half that is charged most intimately with family life, with its stability, with its tone, with its temper, is somehow robbed in public opinion of dignity. This is a serious situation. . . .[30]

The analysis remains apt, and the only thing that has changed is the disposition of women to go outside to find the dignity and acceptance that they have not been able to get inside.

THE DEVALUATION OF MOTHER

If, somewhere, there is a strong-minded, lucky woman who is not affected by the pressures thus far detailed, if, let us say, she is a college graduate with a liberal arts degree, getting her kicks from modern American literature and tennis, married to a devoted young man with a large and steady income, living in the same small city in which they both grew up, and thoroughly convinced that she and her husband owe the world four or five children—if, somewhere, this woman exists, there are further pressures against the whole idea of motherhood that she will have to combat or ignore.

Motherhood used to be honored. That's why we have Mother's Day. Mothers brought forth children in pain and suffering, nursed the sick, buried the dead, raised the survivors, stood by their husbands in bad times and good, looked well to the ways of their households, baked apple pies, and were always there to come home to. Of course this was fantasy, but the fantasies of a society are one way of gauging its temper. Today the measure of their worth is not how much they sacrifice for others but how successful they are in building a satisfying life for themselves. Motherhood is not honored any more.

The most serious charge against mother, presented tellingly by Philip Slater, invokes a picture of an energetic, ambitious, and educated woman who is given only one outlet for all this energy, ambition, and education—her children. Once upon a time she could expend this vitality in feeding, clothing, and sheltering her large family. Child caring was almost incidental to her working life. Today the work of running a home has been mechanized, merchandised, and prepackaged until it has virtually disappeared. Erma Bombeck is the only writer left on the contemporary scene who acknowledges that it exists at all—and she's a *humorist*. The children—the one or two that there are—who used to scamper happily through the interstices of the mother's busy day are now impaled upon the focused point of her entire life force. All of her energy, vitality, ambition, and frustration are poured into them. They become the symbiotic extensions of the mother. And that is bad. The weight gain of a seven-pound baby was never meant to sustain the self-image of a 120-pound woman. The age at which an infant is toilet-trained cannot be the measure of adult ability. The independence of a two-year-old cannot demonstrate the self-sufficiency of his mother. And the frustration the mother feels when she realizes that nothing she is doing provides any reflection of herself as a human being cannot be borne by a small child.

Not all mothers are energetic, ambitious, and educated. Given that life is unfair, some mothers are apathetic, withdrawn, illiterate, hungry. All the love in the world cannot enable them to provide the intellectual stimulation that we increasingly recognize to be vital in the first years of a child's life. Nor can it provide the physical environment, rich in sights, sounds, tastes, and objects, without which the cycle of poverty is endlessly perpetuated. Caught in the quicksand of their own misery, these mothers cannot be expected to extricate their children.

Granted these are the two extremes in mothering. But the attack on mothering covers the whole spectrum. Few mothers can rebut the charge that their baby boys spend most of their waking time in the care of women and have very little exposure to male influences. Not only do sons lack the male influence, frequently they have to contend with their mothers. Slater tells us that the mother is "a molder of live persons":

This is a task for which she may or may not be suited, but into which some frustration and resentment must inevitably creep, since she is unable . . . to realize her talents and is barred from the kind of stimulation which her husband obtains through his work . . . the male child is the logical vehicle for these frustrated aspirations as well as the logical scapegoat for her resentment of the masculine monopoly in the major professions.[31]

Baby girls also get little time with their fathers. While the reasons for the bad effects mothers may have on their daughters are not clear, one study indicates that less nurturant mothers will have daughters who are more academically successful. Or, to turn it around, the heavier the mothering, the lower the daughter's achievement.[32] That would give anyone pause.

Who among us can defend herself against the allegation of occasionally exhibiting bad temper? Of being cross, irritable, downright unfriendly? Of being, in a word, *human*? How many of us can say that we are professionals in the child-care line? That we know what to do and how to do it because we've been trained? When someone tells us that we are providing lots of quantity in our care but asks if it is good *quality* mothering, who could be so deep-down sure as to answer in the affirmative?

Mothers are no longer armored in innocence, protected by ignorance from the suspicion that they could hurt the children they love so much. There used to be a time—it began to come to an end in the 1920s—when people felt that their burdens and blessings were sent to them. Life could be easier or it could be harder, but either way they were not responsible for what it was—only for the way they handled it. Somebody else dealt the cards; their only job was to play them. And they played them one way, the way they and their parents and their parents before them had been taught. If, back in those easier days, you had a rotten kid, a stupid kid, or a lazy kid, you had a problem; *but it wasn't your fault*. It was bad luck, or bad blood, or bad companions. Your job was to do your best with what fate had handed you.

Today we all know, with certain gross exceptions, that the way we give birth, the way we nurse, the way we toilet train, the relationship we have with our husbands, the way we talk or don't talk to our babies and play or don't play with them, the toys we provide and the ages at which we provide them, the vacations we take, the sitters we hire—everything we do is affecting our children. What isn't clear is exactly *what*, in each of these cases, we should be doing. There is much conflicting advice and precious little guidance in picking a path through it. What is absolutely certain is that as parents we will be held to account for our children. When Johnny steals a car and smashes it into a plate-glass window, and Janey turns into the youngest alcoholic the town can remember, there'll be no neighbors tracing the children's behavior back to great-uncle Saul who was never any good. Instead, neighbors will be trying to figure out where you went wrong so that they won't repeat your mistakes. John Anderson, a director for the Family Service of Detroit and a father himself, says, "Parents have lost control over their families. They feel inadequate, overwhelmed—I know I do."[33]

Parenting is a heavy responsibility for young people to accept. Who can blame those who try to get out from under by shifting the responsibility to trained professionals who will be in charge of their children for eight or nine hours a day?

INFLUENCE OF THE FEMINISTS

All of these pressures that are driving us toward an acceptance of day care would exist whether or not Betty Friedan had ever written about "the problem that has no name" and thereby launched the women's liberation movement. But without the movement the pressure would have remained diffuse and vague as each woman struggled separately with her own problem or peculiar combination of problems. The movement changed all that, with results that are mixed. It is not necessary to plead the case of women's liberation. Movement spokesmen do that brilliantly. It *is* necessary to note that, as Willard Gaylin has it, "The cure to one problem usually comes packaged with the cause of another."[34] And one of the results of the movement to liberate women is the fact that, for the first time in history, an entire society seems to be coming to a general agreement that the interests of mothers and children are antagonistic.

A lot of women have read *The Feminine Mystique*, *Sexual Politics*, *The Female Eunuch*. A lot more have read *Cosmopolitan*, *The Ladies Home Journal*, *Redbook*, *Good Housekeeping*, and their daily papers. The message is spread even more widely by television and radio. The words of the pregnant few have given birth to millions, and the ideas of the women who started it all are refined, amplified, reworked, rephrased, and broadcast throughout the land.

It is interesting to those of us concerned about infants and young children to note what these original writers said about parents and children. Betty Friedan in *The Feminine Mystique*, written in 1963, didn't deal at all with the subject of raising infants and young children—at least not positively. Friedan's book still hits the reader with a force and immediacy that is stunning:

> Since the human organism has an intrinsic urge to grow, a woman who evades her own growth by clinging to the child-like protection of the housewife role will—insofar as that role does not permit her own growth—suffer increasingly severe pathology, both psychological and emotional. Her motherhood will be increasingly pathological, both for her and for her children. The greater the infantilization of the mother, the less likely the child will be able to achieve human self-hood in the real world.

Mothers with infantile selves will have even more infantile children, who will retreat even earlier into fantasy from the tests of reality.[35]

Ms. Friedan suggested that the symbiotic relationship of mother and unborn child, a relationship in which the two organisms live as one, cannot be continued beyond birth. If this exclusive dependency, which becomes more emotional and less biological over time, does continue, it will result in child pathology and virtual destruction of the child. It will produce clinging infants, temper tantrums in toddlers, school phobias, withdrawal to the point of schizophrenia, inability to learn, aggression, and theft, leading to full-blown cases of juvenile delinquency, immaturity, precocious sexuality, homosexuality, no sexuality, and early marriage in an attempt to recreate in acceptably adult terms conditions of passivity and dependency. Ms. Friedan laid the blame for autism, perhaps the most frightening and least understood of childhood mental disorders, squarely at the feet of mothers who are deficient in maturity and strength of ego. And her measure of maternal maturity and ego strength is clear. Mothers who meet strong personal job commitments are mature and ego-whole. Unpaid work doesn't count; volunteer work doesn't count; community involvement is fragmenting; and service to others is self-denial. A job—which means that the work you do meets standards for which someone else is willing to pay—*that* counts. *That* makes you emotionally independent and secure and less likely to cripple your child.

Kate Millett would prefer to do away almost entirely with the mother-child relationship. *Sexual Politics*, which draws heavily on Friedrich Engels, one of the most important German theorists and organizers of the Marxist movement, sees the family as the source of the exploitation and degradation of women. Women's lives would be improved by doing away with the patriarchal proprietary family. As for the children, in what is one of the few acknowledgments of the existence of children in the entire book, Millett writes, "The collective professionalization (and consequent improvement) of the care of the young, also involved, would further undermine family structure while contributing to the freedom of women."[36]

Germaine Greer was the first of the original writers on women's liberation to attempt to deal with the raising of children in a world of career-minded mothers. Unfortunately, the solution she put forth, an updated, upgraded version of the old English baby farms, was no solution at all:

> [I] hit upon the plan to buy, with the help of some friends with similar problems, a farm house in Italy where we could stay when circumstances permitted and where our children would be born. Their fathers and other people would also visit the house as often as they could, to rest and enjoy the children and even work a bit. . . . Perhaps some of us might live there for quite long periods, as long as we wanted to. . . . The house and garden would be worked by a local family who lived in the house.[37]

But not many women are in a position to jet back and forth to Calabria in southern Italy to visit their offspring. There are 6.1 million working mothers with children under six in the United States at last count. A villa in Calabria will not answer for very many of them.

From these three women came the initial drive behind the women's liberation movement. But when the second string came in—the magazine writers, newspaper people, and radio and television talk masters—and began to bring the word to us common folk, they knew they had a problem. Above all, these writers knew their audiences, and their audiences were elbow-deep in diaper pails. They were ready, willing, and eager to leave the diaper pails, but they could not be bemused by visions of villas in Calabria. They loved deeply those children who, they were told, were blighting their lives and whose lives they were blighting. So when it came to addressing the millions of women who were going to have to leave their babies, the problem of how to care for the children in the mothers' absence in a way satisfactory to the mother became paramount. Day care was an answer.

THE DAY-CARE PROFESSIONALS

Still another pressure accelerating the growth of day care comes from the people who work in day care. Anyone who earns money from day care has a vested interest in seeing it expand. We're talking about directors, teachers, paraprofessionals, aides; about people who run nonprofit and for-profit centers and all those engaged in franchising day care. We're including college professors offering degree programs in day care at the associate, bachelor's, and master's degree levels, as well as the day-care associations and the people who work for them. We're also talking about the real estate developers who regard day-care centers as amenities that can help them rent apartments and sell condominiums and houses. And last but not least, we're talking about the people who are writing and publishing to promote day care.

These accumulating pressures that separate mothers and children and send the children in a swelling tide to be raised by others will soon become irresistible. Before they also become irreversible, it is time to stop and ask ourselves if day care is what we really want and, if it is, what *kinds* of day care will we demand?

NOTES

[1] Carolyn Bird and Barbara Ashby, "Do Working Wives Have Better Marriages?" *Family Circle*, November 1976, p. 62.
[2] Howard Hayghe, "Family Characteristics of Workers," *Monthly Labor Review*, U.S. Department of Labor, Bureau of Labor Statistics, January 1975, p. 60.
[3] Elizabeth Waldman, "Children of Working Mothers," *Monthly Labor Review*, U.S. Department of Labor, Bureau of Labor Statistics, January 1975, p. 64.
[4] Paula Weir, "Urban Family Budgets," *Monthly Labor Review*, U.S. Department of Labor, Bureau of Labor Statistics, Autumn 1975, p. 3.
[5] Elizabeth Waldman, op. cit., p. 65
[6] Kenneth Woodward and Phyllis Malamad, "The Parent Gap," *Newsweek*, September 22, 1975, p. 53.
[7] Nathan B. Talbot, "This Country's Most Neglected Asset," *Harvard Magazine*, July-August 1976, p. 20.
[8] Peggy Simpson, "Ex-Wives Getting Less Money Under No-Fault Divorce Laws," AP Report, *South Middlesex News*, July 7, 1976, p. 1.
[9] Stanley Lanzet, "Gerber International Foods," *Investor Services*, March 9, 1977, p. 1.
[10] Jeanne Binstock, "Motherhood: An Occupation Facing Decline," *The Futurist*, June 1973, p. 100.
[11] Interview with Freda Rebelsky, May 21, 1973.
[12] Ibid.
[13] Alvin Toffler, *Future Shock* (New York: Random House, 1970), p. 78.
[14] Mary Bralove, "The New Nomads," *Wall Street Journal*, August 1, 1973, p. 1.
[15] Toffler, op. cit., p. 416.
[16] Bralove, op. cit., p. 1.
[17] Philip Slater, *The Pursuit of Loneliness: American Culture at the Breaking Point* (Boston: Beacon, 1970), pp. 67-68.
[18] Lawrence Fuchs, *Family Matters* (New York: Random House, 1972), p. 5.
[19] Ibid., p. 20.
[20] Elizabeth Hardwick, "Suicide," *Mademoiselle*, December 1972, p. 196.
[21] John B. Watson, *Psychological Care of Infant and Child* (New York: Norton, 1928), p. 186.
[22] Gordon B. Blaine, *Are Parents Bad for Children?* (New York: Coward, McCann & Geoghegan, 1973), p. 148.
[23] Toffler, op. cit., p. 242.

[24] Margaret Mead, "The Life Cycle and Its Variations: The Division of Roles," *Daedalus*, Summer 1967, p. 872.

[25] Ellen Peck, *The Baby Trap* (New York: Pinnacle Books, 1972), p. 14.

[26] Shirley Radl, "Marriage, Yes, Children, No," *Cosmopolitan*, April 1973, p. 128.

[27] Lucy Komisar, *The New Feminism* (New York: Franklin Watts, 1971), p. 4.

[28] Nathan B. Talbot, op. cit., p. 22.

[29] Linda Helmstrom, *The Two-Career Family* (Cambridge, Mass.: Shenkman, 1972), pp. 60-61.

[30] Margaret Mead, "What Is Happening to the American Family?" *Journal of Social Casework*, November 1947, p. 327.

[31] Philip Slater, *The Glory of Hera: Greek Mythology and the Greek Family* (Boston: Beacon Press, 1968), p. 451.

[32] Eleanor Maccoby, ed. in *The Development of Sex Differences* (Stanford, California: Stanford University Press, 1966), p. 37.

[33] Kenneth Woodward and Phyllis Malamud, op. cit., p. 48.

[34] Willard Gaylin, "Skinner Redux," *Harper's*, October 1973, p. 48.

[35] Betty Friedan, *The Feminine Mystique* (New York: Dell, 1963), p. 279.

[36] Kate Millett, *Sexual Politics* (Garden City, N.Y.: Doubleday, 1970), p. 62.

[37] Germaine Greer, *The Female Eunuch* (New York: McGraw-Hill, 1971), p. 250.

2

ANSWERS—PLURAL

As we have seen, the tradition that mothers stay home and take care of the children is being broken by such irresistible pressures as the escalating cost of living and the lure of a rapidly opening women's freedom frontier. The old ways and expectations are being shelved, probably for good, considering the swelling strength of the assault on the traditional family fortress.

To be married or not, to be a parent or not, to go out to work full time, part time, or not at all, to share child-care responsibilities between mother and father, to delegate more or less of child-development responsibilities to others—the multiple questions facing young adults are giving rise to a host of alternate ways of raising children.

In this chapter and in chapter 3 we will present an overview of the many solutions that are being tried. Our material was gathered by personal interviews and by visits to group-care centers (unless otherwise noted).

THE SINGLE WOMAN

Susan, 30 years old, bright, aggressive, and independent, has taken a searching look at herself and come up with an option that is increasingly chosen by many young women—that of remaining single and childless.

> I'm an underwriter for an insurance company, and I love it. Ever since I was a little girl, I've enjoyed working with numbers, using my mind. And I'm very organized—everything in its place, five sharpened pencils on the desk, regular hours, that sort of thing. I guess you could call me compulsive. I'm like that at home too. I find it hard to get along with lots of people. I don't like to adjust my plans to something they've got in mind. So I have my own apartment, and I'm living my life just the way I want to. Maybe I'll get married some day—it'll have to be someone very special—but children? I don't think so. I just don't think I was ever cut out to be a mother.

Susan has been freed to choose this life style by the growing understanding in our society that one need not be married to lead a full and rewarding life. Nor need one have children. The promise of expanding career opportunities in the decade of the 1970s has seen increases in the number of single young women. Between 1960 and 1975 the number of persons living alone more than doubled. Marriages are occurring about a year later than they used to, according to the Census Bureau.[1]

CHILD-FREE MARRIAGE

Young women who choose to marry are sometimes choosing not to have children, and the stereotype of just a generation ago, which declared that childless couples were either sterile (in which case they were to be pitied and the subject be avoided) or selfish (in which case they were to be condemned and they themselves avoided), has rightfully disappeared. The Census Bureau tells us that between 1967 and 1974 the number of women aged 18-24 who expected to remain childless increased from 1 to 5 percent.[2] Economist Mary Rowe sees this 5 percent increasing to 10-20 percent by 1980.[3]

Even the vocabulary has changed. Such marriages are no longer "childless" but "child-free," and respected as an alternative life style. The statement by Dr. Lee Salk, famed clinical psychologist, that quality parenthood is so important that more people should consider not doing it,[4] is beginning to have a slightly deprecatory ring to it, implying as it does that many people are not fit to be parents and therefore may not be fit people. Couples may and do decide that having children would disrupt the lives they have chosen, but they do not accept, nor are the rest of us ready to accept, the implication that they are inferior people.

But they are asking hard questions. Are the rewards of parenthood worth the sacrifices? Joanne, 24, wire-service reporter, and Steve, 27, part-time jazz disc jockey, have been married for only five months, but this is how Joanne describes their feelings about children:

> We're in fields where we will never be wealthy. And we've found that there are certain things we like. I love to travel, I love oriental rugs and I love prints on my walls. We like to do things together—that's what made the relationship vibrant and successful.
>
> Economically, a child would end our lifestyle. . . . It was hard for me to find someone whom I trusted and felt comfortable with. And to toss in another variable scares me. It's wonderful that we have something going, but why jeopardize it?[5]

Other couples wonder if adults should give up their own personal growth in hopes the child will be and do what the parent passed up. Some such couples seem to be haunted by their view of the past:

> When my mother was young, she was so much fun—she could tell the greatest stories. But I've seen her slowly close those doors. Now she's no longer the vital and intelligent person she

was, and I think it is because she stayed home with the children. It can happen so easily. Your time and intelligence can be stolen.[6]

Women—and their husbands—who, for whatever reason, have chosen this option to remain child-free but who nevertheless have strong positive feelings toward children have found that there are still many opportunities, within one's extended family and within the community, to initiate and maintain nurturing contact with the next generation. Sunday School teachers, Big Sisters and Big Brothers, Hot-line volunteers, Scout leaders, team coaches, and hospital volunteers are always in short supply. Newspaper and television announcements cry out for interested adults to share a few hours a week with children. And for these children, contact with warm outside adults provides a rich life experience and, in many instances, support critical to emotional and career development.

On quite another level, men and women who have chosen not to have children of their own and who do not have direct contact with the children of others have found that they can function in a watchdog role over such institutions caring for children as hospitals, detention centers, and halfway houses. These facilities all need a concerned citizenry for adequate funding and administration.

These are some of the ways in which men and women are committing themselves to the future without becoming parents themselves.

THE SMALL FAMILY

A rapidly growing number of parents choose to have only one child. Between 1967 and 1975 the percentage of American women between the ages of 18 and 24 who expected to have only one child almost doubled, climbing from 6 percent to 11 percent.[7] A one-child family cuts down on the number of years that a woman who wants to mother her own young child has to be out of the labor force. Equally important, this lessens the family's money pressures.

A mother in her early 30s, an only child herself, summed up her feelings this way:

> My husband and I are trying to decide now whether to have another child. . . . I have serious doubts, and since I'm the one who would have to stay home with it my decision should carry more weight.
>
> I don't really see myself as a mother, in the role of a mother and a suburban housewife. I love my daughter and enjoy being her mother, but I see myself as more than that.
>
> I like the freedom and independence of working. We are also more comfortable financially. So it's not that I don't want another child exactly, but rather that I can't think of enough good reasons for having one.[8]

Reinforcing the one-child decision already made freely by many parents without benefit of counsel come the researchers, population analysts, and psychologists. They point out that "only" children score high in verbal ability, professional status, trustworthiness, and self-sufficiency, and may even turn out to be quite nice people.

Those parents who want two children (in the majority now—58.2 percent of 18- to 24-year-olds wanted only two children in 1975, as contrasted with 37 percent in 1967) are giving thought to spacing them.

Their reasons are various—some mothers must get back to work quickly because of economic pressures, some are anxious to get back to work to fulfill their career goals, some are in their late 30s and they are advised to have their children close together while they can, and some believe a certain space between children is better for child development and for a close-knit, companionable family. We spoke to young mothers who had formed a play group. They agreed with Edith, one of their members, who told us her reasons for spacing:

> I've read that three years is really the best space between children. They say that a three-year-old is more secure, and can accept a new baby better than a two-year-old. But I don't know. If I wait three years for the next one, it'll be a whole year extra that I'll be home, and I'd really like to get back to work as soon as I can, which to me means once the kids are in school all day.

FULL-TIME MOTHER AND SUPPORT PROGRAMS

Some women choose to stay home and be full-time homemakers and mothers. An anonymous respondent to a survey taken by *Family Circle* magazine expresses a popular point of view:

> Most of our women friends work. I do not! My 13 year old has noticed this and told me: "I like you being here when I come home from school." Four of our five children are already in school, and we have a nine month old. But I feel that my 13 year old needs a mother at home just as much as our baby does. I know that housewife bit isn't right for all women, but I sincerely believe it's right for all *children*![9]

Many young women agree that, for infants and toddlers at least, an at-home mother is best. So in much the same determined fashion that characterizes their approach to family planning, young women who have chosen full-time mothering have been finding ways to bolster their sense of worth and self-esteem and to break out of at-home isolation, which for many is the hardest problem they face in their first years as new mothers.

The growing number of women who are electing natural childbirth are making a positive statement about the way they feel about themselves and their role in life months before the baby is even born. They intend to "do" rather than "be done to," and initially reluctant fathers-to-be, doctors, nurses, and institutions are changing long-held attitudes about women's work and women's place (and men's work and men's place) and becoming enthusiastic partners in a venture in which women have the leading role.

Among the things they intend to do is breast-feed, and grandmothers whose own children were dependent on Pet milk and Karo syrup and Polyvisol for survival are ruefully wondering what they and their children missed as they watch their thriving grandchildren who are completely dependent upon mother's milk for nourishment. It is paradoxical that the bottle feeding that was intended to liberate mothers also downgraded their importance, while the breast feeding that was thought to enslave them makes it perfectly clear to everyone, especially the mother, that she is of unique and irreplaceable value.

How do these young mothers react when they read assessments like the following?

> There are some working women we haven't talked about yet. They labor more than 40 hours a week without benefit of minimum wage laws, retirement funds, Social Security payments, paid vacation time, raises or promotions.
>
> They are housewives, homemakers, full-time wives and mothers—and theirs is a back-breaking job filled with repetition and drudgery, which goes largely unrewarded and unrecognized.[10]

Whereas just a decade or so ago our typical young mother might have leaned against the sink, shifted the baby to the other hip, brushed a loose strand of hair from a prematurely wrinkling brow, and murmured "Too true," many young women today are doing what they see other oppressed minorities do with success. They are banding together, finding strength in numbers, and fighting back.

Politically, the results are still only straws in the wind. One example is the Martha movement, founded in the Spring of 1976 in Washington, with Mrs. George McGovern and Democratic Representative Yvonne Braithwaite-Burke of California on the board of directors. The Marthas are organized to elevate the status of homemakers in their own and in society's eyes.

Then there are the grudging beginnings of acceptance by Congress and the Internal Revenue Service of the value of a housewife's service in the home. This is evidenced in a provision of the 1976 Tax Reform Act that allows a contribution to an Individual Retirement Account for an unemployed spouse.

Socially, mothers at home are reaching out to each other. Janie, 24, who follows her construction-worker husband to where the jobs are and who has been in her present apartment just a year, told us about one such effort:

> We've formed what we call a Tot Lot. A local private school gave us a large basement room, and we've cleaned it up and painted it—our husbands helped—and furnished it with cast-offs. We each pay five dollars a year dues, and we use the money to buy toys. The great thing is, we can drop in any morning or afternoon with our children and know that they'll find other children to play with or watch—my baby's just six months old, and he's a watcher—and we'll find someone to visit with over a cup of coffee.
>
> It's a very informal set-up—we each have to be there with our children—but we found it works better than the play group we originally started with. Most of us live in apartments, and they're pretty small, and the older children seem to share more easily when the toys belong to everyone.
>
> And I've made some new friends. Turned out one of them lives just a block away, and I never knew she was there!

The play-group mothers mentioned earlier are pleased with their plan to give mothers time off and children friends to play with. Fran, 27, who worked as a secretary for seven years before her baby was born, described their play group:

> There are five of us and between us we have seven children aged 3½ months to three years. We always have two mothers assigned for any particular day (we meet three mornings a week in each other's homes) and the days that we aren't assigned, we're free to be by ourselves for a couple of hours, and I want to tell you, that couple of hours makes all the difference in the world. Whatever turns us on is what we do. One of us shops and gets her hair done, and one of us tries to get into the city once a week and just walk around and window shop—that's me—and one of us goes back to bed with a cup of coffee and the latest paperback best seller. There's a little friction, sure, between us, but the charge we get from those few hours off is worth it, and then some.

Another answer to at-home isolation is community cooperatives. Cooperatives involve whole families who live in adjacent homes or apartments or within reasonable distance from each other so that getting to each other's homes is no problem. In the heart of one large city Donna and Ernest Cataldo and their two children, who were 5 and 1½ at the time of the interview, were part of such an arrangement. Mrs. Cataldo said:

> This is a wonderfully child-oriented community. We have a baby-sitting cooperative with 25 other families who live [nearby] so that we don't have to pay for a sitter and we always leave the children in top-notch hands when we go out.[11]

Members of cooperatives barter their services. For every hour of child care used, an hour is owed to the group, and so child-care cooperatives provide answers even for those on the tightest budgets.

A more formal solution is provided by YWCAs. The greatest advantage of the Y programs is their availability to total strangers in the community. All one needs to make this contact is a telephone book, and to those for whom Tot Lots, play groups, or cooperative programs are out of reach, the Y is one answer. One Y program, for example, offers a weekly two-hour session for mothers while their children are cared for in a supervised playroom. (Babies under six months stay with their mothers.) The session opens with coffee and with what the Y quaintly calls "confections." Then there is a choice of four or five classes such as Slimnastics, Yoga, Crafts, and Quiltmaking. The Y has found, and millions of young mothers will attest to it, that daily life with an infant is heavy going most of the time, and these young mothers really need some relief. After class there is more coffee and sometimes a speaker or demonstration, determined by the expressed interests of the mothers in the group.

The most valuable asset of the program is the feeling imparted of fulfillment, of being worthwhile. Said one young mother, who had gone directly from her parents' protective home to her husband's protective arms, "It just changed my life when someone came up to me after I'd missed a few meetings and said 'I'm glad to see you back!' and I realized that I was liked for myself alone and not just as an adjunct to my husband!" Feelings of personal worthlessness are very democratic—they cut across class lines and can afflict any one of us who is not getting some support from somewhere.

Y programs are often held in churches. Religious groups have traditionally responded to community needs, and their combination of community concern and available space during the week has made them naturals for programs directed to mothers and young children.

We have been talking about "answers" that afford a central place with some creature comforts where mothers can go with their children. Another way the shut-in nuclear mother syndrome is being alleviated is by the development of supportive programs that have grown up around the country. Gina, 19, with a year-old baby, volunteered for such a program:

> See, I never had any experience at all with babies, and my family's a million miles away, and I was really worried about whether I was doing the right things for Amy. Now I have this teacher who comes to the house once a month, and she visits with us for a couple of hours, and she is *some* comfort to me! I was getting worried about why Amy wasn't walking yet—she just sits and smiles at me—and the teacher told me lots of babies don't walk until a whole lot later, and then I stopped worrying about it. And she showed me a whole bunch of things I could make for Amy to play with, like a Quaker Oats box that we put some empty spools into, and Amy can rattle it, and roll it—and like that!

Such supportive programs are sometimes called intervention programs. They are designed to alleviate all kinds of deprivation—economic, physical, mental, emotional, and social—for mothers and their children. They are an outgrowth of programs of the 1960s, planned by child-development professionals with the best of intentions, that took the child out of the home to child centers and force-fed him with intellectual stimulation. Educators of the 1970s have come to recognize that no child-centered program outside the home can begin to be as effective as one that involves the *whole* family:

> Early learning in school can work, in a limited way, but school will never be home. The complexity of family relationships cannot be reproduced. The bond between mother and child is qualitatively different from the bond between caregiver and baby. No one teacher, no one institution, will see a child from his infancy through all the years of his growth, in chicken pox and scary dreams, lost in a department store, cranky on Christmas morning, fighting for the television, laughing at inscrutable family jokes . . . the core of a child's life is his home; school, no matter how good, is peripheral to his growth.[12]

An outstanding program that developed from this view of the irreducible importance of home life was run by the High/Scope Educational Research Foundation in Ypsilanti, Michigan. The program, headed by Dr. David Weikart, sent visitors into the homes of mothers with infants aged from three to twenty-seven months, and reported that it had made a substantial, positive difference to the families involved.

The key to this approach lies in breaking away from the traditional educational stance in which the teacher is the professional dispenser of all knowledge and the mother is the amateur supplicant. Instead, visitors must come in as sympathetic helpers. They must recognize the difficulties of the mother, common to all of us, in dealing with small children, and work with her to find alternate ways that may make her life easier and more fulfilling. It's a delicate, tricky business—a visitor can't side with the baby against the mother unless he or she wishes to leave behind a household on the brink of war.

This is a situation entirely different from and more difficult than that encountered when a young mother's mother or mother-in-law shares her experience with the new mother. Given the way of the world, most young women battle to get out from under the influence of mothers and mothers-in-law, and can take advantage of any helpful hints without sacrificing their sense of self and natural superiority to the older generation. This natural pull away from dependence doesn't operate when a young mother is confronted with a professional, so professionals must be extremely sensitive in their approach.

A highly ambitious research program that is supportive in nature and that reaches into the home to break down the isolation of mothers of young children is the Brookline (Massachusetts) Early Education Project, widely known as the BEEP program. BEEP began as an effort to cut down on the number of children who enter school with a previously undetected learning handicap, and who then become caught in a spiral of school failure.

The program attracts the attention of many eminent professionals. Its overseers include representatives from Harvard Medical School and the Children's Hospital Medical Center. BEEP provides diagnostic and educational programs for very young children and their families:

> [Its guiding philosophy is] based on the idea that the education of a child begins at birth and is primarily the responsibility of the child's family . . . that the origins of underachievement may often lie in the child's early learning environment, . . . BEEP therefore focuses on assistance to families in their role as the primary educator of their children.[13]

Teachers visit with families regularly, either at home or in the center, and alert parents to the kinds of activity that are suitable for their child at his particular age. They provide professional guidance while leaving the responsibility to parents. In addition, all enrolled BEEP babies are given regular physical examinations and evaluations that include neurologic, physical, and intellectual areas of development.

Parents and children are always welcome to drop in at the center, where there is a professional on hand to talk to them. Between the visiting teacher and the available center, mothers find more interest in their children's growth and more opportunities for support and socializing.

BEEP does not take over from family-chosen pediatricians or health centers, but tries to alert the proper professionals to any departure they notice from normality. It is interesting that one success story to which BEEP can point is the case of a child who suffered from anemia. And who do you think detected the first clue that something was wrong, amidst all these exams? The teacher who came regularly to the home! The baby didn't "feel" right to her when she picked him up and played with him.

By coordinating the efforts of pediatricians, psychologists, social workers, nurses, and home visitors, BEEP provides an interdisciplinary approach that should give a significantly higher level of care than the fragmented care most children receive.

The most exciting intervention program we saw, probably because it makes the most difference in the lives of the mothers and children who attend, was the Parent-Child Center in Boston's inner-city Dorchester section. This is one of 35 programs set up across the country.

It began in 1968, when President Johnson called together a task force, which included a number of prominent educators, to find ways to get to children before they reached the Head Start age of 3½. Head Start teachers were encountering children of that age who came to them with a lot of deficits, including medical, emotional, and experiential problems that severely handicapped them for later formal education. The more direct experiences a child has with the stuff of life—the tastes, sounds, smells, and feelings, the places visited, the objects touched, the sights actually seen—the more concrete a base he has on which to build his speaking and reading abilities and his understanding.

The task force recommended an approach that would reach *families* as well as children, involving mothers in the whole process of development and education. These were mothers whose own life experience, locked into poverty and deprivation from the beginning, left them in a condition of hopelessness, with complete inability to direct their own lives, let alone those of their children.

The center we saw is in a large, modern rented office building. With lots of color, imagination, and muscle, it has become a model for any center that wants to exude warmth and cleanliness and put stars in the eyes of children, parents, and staff alike. In contrast to the aimless look of children just passing time, which we saw in many day-care centers, these children were alive and gorgeous.

The center provides three playrooms for the children, each staffed by a master teacher and two paraprofessionals, work rooms, meeting rooms, and a lunch room for the mothers, who are welcome to come in and work and play with their children whenever they want. But at least once every session they are specially invited into their children's rooms, where they can see a variety of activities appropriate for their child's age and good role models in the persons of the teachers. They are always included in the activities going on. If they are shy about taking an up-front position, the teacher is sensitive to that and asks them to do something that does not threaten them but that includes them in the group in a more retiring situation.

When the mothers are not with their children, they take part in programs designed to teach them skills that, at one and the same time, help them in a practical way to make their own home life richer and also teach them the discipline needed and the satisfaction gained from starting a project and completing it. A woman can learn to cook in the center's kitchen. A washer and dryer have been provided for convenient use. There are sewing machines available, and help in mastering the art. Furniture is provided for refinishing, and materials for doing it—or a woman can bring something from home. There is a staff member who can show a mother how to repair small appliances. Ceramics and painting are offered. Films and discussion groups in child development are an ongoing activity.

Parents are members of the planning committees, which gives them an opportunity to take charge of their own lives. Further, they are encouraged to take part in community affairs. A polling place can be mysterious and frightening if someone doesn't first show you what to do. But once you learn, you can pull a lever and vote for the candidate who you believe will make a difference.

All of this takes place in the company of a warm, supportive staff, many of whom started out as center mothers themselves, and of other young mothers who are facing the same problems. Seventy-five families and 100 children come to the center. Because of space, staff, and funding limitations, the center can serve only half the group at one time, so one-half come on

Mondays and Tuesdays from ten to two-thirty and the other half on Wednesdays and Thursdays at the same times.

Friday is devoted to staff meetings, in-service training (both in the center and in community colleges), and an outreach program that serves mothers who are not ready to participate in the center activities. A team from the center brings the program to these families who are overwhelmed with problems that freeze and immobilize them. Initially the team consists of one child-development person who is responsible for materials and continuing help, plus a nurse and psychiatric social worker.

Their main goal is to help the mother be the best teacher for her child. An at-home activity might include cooking—perhaps baking a birthday cake, a project in which everyone participates. A lot of learning takes place. With the help and encouragement of the center teacher a mother learns to enjoy her child. She learns to make use of everyday things in the house for teaching tools, and perhaps there is a shopping trip involved. Of course, at the end everyone can have his or her cake and eat it, too.

Eventually this support gives the mother confidence to join in the program at the center, where more learning goes on. Mother and child are urged to be ready on time when the van arrives to take them to the center. They are encouraged to have breakfast before they leave home, and are applauded when they arrive fed, clean, and shiny. Young mothers (the youngest was only 13, while the average age is 22) who have not had regularity in their own lives and who often grew up in chaotic circumstances are prepared neither to raise their children differently nor to fit into a working world when their children are older. This program makes the difference.

An important adjunct to the center was a child-advocacy program that lasted for 2 1/2 years. Its purpose was to identify all the families in the target area, become aware of their needs, and at the same time identify and become familiar with the resource agencies in the area. In this way duplication was eliminated and gaps uncovered that, by the use of lavish doses of tact and diplomacy, could be filled by minor changes in programs already functioning.

As an example of the kind of situation this program uncovered, the director told us about a prenatal clinic that had been open five days a week from nine to five, hours when most young women who were about to become first-time mothers were at work. Now it is open evenings and has Saturday hours to accommodate those who need it. It is a sensible example of what can be done when agencies communicate and cooperate.

So, in a small corner of a large city, lonely, depressed young mothers *are* being touched and given a reason to be strong, courageous, and happy with their children.

COMMUNAL LIVING

"Americans," observed humorist Will Rogers many years ago, "will join anything but their own families." And so today some parents are finding their answers in communal living. The large communal groupings of the 1960s, which sometimes saw as many as several hundred people banding together, sharing living space, incomes, resources, and responsibilities, seems to have dwindled in the 1970s. (The history of communes in this country over several centuries has been that almost no commune has lasted more than one generation.) Instead, we are seeing single parents deciding to share a household and raise their children together as a family. The success of these small communal groupings is as yet unknown. But aside from the obvious advantage of cutting expenses, it does seem that for some parents the presence of two or more adults in one household will help relieve the pressures of child care.

THE HALF-TIME ROUTE FOR PARENTS

It is exciting to realize the number of ways in which young women who choose to be full-time mothers of young children are able to enrich their years at home, broaden their circle of friends, grow in self-confidence and esteem, and enjoy the experience of mothering.

Many mothers, however, are choosing the half-time route—half-time with their children, half-time in school or on the job. In that choice they have plenty of support, as far as their half-time mothering goes, from Dr. Burton White of the Harvard Pre-School Study. His book, *The First Three Years of Life*, filmed as a documentary by Westinghouse Broadcasting Corporation, concludes that the first three years of life are crucial in raising "competent" children,[14] that is, children who grow into mature adults and become contributing members of society. White suggests that full-time day care is unlikely to be as beneficial to the child's early educational development as his own home, that working mothers should postpone their return to full-time employment until the child is three, and that the best solution would be one in which each parent works only half time.

Unfortunately for Dr. White's thesis, the business world—and often the world of education—does not share his enthusiasm for part-time work or his understanding of children and mothers. Terry, a 19-year-old single mother, had an experience that shows just how far business is from a sympathetic view of the needs of mothers and small children:

> I *was* working once since my baby was born. I'm a high school graduate and I was working over at [a major nonprofit health insurance company]. And my little boy fell and his tooth cut his lip, and his grandma called me and I had to take him to the hospital. And you know what they did when I got back? They put me on probation for 30 days. Because I left to bring him to the hospital! My super, he said, "If you can't manage to handle your

family problems without it interfering with your work, perhaps you shouldn't be working!" So I quit. I wasn't going to stay no place like that!

American business, more than any other single factor, determines the fate of families and children. We are just beginning to see a few faint signs that indicate our growing realization that people do not exist to serve the needs of business and industry, like so many computers and forklift trucks, but that business and industry exist to serve our needs as human beings.

Here and there can be found small signals of progress. Some young corporate executives, for example, are reportedly refusing to become virtual gypsies as they climb the ladder of success, putting their families' roots in a community ahead of possible promotion. But these signs of progress are being literally wrung from management and administration by determined young parents who know what they want and just how much they will sacrifice to meet their economic needs. Even labor and political organizations, which should be responsive to the needs of their constituencies, have yet actively to demand measures to improve the quality of family life. So far it's a lonely fight that is being waged.

Still, part-time work is sought increasingly by parents. Terry, in the incident described above, simply left a situation in which management was unsympathetic. Betty, we shall see, fought it out, but with mixed results:

> I stayed home the first eight months after Ruthie was born. How did I like it? I guess you could say I was generally miserable. The first four or five months were the *worst*—and Ruthie has always been a good baby. But most of our friends lived on the other side of town, and none of them had children then. They all worked. I felt completely out of it.
>
> Then, when Ruthie was eight months old, a new position opened up in administration where I used to work. I learned about it from someone who had worked with me who had also

left to have a baby. We decided to go after the job together and work it on a shared-time basis.

And I want to tell you, it was a battle! We couldn't get anyone to consider it, and so we went to another company in the same field that *had* accepted shared-time work and they went to bat for us with our own company.

Finally, the boss agreed to give us a chance. They were really terribly pleased with us. They even did a feasibility study on us, and the results were great! So everything was going along well—Ruthie was staying with a lovely woman who had two little children of her own, and she seemed happy there—but then my partner and her family moved out of town, and at the same time, a great full-time job opened up for me somewhere else, and I grabbed it. Now I understand that my old company has gone right back to its old ways. In spite of all our successes, we were the first shared-time employees and it looks like we're going to be the last!

Women have had more luck in education. With the proliferation of community colleges, evening colleges, and adult-education courses, mothers have the opportunity to go to school part time.

But some professions remain hard nuts to crack. Doctors still work their internship and residency on a basis of 36 hours on and 12 hours off, and that's tough for a woman with a young baby. Medical people say, "Of course it's necessary! How is a young doctor going to understand the progress of an illness and observe the effects of various treatments and medications if he or she packs it in at 5 P.M. every day? They have to live through these things with their patients!"

This is hard to explain to an 18-month-old. Mara, a pediatric resident married to a resident obstetrician, found it almost impossible:

My husband and I both have very long hours at the hospital. We have a very good live-in sitter, but the baby cries so when I leave the house, I can hardly stand it. And then the nights when my husband and I are both home together—and that's a real occasion —are awful for me. The baby wraps herself around me and I can't put her down, and meanwhile my husband wants his dinner—we're from Iraq, you know, and he's just not used to doing women's work—and sometimes he and I just want to go out for an evening—an early movie, or a visit with friends for a few hours, and she cries so when we put on our coats that the whole evening's ruined for me.

One solution to the problem of child care is relatively new—the father who either chooses to stay home full time or, more often, part time, sharing housekeeping and child-rearing joys, sorrows, excitement, and boredom with a wife who is working either full or part time herself. Although shared parenting is one of Dr. White's preferred solutions for child care, it seems to be an option largely limited to men in education or in the professions. Most other men are faced with the same rigid employer attitudes toward a part-time work week that their wives encounter.

Earl, 33, an attorney, is one of the men who has been able to take on more than a father's usual share of parenting:

I was working full time in a law firm when Tommy was born, and was becoming totally dissatisfied with the whole set-up. But after Tommy came along, it became pretty clear that my wife was really chafing at the being-at-home-all-day bit, just at the time when I was anxious to chuck my damn job. So we sat down and had a hard talk about all the alternatives available. And we decided that it made sense, for us at least, at that particular time in our lives, for me to stay home, and for my wife to go back to full-time work.

Of course, I think a big factor in our decision was that I'm pretty secure about myself and my abilities, and I never wanted to be locked into that one step at a time climb up the legal ladder of a big law firm.

My wife, on the other hand, has a need to continually prove herself, and her job gives her that satisfaction, which she missed badly when she was at home.

Earl didn't remain a full-time, at-home father for very long:

> I began to get pretty restive at home myself. So I found a part-time job and we put Tommy, who was just five months old then, with a wonderful woman in the neighborhood, who had two children of her own and took in two. She was great with him, but then she sought, and obtained, certification as a licensed day-care home, and then she couldn't take infants any more, which Tommy technically still was. But we found someone else, through a friend of a friend, and Tommy's with her now.
>
> My wife and I are watching Tommy very carefully and so far so good. I'm home with him two and a half days a week and he's with the sitter two and a half days. Actually, we've been doing this for six months now, and my being with him for two and a half days is getting too much for me, and I know it's not enough for him!
>
> But on the plus side, Tommy doesn't seem to be becoming an anxious child, and these last years have given him a chance to have two parents instead of just one.
>
> Long term? I have to say that if push comes to shove, and either my wife or I have to stay home full time, we both agree that my career will have to come first. But for this period in our lives, things are working out well.

Earl has been a househusband, a word coined by James A. Levine of Wellesley, Massachusetts, day-care consultant, teacher of a child-development course at Wellesley College, and author.[15]

According to the Bureau of Labor Statistics, there were 219,000 men at home in 1974-1975 taking care of children while the mothers worked outside the home.[16] Although some of these men are divorced fathers who seek and win custody and others are single adoptive parents, there are some who choose to stay home full time and parent while their wives work and others who share income-producing functions with their wives, each working half time and parenting half time. Says Levine:

> Men who choose to stay at home as homemaker-fathers tend to be independent thinkers. . . . While they are sympathetic to day care, [these men and their wives] believe strongly that it is the family's function to raise very young children. Since they respect each other's ability and right to work outside the home, the assignment of child care is flexible. They have no grand plan about who will earn income and who will care for the young; decisions about family functioning are mutual . . .[17]

Some fathers have strong wishes to be involved in their children's early lives:

> However convinced they are that quality of time spent with a child is more important than quantity, they also believe that quality *and* quantity are better than just quality. As one man says, "You put burdens on maintaining the quality the more the time is decreased. The reason you can't be intimate with a lot of other people is that you're not present long enough for the interaction and trust to develop; with a small child, it's especially important that he knows there's a continuing source there."[18]

The subject of househusbands is particularly difficult to discuss because we have no vocabulary with which to discuss it. "Househusband" hardly seems a title of choice at a time when "housewife" has fallen into such disrepute. So some researchers talk about "fathers who mother," a phrase that has all the potential for disaster, especially as some sociologists and psychologists suggest that when the father adopts a "feminine" role the child may become confused.

Other students of the subject believe that "father" is all the title needed. They say that a child's more frequent association with the father enhances all of those traits associated with masculinity such as activity and independence. How this will sit with the feminist mother who is active in pursuing her independence and undoubtedly wants the same for her daughters is still a matter for conjecture. So we are reduced to awkward circumlocutions such as "fathers who parent" and "mothers who parent."

But vocabulary is marvelously adaptable and surely a term will evolve that gives due respect to all involved and puts down no one. Much more serious is the job of introducing sufficient flexibility into our world of work so that fathers *and* mothers can be freed to nurture their young either part time or full time without permanently closing down their options in the labor market.

Over the last 15 years—a long time considering the progress that has been made—a number of avenues to part-time work have been opened to women. In 1962 five college presidents founded Catalyst, an organization that has been working ever since to promote part-time job options and to counsel women who are trying to reconcile work and family obligations.

Washington Opportunities for Women, which opened its doors in 1967, had grown by 1974 to include 22 paid full- and part-time staff, 35 regular volunteer counselors, and offices in six East Coast cities. It had been in touch with over 10,000 women and 1,500 employees.

Newtime, Inc., a New York employment agency, was founded in 1970 to sell businessmen on a 25-hour work week. Their main selling point is that business can increase its pool of highly motivated and talented employees.

An act introduced by former California senator John Tunney and passed by the United States Senate in 1975 would have mandated that after a five-year phase-in period, 10 percent of all government jobs up to the $36,000-a-year level would be available on a permanent part-time basis with prorated fringe benefits and standard civil service protections.

Honeywell, Inc., in 1972 offered Massachusetts mothers short shifts that fell within children's school hours. The program coordinator explained it this way:

We manufacture photoelectric and proximity controls here, and we were experiencing a very high rate of turnover and absenteeism. Our general manager at the time decided that there must be a lot of women at home who would love to get out and make some money, and do work that women are particularly good at. So we started out by hiring 20 women, to work not less than four hours and not more than six hours a day, at times of their own choosing, so long as those times were on a regular schedule.

In 1976 we have 21 people, each working a five-hour day. Half of them have children, and so half of them leave us in June when school is out and come back in September. They receive prorated benefits, sick leave, vacation, and basic life insurance coverage.

The company has been very pleased with the program. Our part-time people are skilled and reliable, and the rates of turnover and absenteeism have gone way down.

Honeywell may not have been aware that they were following the advice of a Norwegian sociologist who says, "It makes no sense whatever to bring the mother into the one-sided occupationally absorbed and stressed work role the father is already into.[19]

But if Honeywell was unaware of the Norwegian sociologist, the Norwegians weren't. A Norwegian experiment in 1971 involved 16 families in a part-time work program in which the mother would work in the morning while the father stayed home, and then the two would switch roles, the mother coming home, and the father going off to be a wage earner in the afternoon. In a possible variant, both parents would work in the morning while the children were cared for in a state-subsidized center, and the whole family would be home together in the afternoon. So much satisfaction was expressed by participants in the small-scale experiment that by 1974 all major Norwegian political parties were calling for reduced work time for parents of young children.

In Sweden the approach has been a little different. Insisting that both men and women are entitled to work full time, the thrust of Sweden's political parties and labor unions is to reduce full-time work to six hours a day.

"Flex-time" is another American approach that is different from those mentioned above in that it doesn't allow for part-time work or a substantially shorter day, but gives parents a little leeway in handling child-care duties and joys. In 1974, 85,000 workers in 45 firms were given flexible hours—arrival typically between 7 A.M. and 9 A.M. and departure between 3 P.M. and 5 P.M., with core working hours between 9 A.M. and 3 P.M. during which all were expected to be on hand. While flex-time does offer a little more freedom in scheduling one's life than does the factory whistle that blows at 7 A.M. and regulates workers' lives inexorably, it does not actually give them more time to be with their families and so can only be considered as inching in the right direction.

In 1976 Massachusetts State Representative Lois Pines sponsored legislation that has been enacted by the General Court, dealing with flex-time and part-time work for state civil service employees. Flex-time works as described above except that in Massachusetts the core time is 10 A.M. to 3 P.M. In late 1976 flex-time was already a reality, but the part-time aspect of the program was taking a little longer. The overseer of Chapter 500, which is the Pines bill, said that her department "was in the process of working to define jobs that can be split because the intent of this program is to provide opportunities that don't require a 37-hour week."

Even though this program was initially directed toward women, it now encompasses men, handicapped people, and welfare recipients who have not had experience with full-time work and for whom part-time jobs can be a step toward reentry into full-time employment. All benefits will be received on a prorated basis by the part-time workers. As in the Tunney bill, it is expected that in five years 10 percent of all state civil service jobs will be offered on a part-time basis.

Job sharing is still another option being explored, and

although we have referred to it before as it contributed to part-time work, it does have another dimension. A Palo Alto nonprofit organization called New Ways to Work trains individuals to apply as teams for jobs. Among the single positions filled by two-person teams are medical receptionists, librarians, administrators, probation workers, city planners, and program developers. The Women's Industrial Union in Boston, always ahead of its time, was offering teachers to employers on a shared-time basis as early as 1964.

Hewlett-Packard introduced an experimental shared-time program at its Loveland, Colorado, plant in 1976. Six pairs of employees, including two men, shared jobs on a ten-hour shift. The advantages to the employees are a five-hour shift and all standard company benefits except long-term disability. And the advantages to Hewlett-Packard include saving money on overtime and getting ten hours of work from each station rather than eight.

All of these programs have a few things in their favor and a few working against them. Half-time workers have been found to keep up a much faster work pace for four hours than workers who are on the job for eight hours:

> Offering part-time work . . . gives a company a personnel-management lever to use against competitors, especially larger ones in attracting . . . high-quality workers. Secondly, the firm that broadens part-time opportunities will probably experience greater productivity and lower unit costs, due to rapid and dramatic decreases in absenteeism, turnover, recruitment activity and overtime pay. . . ."[20]

Mitigating against the shared-time work week is the traditional work-ethic principle that says the 40-hour week is the way to work, the added cost of training more people, the fear of greatly increased paper work and record keeping that would result from doubling employees, and, particularly in many unionized companies, resulting higher fringe-benefit costs.

Perhaps more important than all of these reasons is the state of the economy. In times of recession, when a company, itself possibly fighting for survival, can get all the good employees it wants simply by hanging out a "Help Wanted" sign, the company is not disposed to take additional risks with unknown ventures or to commit itself to additional expense for some ephemeral future "social good."

All in all, parents who are trying to ease their child-care burdens by demanding cooperation from employers are making very slow progress.

CHILD-CARE ARRANGEMENTS

In Your Home

When parents are at work, what kinds of care can they find for their children? One of the preferred answers for those who can afford it, particularly for mothers of infants, is a woman who comes into her home every day and cares for her baby while the mother is away. Ruth, who is a social worker dealing in family counseling, told us, "There just seems to be something more normal and less disruptive about a situation where the baby remains in its same familiar home environment and the same familiar person comes in every day to care for him."

Recognizing that a good substitute mother figure is not easy to find and shouldn't come cheap if she is to have a feeling of worth and dignity and a reasonable living wage, some programs have been developed to fill the need for well-trained caretakers. One such program is run by the Women's Service Club in Boston. Called the Homemaker Training Program, it offers a 12-week course given four times a year and funded by the Comprehensive Employment Training Act (CETA). Women enrolled in the course learn the most efficient ways of doing housework, basic nutrition, care of children and the elderly, and other specialized knowledge necessary to a homemaker.

Graduates are certified as Home Help Aides, with special certification by the Red Cross in Modified Home Nursing. They are guaranteed a minimum salary of $2.30 per hour plus the cost of transportation to and from work. In 1976 aides were averaging $2.75 per hour, and the record shows that 98 percent of the graduates find immediate employment. The problem is, of course, that a Home Help Aide who works 45 hours a week earns only $123.75 gross plus transportation, and that is a very minimum wage for a long work week. On the other hand, most working parents are so far from being able to pay $123.75 plus transportation every week as to make the whole subject laughable. In fact, most trained aides are now working with the elderly rather than with children.

There are, of course, some homes in which the mother pays out most of her salary to the baby-sitter. If her husband is providing enough income to keep the family going, the wife can then look on her work as an investment in the continuity of her career, and she may find that the satisfaction of her job more than compensates for what, during her child's early years, is probably a no-profit situation in terms of earnings and expenses.

There are cheaper ways of finding care. Many mothers, like Cathy, make their own private arrangements. We answered Cathy's advertisement in a local paper that read "Wanted, woman to care for three-month-old girl in my home five days a week, Monday through Friday." Cathy told us:

> I'm a teacher, and I didn't make any plans to go back to work till the baby was born. I wanted to see how I'd feel about it. Well, I love being home with her, but I love teaching too, and you don't just give up a job in elementary school these days without thinking twice, what with so many unemployed teachers. So I put this ad in, and the phone hasn't stopped ringing. I haven't started interviewing yet, but when I do, the most important

thing will be to find someone who'll take care of the baby like I do. I'm hearing basically from three kinds of people—women who have a small child of their own who they'd bring along with them, women with children in school all day, and older women, in their 50s and 60s, who don't want a job in an office or a store or a factory. What will I pay them? Oh, the going rate seems to be $40 a week, or a dollar an hour. That's what I understand the Office of Child Development suggests as a guideline, and that seems to be what most people I've talked to are thinking of.

Caretaker's Home

Some women arrange for care for their children outside their home, and here relatives head the list. Ellie, a 28-year-old kindergarten teacher, brings her baby over to her mother:

My folks live right down the street. I'm the oldest in a large family, and Ma still has kids in elementary school—and in junior high *and* in high school for that matter. So she's home every day, and I just bring the baby over to her, and I know she's getting the best care in the world, and the most loving. Ma hates the way I wear my hair, parted in the middle like this, and I think she's an awful housekeeper, but we pretty much agree on how to raise a baby!

Other mothers whose parents may live half a continent away, or who agree with their own mothers on hair styling and housekeeping but disagree violently on child care, or whose own mothers are working full time, look to friends for help.

Sandy, a 19-year-old single mother who is periodically on and off welfare, doesn't have much, but she does have a friend:

This girl, she and I been friends for a *long* time, and she has two little kids of her own and can use some extra money. So I bring Ruby over to her five mornings a week, you know, and I work as a supermarket checker. Maybe some day, we'll change places, and I'll stay home and take care of the kids, and she'll go to work. But for now, it's working out good for both of us.

Family Day Care

A more expensive and more widely used solution to the problem of child care is the baby-sitter to whom you bring your child and who cares for several children in her own home. This is what is known as a family day-care home. Sal, 32, single mother, law-school student, secretary, and political activist, finds an answer here:

Those first few months were really rough. I knew I had to get back to work fast—without a husband, there was no question about *that*—and you know, I had just about finished my first year at law school nights, and I certainly didn't want to lose that whole year. I had made arrangements for a sitter months before the baby was born. But then everything fell apart. A week before I went into labor, the sitter canceled out. Then I had a difficult delivery and complications—as if I needed complications!—and I ended up spending almost a month in the hospital. I had a friend who had a baby in family care, and so I called her woman as soon as I could pull myself together. But she had no room for Julie.

You know, I was 30 years old when Julie was born. I think if I hadn't had all the work experience and living experience and maturity that I did have, those first months would have really finished me.

I finally got a line on the Child Care Resources Center, and they gave me the names of several women who took in infants. The very first one Julie and I visited turned out to be just perfect.

Mrs. Campbell has seven children of her own. The oldest is 19 and the youngest is 10. I know their apartment would never pass any kind of state inspection, but they are such loving people! Julie's been part of their family days ever since.

How much does it cost? Well, I started paying $40 a week

two years ago, and now it's up to $50 a week. I'll tell you, I make $190 a week, and if my mother wasn't sending me money every month, I'd have to go on welfare. There'd be no way I could finish school and pay Mrs. Campbell, and give $5 a night to a baby-sitter the times I go to school!

Family day-care homes such as the one Julie is in can vary widely in quality. Just as in the old nursery rhyme, "When it is good, it is very, very good, and when it is bad, it is horrid."

There is ample documentation of the really bad ones. In some cases the care is barely custodial, as in the documented case of the woman who, all by herself, cared for 47 children each day. The basic problem, of course, is that once the mother leaves in the morning there is no supervision of the day-care provider during the day. With a little luck she'll do a good job, but if she doesn't have a real sense of responsibility she could spend a few hours on the phone, take a nap, turn on the TV and plunk the children down in front of it, and no one will be the wiser. And these are the *best* of the bad things that she could do. Infants may be screamers, but they're not squealers.

Some mothers have found a solution to this problem in family day-care programs. A family day-care program is one in which a community agency takes the responsibility for coordinating and acting as a resource for a number of individual day-care homes. The program with which we are familiar was founded in 1970 by the Women's Educational and Industrial Union of Boston, which was in turn founded in 1877 to help working women.

This day-care program finds the family day-care mothers. They don't look for education or even training. They look for warm, empathetic, steady women with a sense of humor and a decided preference to spending their working days working with children rather than with machines. They then give these selected day-care providers a training program that consists of four five-day weeks during which the future day-care mother is exposed to a rigorous course of study. In broad outline, she studies stages of child development from birth to six years and various techniques of play (art media, music and dramatic play, nature and science, children's literature, activities for a mixed-age group, use of everyday toys, infant stimulation, and language development). Other topics include discipline, separation, relationships, organizing time, space, and equipment, nutrition, health and safety, cardboard carpentry, and business problems.

Alternatively, the program offers a two-week mini-course and encourages the day-care provider to supplement this experience with a series of seminars. During the courses the children of the day-care provider and any children for whom she may be caring are taken care of in a children's room with trained teachers in attendance. The courses are taught by a social worker and educators, plus visiting specialists including early childhood educators and a pediatric nurse practitioner. Each day-care home can have a maximum of five or six children, including the children of the day-care provider.

Once the course is completed and the children have been referred to the day-care home, there remains a network of support services. Each day-care provider receives basic play materials suitable for the children for whom she cares. Each day-care mother gets vacation and sick pay. Education consultants visit the home regularly and bring material for working with the children on a play project. A psychiatric social worker comes in when needed, typically to help the day-care mother work with a child who is having a hard time adjusting comfortably to the situation, or with a child who is having some developmental difficulty, or to help when day-care provider and parent are having difficulties in their relationship.

There are evening meetings organized around a workshop or a speaker for the day-care mothers. Once a month there is a large group activity for all day-care mothers and their children —a puppet show, a movie, or a picnic, for example.

Local child-study students from area colleges spend several hours each week in the day-care home lending a second pair of adult hands, presenting new activities for the children, or giving one-to-one help to a child who may need it. A child psychiatrist is available to consult with parents or day-care mothers when necessary.

For this full-day care a day-care provider can earn, depending on the number of hours she works and the number of children she cares for, as much as $159 a week, paid to her by the family day-care program.

A parent who wishes such care for a child or children first contacts the family day-care program. She is referred to a day-care home that is available and that seems to suit her needs best. Either parent or day-care provider can turn down a particular placement if it does not seem the proper place for the child. Parents and day-care mothers are encouraged to meet frequently and informally to discuss the child's progress. Staff members meet with parents twice a year to talk about the child's adjustment and any problems that may arise. Twice a month the parent-day-care provider council meets to discuss program policy, and new parents are urged to participate. Staff members are available to talk to parents.

The 1976 cost of care was $59 per child per full-time week. This includes payment to the day-care provider plus a share of the program's expenses. The majority of parents pay about $30 a week. The difference between what the parent pays in and what the program pays out is made up by a cash donation from the Women's Industrial and Educational Union, Title XX funds from the Department of Public Welfare, and a Federal Mental Health grant that pays staff salaries.

Currently this Boston family day-care program cares for between 60 and 90 children in between 25 and 30 homes. They receive many calls about newborns, but not many parents seem to pursue it. The agency is not sure why, but is just as happy that the demand is not greater. Many day-care providers don't want infants because they feel they won't be able to give them enough attention. One grandmotherly type, however, specifies babies. She'll take two at a time, bring them up together, and prefers them to the older children who run around so much.

In chapter 8 we will evaluate different kinds of care, and will have more to say about family day-care homes.

Finally, of course, many parents are turning to group day-care centers to care for infants, toddlers, and preschoolers. In the next chapter we shall look at a number of these centers.

NOTES

[1] U.S. Bureau of the Census, *Current Population Reports*, Series P-20, #287, "Marital Status and Living Arrangements: March, 1975" (Washington, D.C.: U.S. Government Printing Office, 1975).

[2] U.S. Bureau of the Census, *Current Population Reports*, Series P-20, #277, "Fertility Expectations of American Women: June, 1974" (Washington, D.C.: U.S. Government Printing Office, 1975).

[3] Mary Rowe, "Child Care: Many Options, Many Changing Patterns," unpublished paper, 1976.

[4] Lee Salk, *Preparing for Parenthood* (New York: McKay, 1974), pp. 192-93.

[5] "Child-free Couples: Parenthood Is Not for Them," *Boston Phoenix*, November 16, 1976, p. 34.

[6] Ibid., p. 38.

[7] Diana Loercher, "One Child Family Trend," *Christian Science Monitor*, June 28, 1976, p. 22.

[8] Ibid.

[9] Carolyn Bird and Barbara Ashby, "Do Working Wives Have Better Marriages?," *Family Circle*, November 1976, p. 58.

[10] Niki Scott, "Working Woman," *South Middlesex News*, October 26, 1976, p. 2C.

[11] Estelle Bond Guralnick, "The Cataldo's City Oasis," *Boston Globe*, December 7, 1975, pp. 68-69.

[12] Sara Stein and Carter Smith, "Return of Mom," *Saturday Review*, April 1973, p. 37.

[13] The Public Schools of Brookline, Brookline Early Education Project, Donald E. Pierson, Director, *The Second Year of the Brookline Early Education Project*, Report, October 31, 1974.

[14] These conclusions actually came from Barbara Kaban and Bernice Shapiro, "How to Raise a Competent Child," *Harvard Magazine*, July-August 1975, pp. 14-20. Kaban was assistant director of the Harvard Preschool Project; and Shapiro was administrative research coordinator of the project. White is director of the project, and these conclusions are in his book, which had not yet been published at the time we wrote this passage.

[15] James A. Levine, *Who Will Raise the Children? New Options for Fathers (and Mothers)* (Philadelphia: Lippincott, 1976).

[16] U.S. Bureau of Labor Statistics, *Employment & Earnings*, 22, No. 4, October, 1975.

[17] Levine, *op. cit.*, pp. 126-27.

[18] Ibid., p. 71.

[19] Ibid., p. 92

[20] Ibid., p. 95.

3

DAY-CARE CENTERS

Parents in increasing numbers, with the figure now over 10 percent, are turning to group centers to provide day care for their children. The most expensive kind of other-than-mother care, if properly run, the day-care center nevertheless seems destined to provide for more and more of our children. Between 1965 and 1973 licensed day-care center spaces more than doubled, from 475,000 to about one million. At that same growth rate, the 1976 figure (for which statistics are not available) would be close to 1,200,000. Two factors account for a prediction of even greater growth in the future.

First, the grandmothers, aunts, and neighbors who could formerly be depended on to take up the slack when mothers joined the ranks of wage earners are also going back to work for a paycheck. Perhaps more significant is the fact that the center is a discrete and visible institution that lends itself more easily to government funding and government regulation than do private child-care arrangements. The increasing strength of organizations dedicated to the growth of day-care centers, the number of publications writing about them, and the proliferation of schools producing professional staff for day-care centers lend weight to the idea that, for better or worse, day-care centers are here to stay, and are accelerating as a prime method of alternate child care.

Federal- and state-supported centers, industry-based centers, university and teacher-training centers, parents' cooperatives, and private, run-for-profit centers are some of the more publicized types of centers to which parents are turning for help. It is comparatively rare to encounter a center that is not supported in some measure by state or federal funding. Even private centers reserve some facilities for needy children, paid for out of welfare funds.

It is not easy to categorize centers by location, facilities, clientele, staff training, child-teacher ratios, or indeed by any other quantifiable means. Its sensitivity to the needs of children and parents can make the most unlikely center a warm, nurturing, stimulating environment for children and families. Lack of this sensitivity can turn a center that comes out ahead on paper into a sterile, cold environment that for all its expensive facilities provides merely custodial care, nurturing neither children nor families.

We present, as impartially as possible, a reporter's view of eight typical centers. Our report includes excerpts from interviews with mothers using day-care centers for their children:

> I have two kids here at the center. My big boy, he's three, and I got one in infants, he's 11 months old. And then I got another one coming in a couple of months, you know. The center's good because they teach my kids a lot. They taught my baby how to walk, and they taught him how to eat. This summer they taught my big boy how to swim! We live in an apartment, and I don't know nobody in the apartment. And my parents are gone, and my husband's parents, they live the other side of the city, and they don't bother us none, and we don't bother them.

GOVERNMENT-SUPPORTED PROGRAMS

The Castle Square Day-Care Center is an example of a program supported by state and federal funds. Castle Square has been in operation since the late 1960s. It is located in Boston's South End, on the ground floor of a large housing complex, and cares for 100 children aged from three months to five and one-half years. The children are divided into three groups: 20 infants cared for by 7 teachers, 32 toddlers with 12 teachers in two rooms, and 48 preschoolers with 10 teachers. Six of the teachers have their own children in the center.

As is the practice in many centers, the center hours are long—7:45 A.M. to 5:30 P.M.—and the teachers' work staggered seven-hour shifts so that during the greater part of the day, except for the overlap of shifts, the teacher-child ratio is less than that given above.

However, teacher care is supplemented by student teacher aides from Action for Boston Community Development, adults from Career Opportunities, which is a work-study program, and senior citizens. The idea of bringing together foster grandparents and foster grandchildren works well at Castle Square. The director estimates that at any one time the adult-child ratio is roughly one to three in the infant group and one to three or four in the toddler rooms.

The children receive breakfast, hot lunch, and two snacks during the day. The cost is subsidized by the State Bureau of Nutrition, and the center employs a cook and assistant cook.

The goal of Castle Square is to provide a rich environment of books and music and dance, blocks and toys, water and sand play and conversation, paper and paint and crayons, and all the materials and opportunities that are socially and educationally satisfying for this age. The child's health is stressed. Screening for lead-paint poisoning and sickle-cell anemia are two major concerns, as is dental care. Tufts Medical School handles medical and dental problems.

The infant room is large. In addition to a crib room, which is separated from the main room by a one-way window so that staff can keep an eye on sleeping babies, the room is divided into two major areas. One is for trucks, wagons, tricycles, doll carriages, running, and climbing. The other, which is carpeted, includes library and play-housekeeping corners. There are two adult rocking chairs. The double-stroller carriages, jump seats, and other equipment that one would expect to find in a room where infants and toddlers are cared for are all there.

There is also a wall kitchen with washer and dryer, range, refrigerator, and cabinets. Parents bring formulas for infants and the kitchen has a blender that is used to prepare baby foods. The staff feel that they can prepare food that is more nutritious than jarred foods.

Seventy-five percent of the families who use the center are on welfare, and most of the parents are either working or in school. As in all but private run-for-profit centers, the balance sheet doesn't balance. The center has an income of $12.66 per infant per day, against a cost of $17.58 per infant per day, for a net loss of $24.60 per child per five-day week. The amount allotted for food, for example, was frozen two years ago, and none of us need to be told how inadequate a two-year-old figure can be at present prices. The figures are no more encouraging for older children. The center takes in $14.51 per day for toddlers and pays out $21.60. For preschoolers they take in $11.18 and pay out $14.90.

In order to survive with such unbalanced figures, the center cuts corners. They have, for example, no secretarial help—a major responsibility when you consider the record keeping involved for 100 children, 29 teachers, a director, cook, and varying numbers of volunteer staffers. Filling the paperwork gap is extra duty for the social worker, who is trained to handle more pressing human problems. Teacher salaries start at $6,000 a year for apprentices, $7,500 for teachers, and $8,000 for the head teacher.

Of course, every center is different, but Castle Square is representative of solutions that some parents have found for other-than-mother care for their youngest children:

> If I had another baby, I'd want him to go to this center. My big girl was with this woman, you know, and she took care of a

couple of kids. It was just an awful place! Just a house, and it smelled bad, and my little girl kept getting sick, and she had this like skin rash all over her? And every day when I left her off she cried and cried. Of course, I'd keep my next baby home with me for the first year. That's what they teach us here at the center.

INDUSTRY-SPONSORED PROGRAMS

Stride Rite Corporation, a shoe manufacturer in Roxbury, Massachusetts, provides an industry-sponsored day-care operation in their factory. The three main objectives of their Children's Center are listed as follows in a company brochure:

1. To provide quality day care for the children of Stride Rite employees.
2. To meet [the needs of the surrounding community] for quality day care for children whose parents work or attend school.
3. To maintain a sound program geared to young children's social, emotional, physical, and intellectual needs at various developmental stages.

Stride Rite opened its center in 1971. It is one of the earliest and most successful of industry-based centers. So encouraged is management by its success that there are plans to open other Stride Rite Children's Centers in three other Massachusetts communities as well as in Maine and Missouri.

The Boston center we visited has 45 children aged 2 3/4 to 6. ("They can come as soon as they're toilet trained," one mother confided to us.) The staff included a director, two shared-time associates, one serving as assistant director-head teacher in the morning and the other filling the same two positions in the afternoon, six teachers, a work-study intern, and a cook. This staff, which includes men as well as women, is supplemented by volunteers and students from nearby high school intern projects and from teacher-training programs at local universities.

The center is located in what was formerly office space on the first floor of Stride Rite's Boston plant. The start-up cost of renovation and equipment was $25,000, but that was for the original space, which had been expanded considerably when we visited. The total area of the center is 2,337 square feet, divided into two large rooms connected by a large open hall in which the woodworking area is located, and by the kitchen, bathroom, laundry room, and storage area.

A federal program financed 75 percent of the cost of installing the kitchen, and a contract with the Massachusetts School Lunch and Nutrition Bureau provided $.78 a day per child for food. Breakfast, lunch, and morning and afternoon snacks are provided.

The Center is open from 7 A.M. to 5 P.M. each day. The children are divided into three age groups. In the mornings each group has its own activities, which could include a cooking project, drama, block building, science, math, and reading readiness. After lunch and a long nap the children are free to go to activities that particularly interest them. The long nap was disturbing to one of the parents to whom we spoke. "He sleeps the whole afternoon," she said, "and around 10 P.M., when his father and I are worn out, he's just getting started! We can't get him to sleep until after 11 sometimes!"

An indoor sandbox and the woodworking table, both of which were supervised by men, were getting most of the action during the afternoon of our visit. In the other room contented children were involved in storytime. There was a cubby corner (a small area with individual compartments for each child to keep his belongings), a raised and carpeted library area, and a plant table complete with grow lights.

Stride Rite, in its brochure, says "Lunch time makes industry-sponsored day care unique. Because lunch at the center coincides with the factory break, parents can come in and eat with their children. The family atmosphere this creates is largely responsible for making the center such a positive experience." But the two mothers whom we asked said that they don't come down to the center for lunch. "I work up on the third floor with the cripples," said one, explaining quickly as she noticed our concerned faces that the cripples are damaged shoes, "and I only have a half hour for lunch, so by the time I'd get down here and back to my place, my whole lunch break would be over." "No, I don't come down" said the other. "I think he does better if he don't see me. When he sees me, he thinks it's time to go home."

One highlight for the children is their visit to the dentist. Once each week Director Miriam Kertzman gathers together eight of her "babies" and they troop off to the Pedodontic Department of the Boston University Graduate School of Dentistry, just down the street. In addition to regular dental care the children receive regular medical and mental-health care.

The Massachusetts Department of Public Welfare pays $47.75 a week per child for approximately 50 percent of the children. Employees of Stride Rite using the center pay 10 percent of their salaries. The actual cost of the center comes to $54 a week per child, with the difference paid by the Stride Rite Charitable Foundation.

For those working parents who would like to bring the data and budget of the Stride Rite operation to the attention of their own employers, the accompanying table supplies that information.

We have gone into so much detail about the Stride Rite center because *Newsweek* reported in its December 6, 1976, issue that most companies have dropped the day-care centers that they opened in the late 1960s, although Xerox had just begun an experimental, limited day-care program in one of its plants in Arizona. According to researcher Susan Beresford of the Ford Foundation, who studied 100 corporate day-care

Cash Basis

RECEIPTS	1975
Company	$31,200
Welfare	42,300
School lunch	6,900
Participants	6,000
Total	$86,400

EXPENDITURES	
Salaries	$59,000
Payroll taxes	3,300
Supplies	900
Food costs	7,700
Special services-subs	200
Depreciation	4,300
Rent	9,300
Repairs	0
Cleaning	300
Work study	800
Legal	100
Miscellaneous	1,000
Medical insurance	500
Travel	300
Mass. unemployment	3,000
Total	$90,000
Average number of children	32
Per child per week	$54.50

centers in urban settings, these centers fail because parents are reluctant to bring their children to work on crowded public transportation.

But Stride Rite has made it work. "We just come on the bus every morning and it's only a little walk from there," said one mother. Stride Rite "has found the Children's Center to be a valuable investment. Day care is undeniably an important factor in attracting and keeping desirable personnel." Stride Rite feels it has proved the feasibility and advantages of industry-sponsored care and finds programs such as the one it runs superior to either government or profit-directed centers in terms of both education and cost.

> School centers like this with their level of training—the way they train the children—the way they handle them is just beautiful. I get a lot of advice from his teachers. Things I wouldn't know what to do about. You can come and talk to the teachers anytime. Very relaxed—I love that part. If I come to pick him up at 3, I can sit down and have a conversation with his teachers. What did he do, what kinds of things is he learning, does he do this to you, how do you deal with his temper tantrums—I get a lot of advice from them. They're always willing to sit down and talk. I've never had the feeling they were pushed for time.

KLH, a Massachusetts stereo-producing subsidiary of The Singer Company, also established a factory-based center. It failed, and thereby offers an unusual success story. KLH started its center in 1968 with the best of intentions and the highest of hopes. But four years later the company was ready to close the center's doors. Management found it uneconomical, and moreover felt sure they could attract the employees they needed without offering on-site care for young children.

Community parents, on the other hand, felt that as much as management didn't need the center, they did. So they took it over. In 1972 the KLH Child Development Center incorporated. Every parent with a child in attendance becomes a member of the corporation. Together they elect the executive director and have a voice in all policy decisions.

On our visit 60 children, aged 2 1/4 to 6 years, were attending the KLH center, which differs from other centers in two interesting areas. First, there is a city-approved kindergarten at the center. This allows children to have their kindergarten experience in the same full-day-care environment that is already familiar to them. Second, by virtue of the fact that the center is housed in a building owned by the Jewish Community Center, the children's hot lunch is kosher. "We observe the dietary laws by all becoming vegetarians while we're here," the director told us cheerfully.

Welfare funds paid the tuition of 54 of the 60 children—$48 per week per child. The money to support the center comes from the state, and center employees have found the state a harder taskmaster than was KLH. "The company was more understanding of the cost of living, and that was reflected in higher salaries than the state authorizes," we were told. Whereas the company had paid the director $15,000 a year, the director now earns $11,000 a year, and that salary has been frozen at that level for three years. Teachers have been frozen at the $7,200 level, whereas in 1972 the company had paid them $8,000 a year.

The staff's lives have been made a little easier by two center-paid benefits—membership in the Harvard Community Health Plan and basic life insurance coverage.

> Me? Oh, I work. In Congo Creations. That's an African boutique. I like work. I been working ever since I was 16 years old. I stopped for a year when the baby was born, but then I just got that *relief* to go back to work. I was going crazy when I was home. I'd feel miserable—my brain—not to talk to anybody but my child. All my friends were working. I just had to go to work. That's all there was to it. I couldn't sit there in that house, do the dishes, mop floors and wash walls and do all the things society says a woman is supposed to do!

THE COOPERATIVE CENTER

Some parents have joined together in cooperatives to solve their day-care problems. The Oxford Street Day-Care Cooperative is located in an old house in a mixed residential-university section of Cambridge. Harvard University buildings dominate the area. Harvard owns the house in which the co-op is located, donates it free of charge, and pays the cost of all utilities, as it does for four other cooperative day-care centers in the area.

The Oxford Street group began as two separate play groups. When it became apparent that day care was needed, the parents formed the one cooperative consisting of the families of 38 center children. One-third are single-parent families; eight children have their tuition paid for by welfare funds. The children range in age from three months to five years and are divided into four age groups. When we visited there were six children in the 3- to 18-month-old group, eight toddlers, ten in the 2 1/2- to 3 1/2-year-old group, and fourteen in the 3 1/2 to 5s.

There are eight staff members plus a full-time coordinator. The adult caretakers work five-hour shifts. There is no formal requirement for the staff in terms of education or certification. The parents look for warmth, stability, intelligence—for people who would care for their children as the parents would and who share their general value system.

Except in the infant group, which has two permanent teachers on each shift, each group of children has one permanent teacher and one volunteer parent on duty at a time. The two caretakers are supplemented by other parents and student teachers.

Decisions are made by vote of all members and staff. Every staff member is paid the same—$6,000 a year for a five-hour day. Each has 32 combined vacation and sick-leave days.

Costs at the co-op, even without rent or utilities, are $260 per month for each infant and $160 per month for toddlers and preschoolers. According to the coordinator, the center could not survive without the substantial support of Harvard University.

The parents work or go to school. They give four hours a week to working in the center with their children, which indicates that when they are working they are not working a regular eight-hour day. In addition to their four hours with the children, they give a certain number of hours to parent's meetings, maintenance, construction of toys and furnishings, and other chores.

I just finished a course in auto mechanics! Right! That's what I am, a mechanic! I was in college a year before my little girl was born. But I didn't want to go back. I couldn't see any results from everything I was learning. But when I learn something about a car, I can fix it, and see it work. When I'm through, something's different than when I started. Something's fixed! I guess you could say I found my match. And as for my little girl, I think that my feeling good about myself is the best thing I can do for her.

THE PRIVATE RUN-FOR-PROFIT CENTER

The Living and Learning Centers have 28 centers throughout New England, and are an example of the private run-for-profit group-care centers that began to proliferate throughout the country in the 1960s and gave rise to columnist Joseph Featherstone's much-quoted phrase, "Kentucky Fried Children," which appeared in the September 12, 1970, issue of *The New Republic*.

Living and Learning offers a nursery-kindergarten program from 9:00 to 11:30, a "CORE" program from 9:00 to 3:00, and an afterschool program from 2:30 to 5:30 that takes children up through second graders.

Their full-day child-care program runs from 7:30 to 5:30, and quotes from their brochure include such phrases as "trained, caring adults," "home away from home," "relaxed family-group time," "being comfortable together," and "time to sit-on-a-lap and get-a-hug." The brochure on curriculum covers a science component, creative arts, music/movement/rhythm, mathematics, social studies, and language development. Their stated philosophy is to develop in children a strong

"I AM" and "I CAN," and they consider flexibility a key word—a flexible program for children and flexible hours for the working mother.

The center we visited has 62 children, 25 of whom stay all day. They are divided into three age groups. The 6- to 17-month-olds are charged $45 per week, with one teacher for every four infants. The 18- to 35-month-olds are charged $40 per week, with one teacher for four toddlers. The 3- and 4-year-olds are charged $37.50 a week, with an 8-1 child-teacher ratio for the threes and a 9-1 child-teacher ratio for the fours.

Teachers are certified. Their salaries are unrevealed but were said to be very low. There are some parent volunteers on a hit-or-miss basis, but no general parent involvement because "the parents are working."

When we asked the director what she saw as the biggest problem in her center, she replied "Discipline." Another Living and Learning director added this:

> The company hires the directors, and we hire the staff. We try for comfortable, relaxed pacing during the day, with intellectually stimulating mornings and more relaxed afternoons. Some children have really had it by 2 or 3 P.M. We turn on "Sesame Street," and serve apple slices, and we quiet down—quieter lighting, quieter voices, you know, that sort of thing.
>
> We've found parent participation really doesn't work. The majority of our children are coming out of recent divorces. They have lots of adjustment problems.

The success of Living and Learning and other run-for-profit centers seems to lie in their perception of what parents need—an affordable cost, accessible location, and spoken and written reassurance that the good of the child is uppermost in the minds of the child's caretakers. The fact that the Department of Welfare has authorized attendance at Living and Learning Centers for children for whom it pays provides additional reassurance.

Largely unanswered is the question of how private centers that pay rent and/or mortgage and taxes, all utilities, and buy the food for the hot lunches and snacks they serve still end up with a profit.

My little boy, he's very smart. He started walking at seven months, and he was out of diapers at 11 months. Now they're teaching him his ABCs and his numbers. The teachers say he stays to himself. He says he don't like to go to school with babies. But he's very friendly. He's not shy like me. If someone don't say Hi to him first, he'll go up and say Hi to them. He's not scared of anything!

THE UNIVERSITY-SPONSORED CENTER

Any place where there are large concentrations of young people is a good bet for a group day-care facility. Massachusetts Institute of Technology has been running a small center since 1973. Anyone affiliated with MIT, whether as a member of the student body, the faculty, or administration, or employed in any of the hundreds of support jobs that keep a large institution functioning, is eligible to use the center for his or her children. If the center is not filled up by August a few places are opened for use by non-MIT families.

The center enrolls 20 children, aged two years nine months to five years. There are five staff members, of which two are full time and three part time. The center is open from 8 A.M. to 5:30 P.M., and there is high parent interest in its doings.

For this full-day care the center charges $48.00 per week. However, it must be remembered that rent, utilities, and janitorial costs are supplied by MIT and therefore don't enter into the center's budget. Further, MIT is not providing infant day care, which also inevitably raises costs. And, like some other industry- and business-based centers, MIT must be an inexhaustible storehouse for supplies that children can turn into playthings.

We asked the director what were her major concerns about full-day group care. She felt that funding was a serious problem, that grants to start centers, to pay for the space and the initial equipment, would be most helpful in allowing more small centers to get off the ground and start operating.

> It's a good center. But I wish I could stay home. I think it all depends on how many kids you have—right? I have enough work at home to do without needing no outside job. Boy, I'm tellin' you. By the time you get through cleanin', washin', ironin', cookin'—it's time for the kids to come home, right? You have to have time with them. I would like to stay home with my kids a couple of years, because we would get to know each other more and I could do more for them and make them to respect theyself [*sic*] more and get ready for the outside world too. That's the way I would feel. But I been workin' ever since my oldest was born, practically. I haven't had any choice.

THE YWCA CENTER

We have mentioned YWCA programs that provide several hours of relaxation and socialization for at-home mothers. The Virginia Howard Ehrlich Child-Care Center, at the Boston YWCA, is the oldest licensed child-care service in Boston, and gives full-time 8 A.M. to 5 P.M. day care. This center has room for 24 children, aged one to six, at any one time, and as it offers half-time care and even hourly care the total number of children served is considerably greater than 24.

Children of mothers who are working or going to school are eligible for the center on a first-come, first-served basis. A director with a graduate degree in social work and three certified teachers make up the full-time staff, which is supplemented by the usual complement of work-study students from area colleges and schools.

Facilities include three large, brightly painted playrooms, which can be subdivided, a "quiet room," and a small kitchen and an office. The center is equipped with the standard play materials, plus terrariums, a miniature ecology system, a gerbil house, and a children's library. Because it is the Y it has access to a full-size gym and a physical education staff that has long experience with toddler gym programs.

Children are given milk and snacks but bring their own lunches. The fee is $35 a week for full-day care, but aside from the fact that the center is located at the YWCA building, which saves it money, it is also supported by a grant from the Samuel Goldwyn Foundation.

> I wanted him to be around kids his own age. If a child is around his mother too much, he gets dependent. That's what happened when he was at his grandmother's. He got to be dependent on her. It's not good for him to depend on anyone but himself.

A CENTER FOR HOSPITAL EMPLOYEES

The Middlesex County Hospital in Waltham, Massachusetts, which is a chronic care facility, opened a free center on its premises to attract nurses and other staff members as employees. The center is located on the ground floor of the old Nurses' Home, which is now unused. The hospital staff takes care of maintenance. Food for breakfast and a noontime dinner comes down from the hospital kitchen. At the request of the mothers their traditional 7 A.M. to 3 P.M. shifts at the hospital were changed. They found 7 A.M. was just too early to arrive with sleepy children and so the regular daytime shift was changed to 8 A.M. to 4 P.M.

When the children come they are given cereal, juice, and milk. They have their main meal at lunch with their mothers, which means they can have a light supper at home in the evening, saving wear and tear both on the family budget and on the tired mother.

A hospital, running as it does seven days a week, has certain problems that business centers don't have, so weekend care is provided for $5 a day. In addition, schoolchildren six to ten years old are taken care of during school vacations.

> I don't understand how anyone knows what's right for a child. If everything you do is right—then why, after your child grows up—why do so many women sit back and say "Where did I go wrong?" All those years she thought she was doing what was right and what was best for the child—and then something goes wrong. And she says "Where did I go wrong?" Evidently, she doesn't feel she put her whole self into it.

CENTERS FOR FEDERAL EMPLOYEES

Day-care centers for the children of government workers are beginning to proliferate. One reason for this is undoubtedly the fact that the machinery for identifying the need and for translating that need into action is firmly in place.

The Federal Executive Board consists of the heads of all federal agencies. The Women's Opportunity Committee is part of the Federal Executive Board, and the Federal Women's Program, in turn, is one of the executive arms of the Women's Opportunity Committee. So it was the coordinator of the Federal Women's Program in Boston to whom women turned when they thought that the need for a day-care center in the John Fitzgerald Kennedy Federal Building should be explored. The questionnaire that was distributed in the Government Center area on the matter returned 324 affirmative answers to the need. Of these responses, 56 women had no children and 139 had children under six.

In June 1977 the coordinator was still looking for space, either in the JFK building itself or in one of the surrounding state and federal buildings.

Some of the federal agencies that already have day-care centers include the Office of Education and the Department of Labor in Washington, D.C., the Department of Social Security in Baltimore, the Department of Agriculture in Beltsville, Maryland, and the National Aeronautics and Space Administration in Goddard, Maryland.

> My mother and father think it's awful that I put him in a center. Well, when you start talking about changing attitudes things get jumbled up because a lot of people—even people you love—are just not willing to change how they think. If they were, then things would be a lot different. Everybody's afraid of a change. You just have to exert yourself and say "Well, maybe it's a change for the better," and if you just see some good points in it, and you don't hold back—if somebody sees you striving for something, somebody else is always willing to give you a hand. I feel if you're honestly trying to make something of yourself and honestly trying to do something, there's always somebody there that is going to help you. You just have to recognize who it is and they have to recognize your potential. You have to be ready to recognize it, too.

Now we know, in rough at least, who is watching the children these days, and we have a good idea about why people and organizations other-than-mother are doing that watching.

But how is all this alternate care affecting the children? And, if one is lucky enough to have the ability to choose, is there one way that is better than another? To help to answer these questions, to be able to choose that style of alternate child care that fits particular needs, to understand how alternate care may affect the future of our society, is the purpose of the rest of this book.

4

PRIMATE TIME

More than once, in the course of our research for this book, we have attended lectures on day care given by renowned authorities in the field, and sat with other people who were anxious to know what effect day care could be expected to have on young children. And as often as our hopes were raised, our expectations were dashed. We learned, for example, that both home-reared and day-care-reared three-month-olds will cry if their mothers dump them in a strange room and ostentatiously leave. Or we learned the square footage per child that is considered just right for the size of a day-care center. Never did we hear anything that would help us—or the young marrieds in attendance—in deciding whether or not a very young child should be placed in day care, and if so, what kind.

So we understand the impatience of readers who are now offered a chapter on animal research when what they are interested in is children.

Why do we turn to animal research for answers? Because there *are* no answers about what will happen in the long run to group-reared children or to their parents. No studies have been made in the United States of day-care-reared children to see what kinds of adults they have become. No such long-term research has been done. We are forced back upon Samuel Butler's nineteenth-century dictum, "Life is the art of drawing sufficient conclusions from insufficient premises." This best-guess method is a procedure very familiar to parents who learn early and late that parenthood is a career of best guesses; who know, for instance, that they should call the doctor when the baby is sick but wonder if *this* baby is *that* sick; or who accept the fact that teenagers must be allowed increasing independence but wonder if *this* teenager is ready for *that* much independence.

This chapter, then, is an attempt to familiarize you with some animal studies that have been made. From these insufficient premises we shall try to draw the sufficient conclusions that are being called for in our lives.

A great deal of research has been done on animals and their young. Often the animals behave as we would in similar situations—in so many ways, in fact, that we are forced to the conclusion that perhaps we have something to learn from them. While some may look on animal studies as a poor substitute for studies on humans, this hardly is the case. In fact, and especially in the study of instinctive behavior, animal subjects offer the great advantage of being culture-free—free from the shoulds, dos, and don'ts with which society burdens humans.

Researchers have long believed that animal studies are pertinent to the way humans behave. They look at the biological ladder on which every living organism can be found and they identify certain attributes common to both man and other species. From this evidence researchers deduce that we may have other attributes in common which are not so readily seen.

On this biological ladder we belong, at bottom, to the kingdom Animal; then to the phylum Chordata, which includes all animals that have a nerve chord and stiffening structure on the back; then to the subphylum Vertebrata, in which the stiffening structure along the back is divided into units called vertebrae that form the backbone; then to the class Mammalia, almost all of whom give birth to live young and nurse them on milk provided by mammary glands; then to the order Primate, which includes men, apes, monkeys, lemurs, and tarsurs; then to the family Hominoidea, made up of men and apes; then to the genus Homo, man; and finally to the species Sapiens, wise.

So when we talk about rats and mice, with which none of us is particularly anxious to claim relationship, we are already talking about fellow members of the animal kingdom who have nerve cords and stiffening structures along the back, as we do, which stiffening structure is divided into vertebrae, as is ours, and who give birth and nurture their young just as we do. The same set of likenesses applies to cats and dogs, and when we get to the monkeys, where the most dramatic research has been done on maternal deprivation, we come to a species so like ours that the youngest visitor to the zoo grasps the similarities immediately.

This concept of man as animal is not new, but continues to meet as much resistance in some quarters today as it did when Darwin originally presented it. Urie Bronfenbrenner tells us:

> In actual practice, science is less concerned with absolutes than with probabilities. This is particularly true for research on human behavior, where crucial experiments, even when they can be formulated, often cannot be carried out for ethical reasons. Under these circumstances, if an investigator can demonstrate that a given relationship or process operates (or fails to operate) in a phylogenetic series approaching *Homo Sapiens*, and the relevant characteristics of their analogues are present for the human species *we must then entertain the probability that the given process operates (or fails to operate) in man. At the very least, the burden of proof for demonstrating that man is the exception surely lies with the sceptic* [emphasis supplied].[1]

If we accept the idea that what we learn from animals may tell us something about ourselves, on what particular animal experiences should we center our interest? The adverse effects of deprivation, the existence of particularly critical periods in development, and the need for close physical contact are three areas that deserve our attention.

Studies of deprivation are especially instructive. When animals are kept from experiencing in early life conditions they would normally experience, they grow up the worse for it. It doesn't matter whether they are, as in the case of rats, mice, and cats, kept from food and water, or whether, as in the case of dogs and the more highly developed animals like monkeys, kept from maternal contact or contact with peers. The resulting distress produces symptoms that are remarkably similar. The animals who are deprived as youngsters tend to grow into adults who are abnormally anxious, hyperactive, disorganized, and vulnerable to stress. They have a heightened desire for that of which they were deprived at an early age and a decreased interest in activities that are not related to the early deprivation.

Then there are critical periods in a young animal's life during which he is more vulnerable to deprivation than he is at other times; there are even some deprivations that affect older animals more than very young ones.

Finally we learn that a lack of tender, loving care—"contact comfort," as psychologists describe it—takes a toll on animals as surely as it does on man.

ADVERSE EFFECTS OF DEPRIVATION

The experiments begin with rats and mice who are deprived, after weaning, of food and water. As anyone who has tried to stay on a diet can confirm, the deprived animals develop an unusually strong desire to *get* the missing food or water. And getting food or water remains an abnormally strong drive even in their adult lives, long after the deprivation experiment. These results are the same as those observed in rats who came from large litters. Having to scramble for sustenance from birth, they retained food as their primary focus, and as adults were observably anxious, overactive, and less exploratory in their behavior than were rats from smaller litters.

Early weaning in cats produced symptoms of distress similar to those noted in the deprived rats—random, generalized activity, persistent but disorganized attempts to get food, aggressive but unsuccessful competition for food, little tendency to share food, general anxiety, and more fear and suspicion.

The same distress was shown by puppies who were forcibly weaned at four weeks. Denied the opportunity to suck, they engaged in more nonnutritive sucking, were very restless, and avoided contact with their litter mates and fought with and snarled at them. (Have you ever tried to live with someone who was giving up cigarettes?) It is with the puppies that we begin to see the distress resulting from separation from mothers:

> It would appear as if the young animal had gradually developed some kind of attachment, or at least adaptation to its early environment—especially the mother—so that removal from this environment evokes not only increased activity but also strong emotional disturbance.[2]

The phrase "adaptation to its early environment" deserves our notice because the concept of attachment of infant to mother causes great controversy among developmental psychologists. Some say that attachment is the very cornerstone of human development. Others say "Nonsense!" with all the articulate authority that a Ph.D. can muster. But even those who deny the concept of attachment to a mother figure *do* allow for the habituation of the infant to a unique physical and emotional environment and its consequent distress when this environment changes.

At any rate, it seems plausible that there is a natural progression from the purely physical need for food and water to the emotional need for the maternal figure who has become either the object of attachment for the more slowly maturing infant or a secure part of its environment.

CRITICAL PERIODS IN DEVELOPMENT

Animal research also indicates that, beyond the lasting adverse effects of deprivation, there are sensitive or critical periods in development. When the readiness to learn and the chance to learn come at the same time, the learning will occur most successfully. Conversely, when an animal is not given the opportunity to learn when he is ready to learn, he may never learn or will learn imperfectly.

For example, a critical period occurs for certain birds immediately after hatching. The phenomenon is known as imprinting. Newborn goslings and ducklings naturally follow the first moving object they see. While this is normally the mother bird, goslings and ducklings have been imprinted experimentally to a box pulled by a string, a balloon, or the experimenter himself. Obviously, the mother duck has more to teach a duckling about becoming a duck than has a cardboard box, and so it is to the duckling's advantage that the moving object that he sees at this critical stage in his development is the mother duck.

The existence of sensitive or critical periods in animals has a human parallel. John Bowlby, speaking of young children, said:

> The organization of perceptual and behavior patterns appears to pass through critical phases during which these patterns are highly plastic and after which they become comparatively rigid.
> There is good reason to think that something similar occurs in regard to social perception and social responses. Children of between six months and three years who are separated from their mothers often undergo intense emotional experiences of rage and despair and then proceed to organize their social relations on a new pattern; often one in which no particular human being is sought after and loved. It would appear that if this new and psychopathic organization is permitted to consolidate at

around the same age of three or four years, it tends to become permanent.

Clearly, this "setting" of the perceptual and behavioral patterns in the third and fourth years of life must have as its base important maturational changes in the physiology and anatomy of the brain. . . . My own guess would be that the cerebral centers concerned complete their basic patterns of growth at this time and thenceforward do not change greatly in their general organization.[3]

There is also a suggestion that mature human beings have critical periods. Dr. Lee Salk thinks that human mothers may pass through a critical period immediately after giving birth. (Those mothers who recognize that they did indeed enter a critical period after giving birth and who are still waiting in hope after 15 to 20 years for that critical period to pass are not reading this in the proper spirit of gravity.) In any event, Dr. Salk's research indicates that whereas the great majority of mothers hold their children on their—the mother's—left side, next to their hearts, irrespective of whether the mothers are right- or left-handed, this preference for the left does *not* appear in mothers who have been separated from their babies for the first 24 hours after birth. Says Dr. Salk:

These results suggest that the time immediately after birth is a critical period during which the stimulus of holding the infant releases a certain maternal response. This process may have some resemblance to the phenomenon of imprinting in birds and mammals.[4]

THE NEED FOR CONTACT COMFORT

We can learn a great deal from animal research about the need for contact comfort. For all of our flaunted freedom in sexual matters, we are a society with such a strong touch-me-not ethic that most of us go through life encased in invisible armor. We shake hands with strangers, a vestigial remnant of a long-forgotten humanity, but if the stranger becomes a friend we may share a lifelong intimacy without ever again so much as brushing up against him, even accidentally. And yet the evidence is strong that in all members of the animal kingdom the comfort received from the sense of touch is crucial to healthy mental, physical, and emotional growth.

Ashley Montagu makes a strong case for the importance of this contact comfort. In his book *Touching* he summarizes experiments and observations with cows, horses, dolphins, rats, woodchucks, lambs, goats, hens, dogs, langurs, and baboons, all of which show positive effects from the early licking, caressing, and skin stimulation that the animal mother gives to the infant. These positive effects include the beginning of function of the genitourinary and gastrointestinal tracts, more activity, less fearfulness, greater ability to withstand stress, greater resistance to physiological damage, greater learning ability, and, for the mother, quicker recovery from childbirth.[5]

Human infants, according to Montagu, receive this early skin stimulation during the birth process, when the contractions of the uterus during the long period of labor provide the massive stimulation of the fetal skin that seems to substitute for the licking and tooth grooming of other mammals. This early stimulation "should be continued in very special ways in the period immediately following birth and for a considerable time thereafter."[6]

Contact comfort appears to be a factor that holds steady across species and is of significant importance. An experimenter named Yarrow, following this lead, studied 40 mother-infant pairs and found that the more an infant was held and cuddled, the higher the infant rated in intelligence, exploratory and manipulative behavior, ability to withstand stress, and social initiative.[7]

A LOOK AT PRIMATES

It is now time to see what man has learned about the primates, that order to which we belong along with apes and monkeys. Many studies have been done on unsuspecting monkey infants to determine the effects upon them of maternal deprivation. Since deprivation is a departure from the norm, let us look first at the behavior of primates in the wild.

Primates live in social groups that can vary in size from a few families to several hundred individuals. The group consists of both males and females of all ages from birth to maturity—"The social group usually remains stable. . . . With few exceptions, individuals spend the whole of their lives in close proximity to other familiar individuals."[8] This togetherness is most pronounced between mother and infant:

> At birth or soon after all primate infants, bar the human, cling to their mothers. Throughout early childhood they are either in direct physical contact with mother or only a few feet or yards from her. Mother reciprocates and keeps the infant close to her. As the young grow older the proportion of the day when they are in direct contact with mother diminishes and the distance of their excursions increases; but they continue to sleep with her at night and to rush to her side at the least alarm.[9]

If we translate the above to rhesus monkeys, with whom much of the experimental work has been done, we are talking about a life span of perhaps 26 years, with puberty coming at 4 and full growth at 6. Until 3 years of age for males, and longer for females, the baby remains close to its mother.

And close means *close*. The infant monkey begins to cling to its mother almost immediately after birth and is in this direct contact over 70 percent of the time until its first birthday. In its second year it is in direct contact all night and 10 to 20 percent of the day, and in sight the rest of the time. The need to be close comes from both mother and infant. If the infant begins to wander, the mother scoops it in again. But the infant is really not disposed to wander. He's a born homebody, and his mother's body is home.

Care of the young is the glue that cements the group together. Whole groups on the move will adjust their pace to a mother slowed down by a clinging infant, or one or two adult males will fall back and stay with her. Although it varies from species to species, adult males often take interest in the young, occasionally holding the infants and taking an active part in the lives of preadolescents and adolescents, whom the male grooms and keeps by his side.[10]

THE MONKEY STORY

Psychologist Harry Harlow and his colleagues at the University of Wisconsin have spent over a decade throwing a monkey wrench into this happy history. The Harlow monkeys were subjected to a number of manipulations. They were reared in total isolation, with other motherless infants, with cloth and wire dummy mothers, and with real mothers but without other infants.

Harlow's most famous experiment involved placing infant monkeys in a cage that contained two dummy mother figures. Both were rectangular in shape and monkey-sized, both had heads with roughly schematic faces—that is, discernible eyes, nose and mouth—and both were sources of food, having milk-producing nipples that protruded from the proper part of their anatomy. But one was a wire-mesh figure, while the other was covered with terry cloth and had a light bulb inside that provided a source of heat. Four babies were fed from the wire mother and four from the cloth mother. But *all* spent much more time with the cloth mother. Gradually the cloth mother assumed all—or so it seemed—of the attributes of a real mother. She served as a secure base that mediated between the infant and the world beyond. She provided nourishment and contact comfort and, more than that, a stimulus to the infants' development as they climbed, clung, and explored her features. A mother's face is a human baby's first playground, too!

If a strange object such as a windup toy bear beating a drum was introduced into the pen, the infant would rush to its cloth mother in fright, cling to her for security, peek over its shoulder at the frightening intruder, bury its head in the mother's terry-cloth body, gradually become more curious and less afraid, and begin to make short exploratory excursions toward the marching bear, retreating at intervals to replenish its stock of courage from the cloth mother figure.[11] (This description of monkey behavior would not have to be altered in a single particular to accommodate human babies.)

When monkey infants were placed in a strange playroom, their behavior was directly related to the presence or absence of the cloth mother. In her absence the infants' behavior became disturbed. They cried a lot. They crouched down, held themselves, rocked back and forth, and sucked furiously on anything that came to hand. The animals "would rush to the center of the room where the mother was customarily placed and then run from object to object screaming and crying all the while."[12] When the cloth mother was present the infants would run to her, climb aboard, and hang on tight—a response so strong that it can be depicted adequately only by motion pictures.[13] Gradually reassured, they would begin to make tentative exploration of the playroom, checking in periodically with the mother for their dose of needed security.

The wire mother provided no such security, which led Harlow and his researchers to conclude that contact comfort is the most important requirement for the formation of an infant's attachment to its mother—more important than the provision of food, which had been long thought to be the original tie of infant to mother.

All in all, the cloth-mothered babies behaved like monkey babies everywhere, and indeed like human babies everywhere, and for a while Harlow understandably prided himself on surpassing nature. He had created a mother "soft, warm and tender, a mother with infinite patience, a mother available twenty-four hours a day, a mother that never scolded her infant and never struck or bit her baby in anger."[14] Said Harlow proudly, "It is our opinion that we engineered a very superior monkey mother, although this position is not held universally by the monkey fathers."[15]

Later work, however, indicated that Harlow's pride in his well-engineered dummy mother was premature. The cloth-reared monkeys *had* been severely deprived, but it was not until the infant monkeys matured that the deprivation became apparent.

By 1962, of 60 monkeys raised on cloth mothers, not one male had mated successfully. Four females were unwillingly impregnated by normally raised males. In this group, and in other studies of mother monkeys who were themselves raised either in total isolation or on cloth figures, the motherless mothers turned out to be "hopeless, helpless, heartless mothers." They ignored their infants, hit them, bit them, and ground their faces into the floor of the cages. A chagrined Harlow came to believe that monkeys which have known no affection can never develop either normal sexual behavior or normal maternal behavior, and are bound to live out their lives as social failures.[16]

Do not mistake our point. We are not comparing day-care workers to terry-cloth-covered wire figures. We are pointing out that intelligent people can be misled by short-term observation, and that unanticipated difficulties may become apparent in maturity that are not observable in early life.

The monkey story continues. If cloth-covered monkeys cannot successfully socialize infants but can provide security and comfort, what happens if groups of infants are raised together by terry-cloth mothers? Will the infants socialize each other and develop into mature, sexually competent individuals?

Before 1965 Harlow was beginning to believe that cloth-reared monkeys *would* develop perfectly normal social and sexual behavior if they were permitted each day to play in the stimulating presence of other infant monkeys. Later findings have clouded even this hope. Research has produced contradictory results and there is still no clear evidence that infant monkeys can raise each other. Harlow wrote to Bowlby, "I am now quite convinced that there is no adequate substitute for monkey mothers early in the socialization process."[17]

How can infant monkeys learn maternal and nurturing behavior in the absence of a maternal, nurturing figure? Bronfenbrenner points out that infant-infant interaction has nothing nurturing in it,[18] an observation that will come as no surprise to anyone who has tried to keep two or three two-year-olds in the same room for any length of time and learned to settle for behavior that, far from being nurturing, is merely not destructive.

LOVE SYSTEMS

Some of the conclusions drawn by Harlow in his book *Learning to Love* will be as helpful to you as it has been to us, as he relates his animal research to human behavior. He speaks of five kinds of interactive, interpersonal love.[19] The first is maternal love, the love of mother for child. The second is infant love, the love of child for mother. The third is peer-age mate love, the love of child for child. The fourth is heterosexual love, and the fifth, paternal or father love.

Harlow believes that each love system prepares the individual for the one that follows, and that failure of any system to develop normally deprives the individual of the proper foundations for subsequent and increasingly complex love systems. The first two stages, the love between mother and child and between child and mother, provide the security and trust that enable the child to face the difficult adjustment to normal peer competition. The ability to interact with peers prepares him for the affection, rough and tumble, and competition involved in heterosexual love. This in turn paves the way for paternal love.

It is in this concept of a natural development of increasingly complex abilities that we find a partial answer to the question of what happens if an infant is never allowed to learn to be dependent on a mother figure. With lower animals the problems of lack of contact comfort and lack of stimulation seem to be paramount. As we move toward the primates in whom, because of slower maturation, learned maternal dependency becomes a very strong drive, denial of the ability to develop this dependency may fundamentally skew the development of the mature organism. Harlow suggests that by removing the first two steps—mother-infant love and infant-mother love— we weaken seriously the ability of subsequent steps to develop as they should. And in fact, Bowlby tells us that children who are subjected to early maternal deprivation find it difficult to make lasting emotional attachments as they mature into adolescents and adults.[20]

What have we learned from animal behavior that may be pertinent to an investigation of day care? Animals need to behave in certain ways, and if these needs are not met, particularly in their early lives, the course of their future development is uncertain. An intimate relationship between mother and baby is the most basic of these needs and becomes more important as one moves up the developmental ladder. The effects of this relationship extend to future generations.

While we know beyond question that human intelligence can work to improve the human condition—God helps those who help themselves, we say—we are no longer as boundlessly confident as we were a generation back that with every new discovery we are lighting another candle to illuminate the darkness. It has become sadly apparent that, all unknowing, we may instead be starting the conflagration that will destroy us. Rachel Carson, in *Silent Spring*, made us very aware of the interdependent nature of our world and the way in which disruption of any part of it may have unforeseen and unwanted consequences.[21]

Understanding this, it is time to look at Man. We can follow the same basic course that we did with the monkeys. What happens to mother and baby when they remain together? What happens to them both when they are separated? And, a problem with which the monkeys cannot help us, what then may we expect to happen when infants are placed in full-time day care?

NOTES

[1] Urie Bronfenbrenner, "Early Deprivation in Mammals: A Cross-Species Analysis," in Grant Newton and Seymour Levine, eds., *Early Experience and Behavior* (Springfield, Ill.: Charles C. Thomas, 1968), pp. 627-28.

[2] Ibid., p. 640.

[3] John Bowlby, from 1951 Oxford Conference on Mental Health, quoted in Muriel Beadle, *A Child's Mind* (Garden City, N.Y.: Doubleday, 1970), p. 62.

[4] Lee Salk, "The Role of the Heartbeat in the Relations between Mother and Infant," *Scientific American*, May 1973, p. 29.

[5] Ashley Montagu, *Touching: The Human Significance of the Skin* (New York: Columbia University Press, 1971), pp. 11-21.

[6] Ibid., p. 63.

[7] Leon J. Yarrow, "Research in Dimension of Early Maternal Care," *Merrill-Palmer Quarterly*, 9 (1963), pp. 101-14.

[8] John Bowlby, *Attachment and Loss*, vol. 1 (New York: Basic Books, 1969), p. 62.

[9] Ibid., p. 184.

[10] S. H. Barnett, *Apes and Monkeys: Social Behavior* (New York: Harper & Row, 1971), p. 61.

[11] Harry F. Harlow, "The Nature of Love," *American Psychologist*, 13 (1958), p. 678.

[12] Harry F. Harlow and R. R. Zimmerman, "Development of Affectional Responses in Infant Monkeys," in B. M. Foss, ed., *Determinants of Infant Behavior II* (New York: Wiley, 1961), pp. 501-9.

[13] Harry F. Harlow, "The Nature of Love," op. cit., p. 683.

[14] Ibid., p. 676.

[15] Ibid., p. 676.

[16] Harry F. Harlow, "Love in Infant Monkeys," *Scientific American*, June 1959, pp. 68-74.

[17] John Bowlby, op. cit., p. 165.

[18] Urie Bronfenbrenner, op. cit., p. 685.

[19] Harry F. Harlow, *Learning to Love* (San Francisco: Albion, 1973).

[20] John Bowlby, *Maternal Care and Mental Health* (Geneva: World Health Organization, 1951), pp. 30-36.

[21] Rachel Carson, *Silent Spring* (Boston: Houghton Mifflin, 1962).

5

ONE PERSON—ONE VERY SPECIAL PERSON

A fervent young advocate of infant day care told us recently, in tones ringing with conviction, "There is no reason why women, any more than men, should feel tied to their babies!"

And a middle-aged mother of three adolescents, speaking from a more traditional background, a more conservative outlook, and a longer perspective, echoed her sentiments. "I think," she said, "that *anyone* can take care of a baby. The important time to be available to your children is when they're older and there can be some communication with them. That's when a mother is really needed."

Well, they're both wrong because they're proceeding on the assumption, widely held and long believed, that a newborn is essentially passive—that it eats, sleeps, and cries according to its inner dictates, and that it is unaware of its surroundings. This assumption is false.

Actually, newborns are actively engaged in learning. Researchers recognize now that they are seeing and reacting to people and objects, hearing and reacting to sounds, discriminating and reacting to odors virtually from the moment of birth. In their first four weeks they are capable of seeing complex patterns, and in fact show a preference for such patterns over solid blocks of color. An infant would rather gaze at an eyes-nose-mouth drawing of a face than at a solid black patch. Given a choice between a representative drawing of a face and one in which the features are jumbled, he'll prefer the one that most closely resembles a real face. Two- and three-*day*-old infants have been conditioned to turn their heads in response to a sound after the sound has been paired with a gentle stroking of the baby's cheek and a bottle of sweetened water. Babies have learned to turn their heads to musical tones but not to buzzers, and they have learned to reverse the response, turning to buzzers but not to tones. There is some evidence that infants respond more readily to adult female voices than to adult male voices. Certainly there is evidence that they respond more readily to higher tones than to lower tones.

So we must understand from the beginning of this discussion that we are not dealing with lovable bundles of unconscious innocence but with six or seven pounds of an already formidable intelligence that, whatever its surface appearance, is actively and determinedly engaged in making sense out of the new world in which it finds itself. Given this understanding, we can then proceed to tackle the question that concerns us. Is mother-infant intimacy only a cultural hang-up? If it is, let's do away with it and turn to the day-care centers or to other alternatives. But if, on the other hand, mother-infant intimacy is fundamental, if the way mankind rears its children and forms its values has a firm biologic and genetic base, then let us recognize *that* and work from it as we try to redesign our lives.

There are four aspects of infant development of which we must be aware when we consider other-than-mother care: symbiosis, reciprocal learning, trust, and attachment.

SYMBOSIS

Symbiosis is the bonding together of two organisms, in this case mother and child, in a relationship that is mutually beneficial. A process that does good for mother and child would not be expected to evoke brickbats and scorn, but it does. Betty Friedan, mother of three, condemns symbiotic bonding as unhealthy and unnecessary. Feminist Lucy Komisar denies the need for a close relationship between mother and infant. Germaine Greer talks about women settling down to "breed." A prolific author and lecturer, Greer is sensitive to language, and when she says "breed" we are to think of mindless, animalistic, bestial behavior.

Well, most women won't buy this particular feminist viewpoint. All over the country, future mothers and fathers are learning in childbirth classes that if they work with nature and return to older and simpler ways, both mothers and babies will be stronger and healthier, and fathers, by being supportive, will be preparing for the active role they will soon be able to assume. Prospective parents are learning that babies who are delivered naturally are more alert and less traumatized. There is a growing recognition that traditional medical practice has made birth an unnecessarily shocking experience for newborns. The air-conditioned, floodlit, cold surfaces of the delivery room stand in too sharp contrast to the warm, dark, fluid environment that the baby has known for nine months. But if babies are delivered into a quiet, well-heated, darkened room, handled gently, stroked softly, immersed in a warm bath, placed skin-to-skin on the mother's stomach, and put to nurse directly, they may even muster up newborn smiles of contentment.[1]

Doctors and nurses are telling parents that a just-delivered baby placed on its mother's stomach will squirm its way up to the mother's breast—that breast milk is sterile, comes at the right temperature, and is handily packaged. Parents learn that the best minds in the world of science have never been able to duplicate mother's milk, that this milk confers immunities to babies beyond those with which they are born, is more easily absorbed by the infant's immature digestive tract than is any substitute, and that this natural fitness of mother's milk is so dramatic in some cases that mothers' milk banks are being established in many hospitals. Doctors are reminding parents that the warmth of the mother's body, the familiar heartbeat, and the familiar voice that the baby has known for nine months in utero is uniquely soothing to the baby.

On the other hand, deprivation of mother's milk may even lead to baby's discomfort. For example, early feeding of solids is more common in bottle-fed babies and early introduction of solids seems to go along with colic.

Yes, an intimate mother-baby relationship results in an impressive list of pluses for the newborn. But a symbiotic relationship is one that is *mutually* beneficial. What are the benefits for the mother? Our prospective parents learn that there is real joy in delivering a baby rather than being painfully delivered, that the physical feeling of nursing is pleasurable, that the uterus of a nursing mother firms and contracts and returns to prepregnancy normalcy faster than the uterus of a nonnursing mother. Doctors tell parents that the return of the menstrual flow is delayed or lightened, meaning that the mother loses less iron in the early months when she needs all her strength. Animal research with application to humans has spotlighted a hormone, prolactin, in nursing mothers that makes animals with poor motherly instincts become more motherly. New knowledge indicates that pills and shots that dry up the nonnursing mother's milk contribute to increased hairiness because they contain a male hormone. Therefore doctors are returning to icebags and aspirin to relieve the discomfort of mothers who don't nurse. Evidence is building that the incidence of breast cancer is lower in women who have nursed than in those who haven't.

All in all, it is hard to deny the mutual benefits to both mother and child of a symbiotic relationship in the early months.

RECIPROCAL LEARNING

The second step, the development of a sensitive interaction between mother and child, is dependent upon their early intimacy. No professional, however well trained, will know a particular baby as well as a mother will know the infant she has cared for. And any professional, no matter how skillful, will be strange to a baby who from birth has been banking information like a miniature computer on the sights, sounds, smells, sensations, and tastes that have consistently and repetitively been part of its existence—and that have emanated mostly from its mother.

In every new interaction, mother and baby are communicating. The language may consist largely of body movement, gesture, facial expression, touching, and cries on baby's part, but it amounts to successful, extraordinarily precise communication nonetheless. The baby is saying, "I like this. It makes me feel good. I don't like that. It doesn't suit me." The mother is saying, "I understand. You can affect your life by letting me know what you want. I will, within reason and with more consistency than not, make you comfortable and happy. Certain things are predictable. When you are being fed, you will see my face. When you are being changed, you will hear my voice. What happens to you will be, by and large, comforting. There will be regularity in your life that you can count on."

A 17-year-old, wise in the ways of babies from years of baby-sitting, was called in to sit with a five-week-old. The five-week-old screamed. Nothing the sitter could do would placate that baby. An hour later the mother popped in to check on baby and sitter. "Oh, I forgot to tell you! Debby likes to be held sitting up in your lap so she can look around. And if that doesn't work, she likes to lie on the floor with her diapers off and kick her legs." When the mother returned a second time she asked, "Well, how'd it go?" "Fine," said the sitter. "She sat in my lap for a while and looked around, and when she got fussy again, I took off her diapers and put her on the floor and she's been good as gold." In a short five weeks mother and baby were communicating and reinforcing each other in significant ways.

But when an infant is placed in full-time day care, whether it is a center or care by someone other-than-mother, communication efficiency falls off sharply. The problem is a little different when the baby is cared for by a single other-than-mother than it is in the more structural setup of a group center, but the principle is the same. The first day that the mother takes her baby to the center, the mother and baby will know each other well. In a good center the staff will ask for all the mother's cues about the baby's behavior and for its special likes and dislikes. They will then transfer this information to cards that serve as initial guides to the day-care workers. But cue cards have limitations. The two cue cards shown are in use at the Demonstration Nursery Center, University of North Carolina.

While these cues are certainly more helpful to the day carers than no information at all, they are very general in nature. It is impossible to translate the important subtleties of body language, facial expressions, and cries into a communication system that can be read by strangers. And as minimal as the information is on the cue cards, the baby has even less to go on. *His* adult-to-baby cues have gone off to work with his mother. He has been dropped into a foreign country where he knows neither the language nor the customs.

But from the first day he is spending most of his awake time in the center, and a new communication network, with one adult or with many, must be built. From that first day a reversal of roles between mothers and day-care center begins to take place. Increasingly, it is the care givers who write the cue cards and pass them on to the mother. The problem here is that, while it seems likely that the center staffers will receive helpful information from the mother gratefully and without any emotional reaction, it does not seem plausible that this information exchange can take place unemotionally when the

SAMPLE CUE CARDS

CUE CARD

CYNTHIA   BIRTHDATE: 3-17-69   NURSERY DAY: 8:00–5:30

5:30–6:00	Awakes
	Breakfast—1/2 jar fruit & formula
8:00	Arrival
	Nap
10:00	Snack—offer juice or water
	Play
1:00 or 1:30	Lunch—Meat, vegetable, and fruit (about 1/3 jar each), formula
	Nap
4:00 or 4:30	Formula
5:00	Departure
	NOTES: is rocked to sleep
	hold to feed
	cries when wet
	Mother and Father left-handed

(3-month-old—long day at Nursery)

CUE CARD

ROBERT   BIRTHDATE: 12-20-69   NURSERY DAY: 7:45–4:00

6:00	Awakes
7:45	Arrival
8:00 or 8:30	Breakfast—cereal and formula
	Nap
12:00 or 12:30	Lunch—some table foods, junior foods, milk from cup
	Play
	Nap
3:00 or 3:30	Snack—fruit or juice
4:00	Departure
	NOTES: refuses early breakfast on hom. milk
	offer milk from cup
	junior foods
	cries self to sleep

(6-month-old—leaves Nursery at 4:00 P.M.)

positions are reversed. How does a mother feel about being told by strangers what it takes to comfort her baby? What happens to her sense of being special, of having more to offer her child than anyone else? Many centers complain that mothers pick up their children at the end of the day and rush home without waiting to talk to the day-care people. Is it, as the day-care centers may choose to believe, simply because the mothers are too tired and have such a full evening ahead of them before they can rest? Or is it because a mother doesn't *want* to have to learn about her child from strangers? Or because such confrontations stir a latent sense of guilt about having abandoned—part time—her inherited responsibilities for child rearing?

Whether or not a mother has any nagging doubts about her decision to go to full-time day care, there is *no* doubt that the shift of baby's dominant focus from home to day care undercuts the opportunities for mother-baby interaction. Since such opportunities comprise the raw stuff of reciprocal learning, we must assume that the quality of this learning—for both mother and child—is somehow altered and lessened by the transfer of learning responsibility from mother to others.

Having explored the potential emotional upset of mother, it is time to ask what can happen to baby's composure when a substitute stands in for Mom. Let's go back to our 17-year-old baby-sitter and young Debby. By the time Debby was seven weeks old another phenomenon became evident. Debby had developed a fussy period between 7 and 10 P.M. It was her mother's practice, all else failing, to put her to the breast, and while the baby didn't actively nurse, she did seem comforted and able to get through those hours with less distress. Enter our sitter, called in to pinch-hit while the parents took in an early evening movie and presented with a well-fed-but-beginning-to-be-fussy baby and a bottle of formula. The parents left; the baby screamed. Walking, talking, rocking, holding, singing, diapers on, diapers off, all availed nothing. In desperation the sitter warmed the bottle, sat down in the rocking chair, shifted the baby into position to nurse, and offered the bottle. The reaction? Pure rage. The baby felt for a moment that it was going to get the breast it was after. But everything was wrong. The bottle was wrong, the taste was wrong, the sitter's sweater was not the bare skin to which the baby was accustomed. The rage was unmistakable. At seven weeks, Debby had learned a lot about what to expect.

The contrast between Debby and an infant in full-time day care is striking. We have visited centers in which any one of six to eight different people may go to an infant when it cries. And they would not even be the same six to eight people all the time because, while there may be two regular caretakers, the remainder are usually students taking four-to-eight-week stints to learn about babies. Add to these six or eight interchangeable people, the natural mother on nights and weekends, the father, if available, plus a reasonable number of baby-sitters recruited to give the full-time working parents an occasional break. Can an infant awash in such a sea of adults learn as much as Debby had in seven weeks about what to expect as responses to her feelings and actions? The difference is, of course, that Debby had been dealt with "on a one-to-one basis, thus permitting frequent selective responses on the part of the reinforcing agent."[2] It is Debby's "one-to-one" experience that Urie Bronfenbrenner and other researchers hold to be *essential* in the development of learning and emotional attachment.

TRUST

If mother and infant continue in their intimate relationship in those months after birth, a third important aspect of child development takes place—the gradual growth within the baby of a sense of trust.

Dr. Erik Erikson stresses that a sense of trust is the first basic need for the development of a healthy personality. He believes that the consistent, continuing, loving behavior of a sensitive, caring person gradually becomes an inner reality and an outer predictability for the infant:

> Such consistency, continuity and sameness provide a rudimentary sense of ego identity which depends . . . on the recognition that there is an inner population of remembered and anticipated sensations and images which are firmly correlated with the outer population of familiar and predictable things and people.[3]

Erikson says that if a sense of trust has been firmly established in a child's early experience, he will more readily face new situations and overcome any initial mistrust.[4]

Note that he does not suggest that exposing a very young child to large numbers of caretakers creates a future sense of trust in large numbers of people. On the contrary, the consensus is that the experience of being raised by one mostly present, consistently loving, sensitive figure best prepares a child to function in a world in which we hope he will be at ease with many people.

Robert Coles, a child psychiatrist and author of *Children of Crisis*, puts it this way:

> We are born with the need for someone to do more than feed us. We need to be held, recognized, and affirmed. We need recognition. We need to gain another person, whose living, intimate presence in turn enables us to become distinct.[5]

And humanist Abraham Maslow tells us that the feeling of safety, which comes from trust in others and trust in oneself, is basic to the ability of a child to grow. Within each of us, he believes, there is a constant tug-of-war between safety and growth:

> Every human being has *both* sets of forces within him. One set clings to safety and defensiveness out of fear, tending to regress

backward, hanging on to the past, *afraid* to grow away from the [mother], *afraid* to take chances, *afraid* to jeopardize what he already has, *afraid* of independence, freedom and separateness. The other set of forces impels him forward toward wholeness of Self and uniqueness of Self, toward full functioning of all his capacities, toward confidence in the face of the external world at the same time that he can accept his deepest, real, unconscious Self.[6]

The importance of Maslow's views for those of us who are examining day care for under-fours lies in his conviction that "growth forward customarily takes place in little steps, and each step forward is made possible by the feeling of being safe, of operating out into the unknown from a safe home port, of daring because retreat is possible."[7] Moreover, he tells us, we on the outside have no way of knowing *when* the child is ready to take the next step forward toward self-actualization. Only the child himself can tell when the impulses to grow are stronger than the need to be safe.

So we ask the experts in affect and cognition: How does this relate to day care? How does a young child retreat to the safety of a mother who is halfway across town? What does management know about a particular child's ability to make it on his own when it lays down decrees about three-month maternity leaves? If a child is placed in a center with many caretakers, on what does he build his sense of safety and trust?

From the experts we hear an answer. The child learns to trust in both his mother *and* the center. But certainly we may presume that his learning to trust in his mother must be circumvented somewhat by the fact that for nine hours a day, five days a week, 50 weeks a year, she isn't there. And his growth of trust in any particular person at the center will, sooner or later in this peripatetic society, be checked by this particular person's sudden, unexplained, and permanent departure. Of course he can trust the center itself—a place, an organization, a staff, a routine. But his trusting experience will be different from that of a young child who spends most of his time in his mother's care. And he may grow into a different adult.

ATTACHMENT

The symbiotic relationship, the reciprocal give-and-take learning, the building of a sense of trust have all been leading to our discussion of the phenomenon of attachment, one of the most controversial subjects in child research. There are many definitions of attachment. This one is representative:

> Attachment is a process by which the child becomes passionately loving of the mother or other main caretaker and devotes uniquely powerful energy to retaining visual and auditory contact with her, shows severe disorganization and emotional distress at separation, and ultimate joy at reunion.[8]

Most mothers are aware of the seemingly sudden onslaught of attachment, although they may not give it a name. But when a mother's friendly, amiable baby, who previously greeted friends and strangers with equal delight, suddenly, in the second half of his first year, turns peevishly suspicious and becomes happy once more only in his mother's arms, a mother knows *something* has happened.

Researchers have isolated a number of specific behaviors that indicate that attachment is developing or has taken place. There is, first of all, a preattachment phase:

> [This phase] begins at birth and occupies the first few weeks of life. From the very beginning the infant is disposed to respond more readily to stimuli within certain ranges than to others, and there is much evidence to support the proposition that the stimuli to which he is most responsive tend to emanate from

other members of the species, and perhaps especially from adult females.[9]

Confirmation of this view comes in a striking experience reported by Dr. T. Berry Brazelton:

> We examined a two-pound premature baby . . . who had been on the respirator for about six weeks and had made no effort to try to live on its own. We wondered whether he wasn't severely brain-damaged. We made an experiment. I took the baby in my hands . . . and I talked to him. The baby . . . turned his head to my voice. Everybody began to gasp. Then I asked a nurse with a high-pitched voice to stand facing me on the other side of the baby. We both talked to him. He seemed to make a decision. He frowned and turned to the female voice three times. By then, everybody believed in him and was ready to fight for him. [He demonstrated] an ability we now know babies have at birth, to make very fine choices and to attach to a female voice.[10]

As the infant matures he shows other signs of attachment. He cries, smiles, and vocalizes differently in his mother's presence than in her absence, implying that he has learned to discriminate his mother from other people and that he responds differently to her. He follows her with his eyes and twists his body to keep her in sight. He cries when his mother leaves the room and follows her if he can. He scrambles over the mother, exploring her face, hair, and clothes. He buries his face in his mother's body. He uses his mother as his secure base and will explore from her, but is distressed if his mother leaves him. He clings to his mother, most noticeably when frightened. He lifts his arms in greeting or spontaneously claps his hands when his mother comes to him.[11] These behaviors were observed in a study of mothers and fathers in a remote village in Uganda, and if you in your tenth-floor apartment in New York or in your farmhouse in Iowa recognize them as behaviors you have observed in infants you have known—and you will—then babies will be recognized to be, in this regard, as culture-free as the monkeys, who behave in the same ways, too. Whether human or anthropoid, a primate infant is a primate infant.

Attachment is of a one-to-one nature and, given current interest in multiple mothering both inside and outside day care, the seriousness of diluting this one-to-one relationship should be understood:

> Regardless of the system of infant-rearing common in a given society, it seems entirely likely that the infant himself is innately monotropic—that is, he tends to attach himself primarily to one specific figure, although he may well subsequently extend his attachments to other supplementary figures. . . . If the human infant is innately monotropic, then a situation . . . which impedes monotropic attachment will distort the normal course of development.[12]

How much time together is necessary for a healthy attachment to be formed between mother and baby? No one really knows. No one suggests, to carry the situation to its ultimate absurdity, that *one* really great, super-quality interaction between an infant and an adult will suffice. Instead we gather that a "sufficient" number of interactions is required. We are on our own if we have to decide whether an hour in the morning and an hour at night and parts of weekends is sufficient. Perhaps it is and perhaps it isn't.

We can be sure that when reliable long-term studies on the amount of interaction necessary to develop attachment are done, they will be able to tell us only that the particular babies studied needed X amount of interaction on average to attach. And we will be left with our own very individual baby and have to ponder just how much interaction he will require after we have factored in his personality and ours.

Having explored the nature of attachment, the signs of its existence, and what is necessary for its development, we must then ask perhaps the most important question of all. *Why* should a baby in this transient world of ours attach? Does it matter? Most researchers think it does.

First, attachment seems to be a basic need. Babies *will* attach to someone or something. If a permanent mother figure isn't available, babies will attach to physical objects such as toys or blankets, or to rooms, peers, or groups. Often they will do this even when the permanent mother figure is there, as we all know. But attach to something or someone they will. Only in unfortunate infants who have made an attachment to one figure and have seen that figure disappear from their lives, then made a second attachment only to have *that* person also disappear, and who gradually learn to invest less and less of themselves in relationships that they begin to understand are not going to last and are going to give them pain, do we see infants who give up, make no effort to attach further, and grow into affectionless, detached adults.

Second, the attachment of a baby to a single adult is tied to the very survival of humanity. Attachment hits the baby at just about that time in his development when his physical ability would otherwise allow him to get away from his mother, and perhaps into deep, irreversible trouble. In that period, from 6 to 18 months, when his locomotive skills are such that he may creep, crawl, or toddle out of an unwary mother's sight, attachment dictates that he is unwilling to get very far out of mother's range. So attachment acts as a protective device to insure the baby's safety—and mankind's survival. We must remember the behavior of infant monkeys who, in strange and fascinating situations, would explore out from their mothers very tentatively, then tag back in for security before venturing out again, no matter how great the outside attraction. Human babies do the same.

Those mothers of perpetually lost children who turn their back on their toddler for a minute when they take him outside and then are heard throughout the neighborhood calling for their vanished child may find this idea of attachment a little difficult to believe. It is not that their wandering child is unattached. His spatial perceptions are not yet developed, and a stray cat or an intriguing noise may draw him away without his realizing that mother is getting out of immediate reach.

Most significant, the attachment of infant to mother is the first of three major attachments that most people make in a lifetime. If this first attachment is warm, stable, and deeply satisfying, the child grows into an adult who is disposed to look for the same warm, stable, and deeply satisfying relationship in maturity. Given the sexual drives of adolescence and early adulthood, this second deep attachment is to a mate. And then such securely mated adults are able to attach deeply to their own children, forming a new and strong family. Of this process comes the strong cement of our society.

Cynics may believe the foregoing is our remembrance of things past. But for those who want rescue from the current cynicism about fickle male-female relationships, we quote Lawrence Fuchs of Brandeis:

> A species which has survived through learning and not by instinct can ill afford to forget its past. The distinguishing characteristics of human families—helpless children dependent on their mothers, long-term sexual bonding between adults who are dependent on each other, and a large-scale investment of energy by fathers in feeding and protecting the young—are what have made human families human.[13]

Those who believe that it is time to throw away mother-infant bonding and the parenting of our own children and turn to a kind of community parenting—those who feel that in narrowly concentrating on me and mine the world has done poorly—had better understand that we will then be challenging not *the way things have always been*, which many of us would like to change, but *the way we are biologically programmed*—and that's a lot more dangerous to tamper with. Put it this way. A student of karate does not try to block an onrushing force of superior strength and oppose to it an immovable object. He steps aside and directs the irresistible force to his own ends. We will do better if we understand the irresistible forces within human primates and then direct them gently but firmly in ways we wish them to go.

In the face of the volumes of work that emphasize the importance of attachment to the entire human species, we naturally find day-care centers insisting that *their* infants are attached, both to their mothers at home and to the day carers in the center. But how do the day-care people *know* this? Dr. Ainsworth, who authored the Ganda study of attachment, tells us that a baby who cries when his mother leaves the room, and follows her if he can, is demonstrating his attachment to her.[14] Not so, says Dr. Kagan, equally eminent psychologist whose work we will detail later. Crying is simply a matter of the baby's developing cognitive ability—ability to understand a new situation and resolve it. The baby, says Kagan, cries because he is beginning to ask questions but is not yet able to answer them. A situation that is different from the one he is used to frightens him.[15]

Dr. Kagan tells us that his research has not made clear what attachment is, but he is sure that "separation protest" is *not* a measure of attachment. Perhaps it isn't. The fact remains that babies between the ages of 6 and 18 months often indicate, by crying, a great deal of distress when their mothers leave them. Whether the baby cries because he is attached or because he has not yet developed the ability to understand what is happening, is he not in either case frightened, anxious, lonely? Dr. Kagan is dealing with the clinical causes of the crying. While this is certainly an interesting question to explore, we are concerned with the *long-term* development of a baby who, whatever the cause, is made deeply uncomfortable day after day. It is frightening, even devastating, for an adult to be in a situation so foreign to him that he has no clues from his past experience on the way to handle it. So why should we subject our vulnerable infants to that which is intolerable to us?

How, then, do day-care people measure attachment? We don't know. We do know that appearances can be deceiving. If an eight-month-old baby parts from his mother happily in the morning and from his day-care center happily at night, is this an indication of his security and of his developing independence and cognitive ability, or is it simply an indication of a lack of attachment? If a baby cries and generally seems distressed when his mother drops him off at the center and greets her with great joy when she returns, is this a sign of his emotional health because it shows he has made a strong attachment? If he is that strongly attached to his mother, what is happening to him during the nine-hour separation, day after day, week after week? On the other hand, has our first baby, who travels back and forth as happily as a little commuter car, perhaps made a dual attachment to a mother and to an institution? Most of our authorities insist that, left to his own devices, a baby will make *one* strong attachment. Well, to whom has this cheerful baby made his? When he holds out his arms for his mother when she dashes in to get him at 5:30 P.M., is that a sign of attachment? Or is it habituation, a secure part of his daily routine, and does it have nothing to do with attachment?

When we are told that a baby who gets hysterical at his mother's departure is really on the road to a healthy emotional maturity and that a baby who couldn't care less whether she's there or not is considered to be at emotional risk, what are we to make of babies who seem to have made happy, healthy adjustments to full-time day care? We don't know yet. But over and over again in the literature this theme is struck.

> Finally we have the need for every child to become the recipient of emotional investment of significant persons. Particularly in infancy the baby needs one person of special significance to him, one on whom he depends for his security in a world which is otherwise chaotic and formless. Once he has such a person, he is upset at losing her. In fact, we are worried if the child is not threatened by the loss of one so vital to his sense of well-being. If he is "promiscuous," forming superficial attachments to any adult who comes, we believe that the child has missed an essential experience.[16]

Of course this state of affairs does not go on forever. While the child's tie to his mother remains strong during the first three years of life, by about the third birthday most children show a new ability to accept temporary separations from their mothers. This is due to the fact that at three a maturational threshold *has* been passed, and the child has a better ability to understand events in the world around him. A three-hour separation does not evoke the doomsday feeling of forever. The trust that his mother's presence afforded him in the past has become so strongly internalized that the three-year-old is able to separate with less anxiety. That is why early childhood educators who believe in the value of good nursery-school experience strongly question the value of day care for children under three. We even question day care for children over three. There is an enormous difference between 9 to 15 hours a week in nursery school and 45 hours a week in day care, even for children of three and four.

In a well-run, carefully staffed infant day-care center a visitor will find bright, healthy, cheerful children, sociable and responsive. But we suspect that these bright, healthy, cheerful children are going to be *different* adults than they would have been had they been brought up at home in a healthy, caring, competent family. Our look at group care in other societies in the next chapter will make that plain. Children seem infinitely adaptable. But they pay a price for their adaptation and it is up to us to see that we exact only that price and ask for only that degree of adaptation that will free them to grow into strong, confident, loving, and trusting adults.

NOTES

[1] Frederich LeBoyer, *Birth Without Violence* (New York: Knopf, 1975).
[2] Urie Bronfenbrenner, *Two Worlds of Childhood, U.S. and U.S.S.R.* (New York: Russell Sage Foundation, 1970), p. 135.

[3] Erik H. Erikson, *Childhood and Society* (New York: Norton, 1950), p. 247.

[4] Erik H. Erikson, quoted in Henry Maier, ed., *Three Theories of Child Development* (New York: Harper & Row, 1965), pp. 31-74.

[5] Robert Coles, *Erik H. Erikson, The Growth of His Work* (Boston: Little, Brown, 1970), p. 287.

[6] Abraham Maslow, *Toward a Psychology of Being* (Princeton, N.J.: D. Van Nostrand, 1962), p. 46.

[7] Ibid., p. 49.

[8] Robert R. Sears, "Attachment, Dependency and Frustration," in Jacob L. Gewirtz, ed., *Attachment and Dependency* (Washington, D.C.: V. H. Winston, 1972), pp. 18-19.

[9] John Bowlby, *Attachment and Loss*, vol. 1 (New York: Basic Books, 1969), p. 106.

[10] T. Berry Brazelton, "Babies to the Rescue," *Harvard Magazine*, December 1974, pp. 15-16.

[11] Mary D. Ainsworth, "Ganda Study," in "Patterns of Attachment Behavior Shown By the Infant in Interaction With His Mother," the Merrill-Palmer Quarterly, 1964, vol. 10, p. 15-16.

[12] Mary D. Ainsworth, "Review of Findings," in *Deprivation of Maternal Care: A Reassessment of Its Effects* (Geneva: World Health Organization, 1962), p. 147.

[13] Lawrence Fuchs, *Family Matters* (New York: Random House, 1972), pp. 194-95.

[14] Ainsworth, "Ganda Study." in "Patterns of Attachment Behavior," Merrill-Palmer Quarterly, 1964, Vol. 10, p. 15-16.

[15] Jerome Kagan, from our taped interview, April 4, 1973.

[16] Laura Dittman, ed., *Early Child Care* (Chicago: Aldine, 1968), p. 9.

6

GROUP CARE IN OTHER SOCIETIES

The belief that other countries have found ways of raising their children successfully in groups is dear to the hearts of some day-care center advocates. But upon close examination, group care presents a mottled picture—one that we may well not be able to buy and would not choose to if we could. In this chapter we will be looking at Israel, Russia, and China. In chapter 8, we will turn to Sweden, which is being closely examined today as a model for expanding day-care centers in our society.

First we must understand that what works in other societies may not work for us. Paul de Florac, a contemporary of Balzac, cautioned, "Do not adopt our institutions halfway," and it remains true today that one society cannot pick a jigsaw puzzle piece from another society and place it into its own national life with any expectation that it will fit. Every society, even one so seemingly diverse as ours, has a history, goals, and a character that set it apart from others:

> Every society, as it brings up the next generation, presents the child at each step of his growing up with the particular demands flowing from the way of life particular to that society. These demands reach the child through the attitudes he encounters in the persons who take care of him most—attitudes that both

enable and compel him to solve the problems brought on by his development. And by problems are meant the repeated crises between personal endowment, aspiration, and what his society permits and requires. The very way he resolves these crises brings him closer and closer to becoming a viable and effective member of that society.[1]

In the United States we have evolved a society that is peculiar to us in its emphasis on aggressive, individualistic, independent behavior. So accustomed are we to these national characteristics that it comes as a shock to learn how different our way of life is from that of others. In many countries cooperation, socialization, and dependency are the goals. In India, Japan, Nigeria, and Uganda, infants are born into large families or tribes, closely mothered and protected, raised to live with, depend on, share with, take part in, put up with. Formal group care of infants is unnecessary because each family or tribe provides a naturally selected group of its own.

A Filipino child, for example, is brought up in a one-room house with many brothers, sisters, aunts, and uncles. He may never sleep alone in the course of his whole life. Much of his growing up involves learning to live with this togetherness. Success or failure is family success or family failure, never sought after and never achieved by an individual:

> From childhood he learns to enjoy being taken care of and realizes that he can make others happy by being dependent on them. There is no age when a child is expected to leave home nor an age when he is expected to become fully self-reliant.[2]

Our goals and life styles have another orientation entirely. Think for a minute about how we feel about married children settling down permanently with their parents, or aging parents moving in with their grown children, or 35-year-old bachelors who have never left home. For better or worse, our goal is to enable our children to grow into a maturity that is independent of us, and to mature ourselves into an old age independent of them.

When we study the day care for children in the U.S.S.R. and China and in the kibbutzim of Israel, we find the disparity between their goals and ours equally striking. There is, however, one important difference between growing up grouped in these first three of our model countries and group upbringing in societies like India, Uganda, and the Philippines. In these latter societies group upbringing is of ancient lineage, closely woven into the fabric of their history and daily living. But in the U.S.S.R., China, and the kibbutzim, it is a patch job, self-consciously stitched onto life styles that have been frayed and torn by horrendous experience. The countries at which we are most often asked to look for inspiration are countries in which group care, as a matter of pragmatic necessity and political philosophy, has been enforced by dictate, fiat, or vote—countries or peoples whose immediate past history had been so unbearable that just about everyone involved was willing to wrench his or her life from its foundations and start anew. The Union of Soviet Socialist Republics set a goal of fashioning "the new Soviet man" from the debased serf of Tzarist Russia. Communist China has seized every opportunity to lift its 800 million out of age-old poverty, inequity, slavery, starvation, disease, and corruption. The classless kibbutzim, Israel's communally run agricultural and industrial communities, were founded by the idealistic children of the ghettoized, persecuted Jews of turn-of-the-century Europe.

In each of these communal ventures the goal was to produce children who put the group ahead of the individual, a goal for which group care is uniquely suited. And in each of these societies there was total top-to-bottom agreement on the way the children should be raised. In the kibbutzim the agreement came by vote of all members of the kibbutz, to which all members thereafter subscribed. In the Chinese commune and the Russian collective Chairman Mao or the Soviet hierarchy dictated. But in all three cases infants were born into what Bettleheim has called a "community of consensus." Trained caretakers might be multiple in number but they were as one in their goals, the values they held, and the methods they used to raise the children.

However, homogeneity is not what most Americans have in mind for their children. We don't have a "community of consensus." On the contrary, we parents would have trouble in finding even one other family of our acquaintance that values discipline and permissiveness in quite the same degree as we do, whose goals for their children are the same as ours, one other family to whom we could entrust the care of our children, if the need arose, with complete confidence that they would raise our children exactly as we would. Rather than a community of consensus, we have an agreement to disagree, a national commitment to diversity.

We could, of course, with modest training produce child carers who, as a group, would espouse the same goals. But the problem of matching the professionals' goals to those of the parents is not so easily solved, and the problem of a child who spends his days living up to one set of expectations and his nights adjusting to another, while not insoluble, is one more difficulty the child must overcome.

So we are faced with an individualistic, independent population and a plurality of goals that does not exist in Russia, China, and the kibbutzim. And then, of course, to complicate matters further, we have the difficulty of endlessly changing caretakers. People don't move around with such reckless abandon in the societies that have chosen to raise their children in groups. The metapelet (child-care worker) in the kibbutz, the auntie in the commune, the upbringer in the collective stay there. So do the children. There is a security for the children in this permanence that is decidedly lacking in our society where, if the child carer doesn't move away, the child probably will. "Multiple mothering," meaning a number of mother substitutes, is the same in United States day-care centers as in the group-care centers of China, Russia, and Israel. But if the substitutes are permanent in the child's life, as they are in China, Russia, and Israel, and if they are all in agreement—as they are—on the way the child should be brought up, it is much more comfortable for the children than U.S.-style "serial mothering," in which one caretaker gives way to another, then to a third and a fourth, each disappearing at irregular intervals to be replaced by still another stranger.

NUMBERS OF CHILDREN IN GROUP CARE

It is difficult to change a society's deep-rooted value system. But it could be done, and whether in macrocosm as in China and Russia or microcosm as in the kibbutzim, adults in the United States who are concerned with the quality of life for their generation and future generations *could* construct stable societies of consensus if there was clear evidence that group rearing of infants improves the quality of life. There is no such clear evidence.

One would think that in societies such as China and Russia, where molding their citizens from birth in the Communist image is to be expected, and in Israel, where the kibbutzim were so essential to the survival of the new state, that group care of infants would be part and parcel of national life. Such is not the case. The number of children in group care is not what one would expect from all the commotion made about this supposedly successful innovation in child rearing. Only 3 percent of Israel's population of 3 million live in kibbutzim and, even given a slightly higher kibbutz birth rate, a similarly tiny percentage of Israel's children.[3]

In the Soviet Union a mere 10 percent of children under two and 20 percent of children from three to seven years are in state nurseries and kindergartens.[4] Nor is the number of group-reared children expected to rise in the U.S.S.R. Khrushchev's 1956 objective of shifting responsibility for child rearing from parents to collectives so that by 1980 100 percent of children would be group-reared has run into strong opposition. A Soviet educator tells us, "I don't foresee any great increase in the number of babies in state nurseries. Parents simply don't want to put babies in nurseries unless there is absolutely no alternative."[5] And in the crowded three-generation households of Soviet Russia there is almost always an alternative—the babushka, or grandmother.

In China the picture is more clouded. But an informed guess would put the number of very young children in state nurseries at considerably less than 40 percent, the rest remaining at home with their mothers, grandmothers, or friendly neighbors. So the numbers of children in group care even in the societies that make a point of group care are comparatively small.

RESEARCH ON GROUP-REARED CHILDREN

Very little research has been done on these children who have been brought up in groups. The U.S.S.R. and China are closed societies, and we learn only what they choose to tell us. Israel is an open society, and the voluble Israeli personality is liable to insist on showing us more than we have the energy to see. But either way, it doesn't seem to make much difference. Much of the material that comes to the notice of the general public, when divested of the sociological jargon, is really of the wide-eyed, uncritically enthusiastic variety. Little of it contains accurate observations of individual children and their families, measurements of abilities—physical, intellectual, creative, and social—control groups in which group-reared children are carefully matched to home-reared children, and, perhaps most important, longitudinal research that follows these children into adulthood and assesses them as mature members of the community and as parents themselves. In

Israel alone, where a third generation is growing up in the older kibbutzim, is there beginning to be a body of long-term research.

The lack of long-term observation of these group-reared children is particularly worrisome. Short-term observation can be very tricky. For example, one could be forgiven for believing that the institutionalized child who rushes up to visitors and is open, confiding, and affectionate toward them is well on the way to a healthy, happy, outgoing maturity. But this behavior may be the mock social promiscuity of the unattached child, which is something to worry about. Researchers Dale Meers and Allen Marans, for example, believe that we must be concerned about the "latent damage to such children's cognitive capacities or their social and emotional health."[6]

While day-care children are a far cry from institutionalized children who know no other home, we still remember with apprehension Harry Harlow's initial optimistic short-term assessment of his superior manufactured monkey mothers and their happy babies, and his later rueful recognition that the babies who had seemed so superbly mothered in infancy had matured into adults unable to function normally either as sexual partners or as parents. Observations of three- and four-year-olds in day care may be deemed only contributary; they are not conclusive.

So we have comparatively small numbers of children who are being raised in groups, and only journalistic commentary on the effects of their group upbringing in Russia and China. Finally, the group-care experience in these societies is not comparable to what we project for our own infants. Soviet mothers, more often than not, take a year's maternity leave while still receiving part of their salaries. Chinese and kibbutz mothers nurse their children, and their working day is so organized that they are with their babies two or three times during the day. The nine-hour day apart, which is the norm here for day-care babies and their mothers, is not the norm for babies and mothers in other societies.

With these important reservations in mind, let us take a look at what the day-care advocates are talking about when they tell us that group care works well in other countries.

THE U.S.S.R.

The modern approach toward group rearing had its beginnings in the Russian Revolution. At that time:

> Many Soviet theoreticians predicted that a socialist society would do away with possessive mother love and exclusive sexual love between husband and wife. This reasoning was simple. Since the child was no longer the property of the family but only of the state, the mother would feel it wrong to have possessive maternal instincts. . . . A system of wide-spread communal infant and child care was begun.[7]

In the words of Makarenko, Russia's Dr. Spock, the child was to be brought up "in the collective, by the collective, and for the collective."[8] A collective is defined as "a group of children united in common, goal-oriented activity and the communal organization of this activity."[9] A child can be placed in a collective at two months. There is a planned ratio of one caretaker to every four children. The caretakers, called "nurse-upbringers," have three years' training in teachers' colleges, reflecting the strong Soviet belief in credentialism. There is great emphasis on uniform instruction and on keeping up with the newest information in journals.

The youngest children are placed several to a playpen and the playpens are elevated to bring the children closer to eye level. A warm and colorful environment is provided. There are strictly prescribed regimes of regular stimulation and a progressive program of physical education that reaches all the way down to the infant. At the appropriate age planned programs to develop speech begin. Nothing is left to chance.

Children are encouraged to cooperate and be helpful to each other. With this in mind toys are specially designed to be worked by two or three children together. As the children get older they learn that they are measured as individuals by the contributions they can make to the group, and condemned as individuals to the extent that their actions detract from group goals.

CHINA

Chinese child rearing of the last several decades, like almost everything else about China today, is still shrouded in official fog. It is virtually impossible to obtain reliable statistics about the numbers of children who are being group-reared from infancy, or reliable information about how these groups function.

One of the most readable sources is Ruth Sidel's *Women and Child Care in China*. One gathers from her book that there are two conflicting strains at work in child care. There is first a tendency toward decentralization of child-rearing methods, a result of the vastness and diversity of the population, a belief in self-reliance, and tailoring of services to meet needs. The Chinese have had to be much more pragmatic than the Russians; they are in a hurry! One will not find the proliferation of manuals, directives, and professional journals that keep the well-trained Russian upbringers in line. For that matter, the Chinese are much more casual in their training altogether. Whereas the Russian upbringer has three years of professional schooling, the Chinese auntie may simply be chosen for child care because she seems to be more patient and more responsible than other available adults.

On the other hand, there is a cohesiveness among the millions of nurseries throughout China that comes directly from Chairman Mao and is transmitted through the Communist party and the revolutionary committees that run the individual child-care centers. For all its vastness and diversity, the Chinese system teaches young children a unified value system that is apparently accepted by all.[10]

Sidel describes a factory nursing room she visited. Nursing mothers, who have returned to work eight weeks after giving birth, bring their babies to the factory with them. There they are cared for in a crowded fourth-floor nursing room by the caretaker aunties. Most mothers come in twice a day to breastfeed their babies, in addition to their lunch period, which they can also spend with their children.

In the nursing room there is a ratio of one auntie to six children, who range in age from two months to one and a half years. In the particular nursery Sidel describes, most of the children were under eight months old. There are too many babies to be picked up every time they cry, so the aunties pair them up, two to a playpen and two to a carriage for company.

Sidel found the rooms dismal, but the babies are supplied with colorful clothes and quilts from home. There are very few toys, blocks, or building equipment, stuffed or live animals—not that toys are unknown in China. On the contrary, they are manufactured in considerable quantity, but only for export. The impression was given that learning in China is a people-to-people process, and toys are considered superfluous.

Aunties do not allow toddlers to walk in the nursing rooms because the floors are "dirty." The children do walk in walkers, however, and their mothers can take them outside at lunchtime.

If you believe that a lower ratio of adults to infants, a carefully designed series of progressive exercises to develop each child's capacity to the fullest, toys that are scientifically selected to make the most of every stage of development, and rigorously trained caretakers are all important, the developmental data from the Russian and Chinese nurseries are going to jar you a little. The babies grow and mature at the same rate in both countries, a rate, incidentally, that is just about what we expect from our children in the United States. They sit alone at six months, crawl at eight months, stand alone at 10 to 12 months, begin to walk at about one year, are toilet-trained at 18 months, speak simple words at 18 months. The major difference in the United States is that our babies are often not toilet-trained by 18 months. One probable reason is that our current focus has moved away from early toilet training toward force-fed intellectual development.

If you are still going to opt for day care, it won't hurt to remember that while gross deprivation of experience can seriously injure a baby, massive, strategically designed programs of stimulation won't necessarily improve him. We cling to a belief that the professional child carer should offer superior knowledge and superior facilities. But if this superiority is as important as day-care advocates would have us believe, why are there similar developmental results between the Russian group-cared child who is given so much and the Chinese group-cared child whose surroundings are so comparatively stark?

THE KIBBUTZ

The third society that is most often cited for its communal child rearing is the Israeli kibbutz, a unique combination of agricultural and industrial settlement, training center, and military outpost. Almost all kibbutz property is collectively owned, work is collectively organized, and living arrangements, including the rearing of children, are largely collective. The kibbutz first made its appearance in Palestine in 1912. The importance of kibbutzim for educators and parents lies in their child-rearing practices. The original kibbutz settlers, who came from Western Europe and Russia, had a strong socialistic or communistic bias. Their precarious lives in an arid, hostile, Arab Palestine demanded the full work-and-fight effort of every adult, male and female. In the early years there weren't any children. Pregnancy was frowned on. When conditions eased enough to go about having babies, there was considerable consternation and soul searching. How were the children to be raised? The most obvious problem was that the women could not be spared from their regular work. In fact, most didn't want to be spared. One view holds that memories of their ghettoized, Orthodox Jewish mothers made motherhood unappealing. The women were caught in a bind, not unfamiliar to many of us, in which they were sure they didn't want to raise their children as they themselves were raised and yet had no other experience on which to draw. Their style of collective living in which they shared work, dining hall, showers, and dormitories provided the answer; they would raise the children collectively. They assigned one woman—and then two and then three as the number of children grew—to take care of the children. Two weeks after birth mothers surrendered their babies to the Infants' House and, as they grew older, to the Children's House, where they remained until they were old enough to take their places as full-fledged adult members of the community.

While in the Infants' House the babies were cared for by metapelot, the kibbutz term for nurses or child-care workers. For the first six months mothers came in six times a day to nurse their babies. Since the kibbutz work day ended at 3 P.M. both parents were free to be with their children of any age from 3 to 7 P.M. every day.

The kibbutz child grew up in a manner that was halfway between Russian and Chinese extremes. The metapelot were trained in child care, but not as rigorously as were the Russian upbringers. Since the members of the kibbutz believed that a child must grow to depend on himself and on his peers, the metapelot took a less active role than one might expect. During the day children who were old enough were put together into large playpens or play yards and left alone for hours at a stretch. A baby who got crawled over, stepped on, or pushed aside cried until he stopped. Eventually the children learned to get along, whether it was by getting out of the way or pushing back, arriving finally at an amicable state of cooperative existence.

At night, with the familiar metapelot asleep in their own quarters and some adult member of the kibbutz taking his or her turn on duty in the Infants' House, the children turned to their peers for comfort. Very young babies would gaze fixedly at cribmates, older children would crawl into bed with a friend for security. Psychoanalyst Bruno Bettelheim, whose *Children of the Dream* is a searching attempt to understand what went on with these group-reared children, finds their early years were difficult as they came to grips with life's problems without a permanent mother figure to buffer them.

But by age six or so the children had adjusted very well, and although Bettelheim feels that they had a hard time again in their teens, the adult who emerged was generally competent, alert, responsible, hardworking, and cooperative—as is his counterpart in China and in Russia.

PROBLEMS IN GROUP REARING

So what is the problem? Should parents want more for their children than that they be competent, alert, responsible, hardworking, and cooperative? Yes, they should want more for their children and more for themselves than infant group rearing allows. Parents have a right to want children who grow into adults capable of independent thought and action. Parents have a right to want to nurture in their children those sparks of creativity and uniqueness that enrich, deepen, and diversify the lives of all people. And parents have a right to hope for the love, warmth, and caring of one human being toward another without which this world of people—however competent, bright, hard working, and cooperative—would be dull and mechanical. In all of these areas societies that have chosen to raise their children in groups are having trouble. With intelligent planning we can profit from their failures as well as from their successes.

INDEPENDENCE

Independence of thought and action are qualities that children learn. Though there certainly may be a genetic propensity for one child to be more independent and another less, the way in which children are raised can strengthen or virtually extinguish this tendency for independence. In the multiethnic United States children are raised in many ways, but the ultimate goal is the child who can stand on his own two feet. But in the societies we are studying, the stated goal is to discourage independence, though it is usually phrased in a more positive manner. The group-reared child, we are told, puts the good of the group above the good of the individual. But it all comes to the same thing. The U.S.S.R., China, and the kibbutzim set out to raise group-dependent children and they end up with group-dependent adults.

The difference in training makes itself evident early on:

> To anyone who has visited nursery schools in the Soviet Union and compared them with those in the United States, the contrast is startling. In place of our noisy, competitive individualism—each child doing his own thing—the Soviet youngsters quietly cooperate in performing the tasks at hand. . . . To the Soviet educator, the capacity to discipline oneself comes from learning how to behave in a thoroughly cooperative manner as part of a larger group.[11]

GROUP CARE IN OTHER SOCIETIES

Chinese officials worry about the babies who are being raised at home by grandparents. They prefer the greater collectivism of group rearing to the individualism that is fostered in the home-reared child:

> They are attempting to fashion a human being who will put the needs of the society before his own, . . . they start with the child in the nursing room, and using a variety of techniques and skills, attempt by the time he is seven years old to inculcate him with these values.[12]

This strong group pressure is equally evident in the democratically run kibbutzim:

> The interests of the individual must be subordinate to the interests of the group. When the needs of the individual and those of the group come into conflict, the individual is expected to abdicate his needs in favor of the group's. This applies to vocational interest, *as well as to ideological conviction* [our emphasis]. . . . Once a formal decision is reached by the kibbutz, he is expected to acquiesce in its decision and to support it, however much it conflicts with his personal views.[13]

That the good of the group becomes paramount as prescribed is a result of the very young child's growth of attachment to that which is secure and dependable in his life. The home-reared child will attach to his mother; the group-reared child, denied the security of a mostly present mother or mother substitute, will attach to that which is securely there, in his case, the group.

The problem in all this is that it makes a difference to whom or to what the child attaches. Having grown through the first attachment to a mother, a child becomes free to function without her. But if the first attachment is to a group it is not so easily outgrown. While mothers accept children because they love them, groups accept members only because they conform. One's feelings, attitudes, and actions are constantly measured against group standards, and one's continued acceptance by the group is always at risk. If the group is one's major source of security and attachment, its power to mold the thoughts and actions of its members is enormous.

The literature on group control is extensive. A young child whose inner security is still tremulous and whose outer security comes from the support and companionship of his agemates is extremely vulnerable to their approval or disapproval. This vulnerability is easily subject to adult manipulation. With the adult ultimately in control of all reward and punishment, the majority of the group will opt for the behavior that results in reward, and the young dissenter who threatens the rewards of all finds their open disapproval focused on him with unbearable force. (This is hardly a technique that is unfamiliar to us in the United States. For example, "Unless the child who threw the chalk comes forward, the *entire* class will stay after school today!" But there is a difference between the irritated teacher who just wants to identify the chalk-throwing villain and the calm professional who, as a result of training, ideology, and goal, uses the technique designedly.)

A kibbutz child may wish to escape this pervasive groupthink, but to no avail, as Bettelheim points out: "The commands [of the group] are more inescapable because there is nowhere a dissenting voice to support one's own doubts or dissent."[14] In adolescence the child is even more deeply enmeshed:

> What pulls the adolescent up short is always group pressure—first and foremost that of the peer group, and secondly the kibbutz, in the person of some adult. Their giving in starts as soon as they feel (or fear) that group opinion leans the other way.
>
> With very rare exceptions they cannot buck the group, not for a moment: it is too threatening. This is where their emotional security resides. Without the peer group they are lost.
>
> It is not just out of closeness to the group, but more a fear of their rejection. Fifteen or sixteen years of living not as an individual but as an integral part of a peer group has made it

nearly impossible for them to conceive of standing up alone against the group. Not only have they been taught this is unpardonable, but they have no experience whatsoever that a single person could go it alone. How, then, can they believe they could do it?[15]

Margaret Mead acknowledged the difficulties of group rearing in an address entitled *A Cultural Anthropologist's Approach*, which was given to the World Health Organization in 1962:

> Children raised with age-peers, with changing and overburdened nurses, who see parents, themselves reared in old style small families, for short intervals every day, combine excessive responsiveness to parental behavior with excessive dependence upon the peer group, and in youth become heavily dependent upon the members of the peer group with whom they were reared. The Hutterite studies . . . in which the parents were reared within the same system as the children, with children isolated for most of the time from association with their own parents, confirm the extent to which children so reared are dependent upon the community and unfitted for venturing forth as individuals. Neither [the material on the kibbutz nor on the Hutterites] suggests that children do not thrive and survive under conditions of group nurturing; they both suggest that their mobility and flexibility are impaired.[16]

Consider, in contrast, the situation of the child who is fortunate enough to be born into a reasonably healthy family situation. First of all, he is not in constant anxiety about being expelled. Those of us who have raised children to maturity know very well just how much rebellion our children, toddlers to teenagers, feel comfortable in expressing. The desire to conform out of fear of expulsion from the family group is not a major motivating factor in a family-reared child's existence.

Second, the child of two healthy, self-respecting parents learns that divergent views are acceptable. He sees from earliest infancy that two people, both of whom he loves and who love him, are often in disagreement about all sorts of things, that they express this disagreement openly, that differences are somehow resolved without the world being shattered or the participants disintegrating. To our mind, the child who witnesses these experiences becomes more flexible, more self-confident, more willing to hold his own, and more accepting of other people; he feels much less pressured to conform than does the child who grows up in a community of group consensus.

We are not after a community of consensus. The wise child who complained to her parents that she didn't think the United States was a melting pot, as she was being taught in school, but was more like a tossed salad expressed beautifully the best that can come out of a pluralistic society like ours. Most Americans really don't want to surrender the strengths and idiosyncrasies of their ethnic origins and genetic inheritance. We prefer to think that the best we have to contribute can be combined with the best contributions of others to construct a strong and healthful environment for all.

A community of consensus is too vulnerable to the possibility of sliding toward a tyranny of the majority, minus the protections of the rights of the minority. In a country where almost everyone belongs to a minority in some sense—if not racial or religious, a minority in terms of conviction, life style, age, or place of residence—the protection of minorities is of concern to everyone.

So, in our terms, a child who is group-dependent poses difficulties. Group dependency is, after all, as good or as bad as the group upon which the individual is dependent. The notorious Hitler Youth of the 1930s and early 1940s were, according to almost all studies, strong, competent, bright, responsible, hard working, and cooperative—the very virtues claimed for group-reared children in the societies we have been reviewing. And yet all of these good qualities served such a horrible end! Of course we want and expect our children to group together to achieve various ends—social, political, and economic—during their lives. There are many times when rugged individualism must give way for the benefit of the larger group. But let us help our children to develop the inner strength to be group participants without saddling them with the inner weakness that makes them group-dependent.

Creativity

Those societies that bring up group-reared children and intend from the beginning that the child should put the group before the individual, adopt group values as his own, and exist as a cooperative member of a larger whole, have every reason to be pleased with the results of their group care in this respect. But there is evidence that they are concerned with another problem—the tendency of this assembly-line upbringing to produce adults who, while fully functional, have lost that spark of unique creativity without which no society may grow and develop in a world of competitive societies.

It is virtually a truism that great new ideas do not come from committees; they come from individuals. Great music is played by symphony orchestras: it is created by single composers. Great painters do not work in tandem; they work alone. With only an occasional exception, our litany of great men and women is almost invariably in the singular, and in more ways than one. The creative geniuses of mankind have usually struck out in their different independent directions at a very young age. While the rest of the kids were out doing whatever was appropriate for kids in their particular circle in their particular place in time, those who were destined to do great things were often doing something distinctly different. Most of that which has been most beautiful, most valuable, most significant in its ability to enrich mankind has come from the iconoclasts of the world, the idol breakers who saw things differently or felt things more intensely and were able to reach deep into their inner beings to discover for the world that which, had it not been for them, might still lie unheard of, unthought of, unused, buried in the collective unconscious of mankind. "Man ascends by discovering the fullness of his own gifts."[17]

The loss of our occasional geniuses would be a sufficiently severe blow. But that open, independent life style that gives men and women of genius the chance to develop their individual gifts also gives each of us the opportunity to nurture our own special and creative gifts. We may think and express our own thoughts, see life from our own individual perspective, and contribute the quality of our individuality to our society.

But what happens to individual creativity when people are subjected from infancy to the multiple mothering of group rearing? Bettelheim analyzes the kibbutz experience:

> The real question is whether, and to what degree, the much and varied stimulation of many persons can replace the greater consistency and intimacy that comes of being cared for and stimulated mainly by one. Because the many of course cannot so easily gear the stimulation they offer to the needs and abilities of the particular child. Nor can the child develop as easily when his development is not directed, first and foremost, toward mastering the one major relationship, with all others being secondary.
>
> While an adjustment by the infant may bring some extra attention from one metapelot, it may fail to do so from another, or even may bring a negative response. Then, since the infant at this early date cannot realize that different persons need different ways of responding to them, all his efforts at specific responding (or "to give in return" as Erikson puts it) will also be extinguished by nonreward. But by adjusting one's response to the other, one does more than learn about others, one also learns about oneself. So from the very first the kibbutz infant has less reason to strive for individuation.[18] (For a corresponding view of infant development see the discussion by Humberto Nagera in chapter 8.)

This diminished drive to work for individuation explains in part what many refer to as the "flat" personality of kibbutz children. Erikson suggests that the flatness comes from the fact that extremes of development are absent—a child feels neither the security he would receive from the inner knowledge that he is at the center of his mother's existence nor the fear that this person who is so important to him may be taken from him. The emotional peaks and hollows of existence are not present for the kibbutz child.

Whatever the explanation, many researchers agree that there is missing in the kibbutz child those elements that contribute in large part to the creative person. As the kibbutz child grows up, group rearing pressures him continually to direct his attention outward. The challenge is to do; there is almost no opportunity to sit, to think, to feel. Adolescents have a real need to think their own thoughts, but they have no experience on which to build this kind of introspective self-searching. Bettelheim finds them more familiar with what the body does than with what the body feels.

The creative spirit of the Chinese people has been a potent force in the world for thousands of years. Printing and paper were invented in China; silk and porcelain were first used there; and in keeping with the idea that the last shall be first, Chinese art in the mid-twentieth century is of interest to many. Ruth Sidel focuses on the problem:

> One of the most common questions I am asked is "Doesn't the lack of individuality stifle creativity?" In our society, where creativity seems so closely linked to finding whatever is unique in each person, to ferreting out the occasional genius, to avoiding the standardization and conformity that occur when the group is emphasized over the individual, it may appear likely that the Chinese will produce uniform, prescribed thinking, and stifle unusual ability or insight.
>
> Before we can adequately measure another society's creativity, we must define the word, because one society's creativity might well be another society's decadence. The Chinese today regard as creativity whatever furthers their cause in an innovative way. . . . I think we shall have to wait another generation

before evaluating the impact of Chinese society on its people's creativity, however it is defined.[19]

We remember with apprehension, however, the effects of the revolution upon the creative arts of the Russian people, and the political dogma that dominated all art for decades afterward.

The Russian experience in group rearing has been longer than that of the Chinese, and they have more to tell us about the effects of this communal rearing on creativity. By nursery-school age the collectivized children already are behaving differently from our children, and the prevailing atmosphere in the Soviet classroom is one of quiet, cooperation, and industry. But as in the kibbutzim, Soviet society, having raised its children just as it wanted, now worries about what it has done.

A Soviet educational expert and researcher, L. I. Novikova, wrote of this concern in a 1967 paper that has received significant recognition in the U.S.S.R.:

> A substantial deficiency of our children's collective consists of the uniformity of the internal relations determining the life experiences of the child. Relations in school are most often limited to the sphere of task-oriented relations. It is precisely these which in the first instance are developed by teachers. These are relations of mutual dependence, mutual responsibility, mutual control, subordination and commanding, and intolerance to persons interfering with the common tasks . . . [but] by developing primarily the task-oriented aspects of human relationships in the children's collective and allowing other characteristics to develop as they may, we in the last analysis impoverish the personality of the child. . . .
>
> If every year we shall be obtaining more highly developed people but all of the same type, then this will be of little profit either to society or to personality. Socialist society is interested in original persons capable of revolution in the spheres of science, technology, and the organization of production. And the personality is interested in developing to the full those

capacities with which it has been endowed by nature. And those capacities are by no means the same in all people.[20]

In their newly awakened concern for individual potentialities, abilities, talents, and gifts, there is now a Soviet emphasis on the importance of encouraging the growth of the individual personality. They are trying to find a better way. And when they've found it and proved it over a generation or two, we can all benefit from it. It really isn't necessary for us to duplicate their mistakes—not when the quality of life for all of us is at stake.

Parental Love

Finally we come to the question of what happens to a society when its adults are denied the experience of raising their own children. Insofar as a human being never has a chance to learn those skills and sensitivities that go into nurturing the young, to that extent will his or her adult development lose a vital dimension.

Urie Bronfenbrenner tells this tragicomic story of a plane trip he took from Tashkent to Alma-Ata. He sat next to a young mother and her six-month-old baby. The mother held the baby awkwardly, its upper body well away from her own. When the baby fussed she popped chocolates into its mouth, all the while telling Bronfenbrenner about herself. She was a chemist, her husband was a mathematician, and both were students at the University of Tashkent. Meanwhile the baby kept fussing, and the mother, who neither spoke to it nor cuddled it, kept stuffing chocolates into the open mouth. The baby, as one might expect, was soon a chocolate mess, and Bronfenbrenner, in almost a reflex action, offered the mother a perfumed moist towelette. She accepted with thanks and promptly used it to clean her own face, ignoring her sticky baby entirely. The purpose of her trip was to enroll the baby in a residential nursery in Alma-Ata, since there were no openings in Tashkent. She had relatives there, and she and her husband could fly in occasionally to visit the baby.[21]

The more one reads the story, the less comic and the more tragic it becomes. Giving birth or fathering a child has never made a mother or father; there must be learning and an investment of self involved. But our society does not commonly value this kind of learning as it values other learning, unless, of course, it leads to degrees, titles, and salaries. For instance, we all know that women who talk about their babies are an old and lightly honored joke. In some circles the joke cuts so deep that a woman wouldn't be caught dead talking about her baby. It would be gauche, and would forfeit her esteem in the eyes of her friends.

But on an absolute scale, is there something intrinsically less worthy about learning to be sensitive to another human being, to moderate one's behavior in an empathetic way that allows two people to give and receive comfort from one another? Is it less laudable to grow in such interpersonal skill, in learning to adjust to the constantly changing environment that a growing child creates? Is there something less worthy about all this than dealing with objects or with theories? When so many people are bleeding for the lack of one other human being with whom they can have a close, loving, open, and dependable relationship, should the very first relationship of all be so deprecated?

So one can worry about the woman chemist from Tashkent whose intellectual development is presumably proceeding apace but whose development in the art of being a human being seems to be atrophying even more rapidly. One *must* worry because there is an issue here that transcends single parent-child relationships. While on an individual woman-by-woman basis each woman should have the right to devote her life to an occupation rather than to children, the problem becomes a little different when we consider an entire society. Many of us believe that a person who invests the major part of her time and energy in raising a child from infancy to school age hones a fine sensitivity to that child. And in learning to be sensitive to one human being she learns to be sensitive to others.

Of course there are mothers who never learn these lessons, just as there are secretaries, plumbers, doctors, and mechanics who should have flunked out but managed to squeak through and inflict their incompetence on the rest of us. But we never make the mistake of thinking that society had nothing to teach these incompetents; we understand that they simply never learned. So it is with some mothers and fathers.

We are, then, faced with a problem. If it is true that woman's greater sensitivity comes from her contact with infants and small children, if this daily schooling in responsiveness, tenderness, and intimacy is the source of woman's fabled superiority in these most human of skills, does a society really want to make a collective decision to limit these opportunities for growth to a small professional class of child carers? In the absence of more stringent evidence on the development of humanity, must we so quickly abandon that which we know in order to embrace that of which we know not? All change is not necessarily for the better, and our society, which is currently somewhere between delayed adolescence and advanced senility, is surely old enough to recognize the advantages of a certain caution in its decisions.

What, for example, can we learn about the women in societies that group-rear their children? Has freedom from child care enriched their lives without evenhandedly impoverishing them? Have they been liberated to develop fully, each according to her bent? If we follow the development of the native kibbutz-born Sabra personality, we find researchers pointing to a striking inability to take part in strong, intimate, one-to-one relationships—an inability that causes pain to those who experience it and do not know how to combat it:

> By 16 the young adolescent has given up hope of forming a strong friendship and settles back into a group life that is devoid

of true intimacy. . . . This, incidentally, worries kibbutz educators, despite their stress on group life. They recognize the importance of serious friendships for the adolescent . . . their own children seem unable to come close to each other. Though leading educators are deeply concerned about it, they do not see that their arranging for the child's life to comprise only group events, so that he is never alone—has no time and no place of his own, is almost never forced back upon his own resources—now prevents him from being intimate with others.

Intimacy requires a great deal of time, but also a great concentration on the other person.[22]

Even marriage does not provide the opportunity for true intimacy that the kibbutz adult secretly yearns for, probably because having been untutored in intimacy in their youth, the adults don't know how to achieve it. But there is a trend toward larger families in kibbutz and it seems that the need to be really close to one other person is operative. Rabkin and Spiro tell us:

Pregnancy provides the mother with some degree of narcissistic gratification in the form of community interest and attention; it provides her with an opportunity for creation denied to or unused by most women; it cements her ties to kibbutz and husband; for some it provides a welcome respite from work; and most important, it allows for an approved one-to-one intimacy not found in any other relationship, including marriage.[23]

But, having had their babies, women are still frustrated in their maternal role. Rabkin and Spiro go on to point out the deficiencies of these group-reared parents who give birth to group-reared babies:

Sabra parents simply do not possess—because there is no need for them to acquire—the range and variety of responses that a mother or father in a nuclear family structure must acquire. They do not know how to discipline a child, and when they (very rarely) do, they are embarrassed by the child's acting up and their own helplessness. Nor do they know how to spend an extended time with their children—longer, that is, than the usual two-hour afternoon play period. They see their role primarily as gratifiers, and they are quite content to delegate the socializing responsibilities to the nurses and teachers.[24]

Rabkin and Spiro conclude by speculating that while the parents may accept the system, they do not get a great deal of emotional satisfaction from it. They find, as many of us have found before, that there is no perfect solution to human problems. They wanted strong, brave children; their children are strong and brave, but their parents feel that they lack a certain sensibility and softness. They wanted rational, scientific, objective children, and they have them, but now they miss a certain human, irrational quality in them. They gave their children everything, but now they worry that, having been supplied "everything," the children have acquired a certain passivity.[25]

Their disappointments with their children have contributed to their revolt against this system that comes between parent and child. The movement in the kibbutzim is now for longer periods of time spent with parents, and for larger living quarters so that from late afternoon on the children live with their parents rather than in children's houses.

A 1975 study in depth, *Women in the Kibbutz*, by Tiger and Shepher, attempts to explain the modern kibbutz woman's return by choice to a traditionally womanly role. Lionel Tiger, professor of anthropology at Rutgers, is the author of *Men In Groups* and coauthor of *The Imperial Animal*. Joseph Shepher has been an Israeli since the state was born and has lived within the kibbutz movement for 28 years. He is a teacher of anthropology at the University of Haifa. Their study is based on the lives of 34,040 kibbutzniks—about two-thirds of the contemporary kibbutz population—living in kibbutzim that vary in ideological affiliation, religious orientation, size, and length of existence.

Interviews, graphs, tables, and detailed computerized data

led Tiger and Shepher to the conclusion that "men and women seemed to live as if in two separate dwelling places. It is almost as if we have been studying two distinct villages."[26] They discovered, "as several previous researchers had in specific kibbutzim, a strong, general, and cumulative tendency of women and men to become less, rather than more, similar in what they do and evidently want to do."[27]

While Tiger and Shepher do not buy the simplicity of the catch phrase "biology is destiny," they do believe that biology is "statistical probability." They discuss the fact that all over the world, and throughout history, "the care of young children is virtually a female monopoly,"[28] and this remains true within the kibbutzim, in societies that for three generations now have been philosophically dedicated to the complete equality of men and women. Their findings indicate that kibbutz women have concentrated increasingly on maternal, service-oriented occupations and left production to the men—by choice:

> Our data show that although some 10 to 15 percent of the women in the kibbutz express dissatisfaction with their sociosexual roles, the overwhelming majority not only accept their situations but have sought them. They have acted against the principles of their socialization and ideology, against the wishes of the men of their communities, against the economic interest of the kibbutzim, in order to be able to devote more time and energy to private maternal activities rather than to economic and political public ones. Obviously these women have minds of their own; despite obstacles, they are trying to accomplish what women elsewhere have been periodically urged to reject by critics of traditional female roles. Our assertion is that the behavior of these mothers is ethologically probable; they are seeking an association with their own offspring, which reflects a species-wide attraction between mothers and their young. Usually women have no choice but to have close contact with their children; in the kibbutz, the opposite is true. So, what kibbutz women *choose* to do may be significantly related to what other women elsewhere routinely do under similar circumstances, if also ap-

parently more constraining ones. A single case cannot define a species, but given the experimental style of kibbutz society, the result is certainly revealing.[29]

Tiger and Shepher deny the theory that women are condemned to child care because men make the rules:

Abraham Maslow noted that most utopias have been created by men. The records available to us suggest that the men who dominated the public life of the kibbutz also strongly influenced basic child-care policy. *Had women been more fully and assertively involved, the severance of the link between mother and child as a matter of theory and then of practice might have been less extreme.* Today kibbutz mothers may be responding not only to their need to be close to their children but also to their children's ability to elicit these feelings from them. [our emphasis]

Russian parents are facing the same problems. There are indications that people resent having their children taken away from them and that they are resisting further encroachments on the family. In this they are supported by a number of prominent Russian psychologists who question the necessity of depriving a family of the joy given by well-brought-up children and who recognize that the family, by virtue of its members' love for one another, has special unique qualifications for rearing children, qualifications that are particularly important in developing the emotional life of a child.[31]

A U.S. government study of day care in the Soviet Union, Hungary, East Germany, Czechoslovakia, Greece, Israel and France found widespread concern over the effects of day care on children and the report noted that there was no recorded case where a senior official running a day care center made use of that center for his or her own children.

In one country, Hungary, the government is moving away from day care and now pays a day care allowance for each child directly to the mother. And Czechoslovakia recently revised its laws to provide for a six-month paid maternity leave.[32]

We have been talking about a fairly subtle problem. The inability to be truly intimate with another, the hidden pain that comes from what Spiro calls the frustration of deep-seated maternal impulses, the lopsided development of adults who become parents in a physical sense but then are unable to parent—these problems do not show up in easily documented statistics. We have to be alert to the problems reported by observers of other societies and assess the likelihood of their occurrence in our society.

Nor can we take comfort in the fact that our day care does not contemplate the virtual 22-hour-a-day separation that was studied in kibbutz (although our care *is* comparable to Russian day nurseries). Bruno Bettelheim has a cautionary word that is as applicable to 9-hour care as it is to 22-hour care:

> But even if the parents are free and present, and try to do a good job, it is the end of the day. After eight or more hours of hard work, and after the two visiting hours with their children, many of them are simply exhausted, physically and emotionally. Here it makes a difference that parents try to crowd too much emotion into the short span of time, because they feel the visit comprises the whole of their relations with their children. They want it to be so good and meaningful, they want to concentrate on their children so exclusively, that they impose a heavy emotional burden on themselves.
>
> So when bed time comes round, to quote a kindergarten teacher, "The parents simply have no more patience. They want the children in bed and to get away as fast as possible."[33]

American pediatrician T. Berry Brazelton describes much the same problem when he tells us of an American working couple whose 15-month-old daughter is cared for during the day in the home of a baby-sitter. The doctor is most sympathetic to the problems of parents. But in his description of the early morning rush, the harried mother, the emptiness and lack of parental contact with their daughter in the too-short morning, the tired mother's irritation and anger at her fatigued and fractious baby in the evening, the inability of either parent to handle the little girl, and their feeling of guilt at having had so little time with her during the day, it is certainly hard to discern much emotional satisfaction and pleasure for the mother and father in their parenting role.[34]

It seems, then, that whatever benefits a woman receives when the "burden" of child care is removed from her, she *does* lose something. Have her gains been enough to make up for the loss?

In China teaching and nursing remain exclusively female occupations. In Russia, after all these years, Sidel finds women still heavily burdened with housework and child rearing. The new equality of the sexes has only piled responsibilities on top of responsibilities. Women have been enabled to hold down tiring jobs in addition to traditional woman's work. In the kibbutz women increasingly have gone into service jobs that, being repetitive in nature rather than productive or administrative, are little esteemed. Instead of the traditional home in which a woman could move at will from cooking to cleaning to child care to decorating to gardening to reading to socializing, today's kibbutz woman, freed from these burdens, can spend eight hours working in the community kitchen or eight hours sweating in the kibbutz laundry:

> No women work in field crops, fisheries, fruit orchards, vegetable gardens, heavy machinery, and the garage; but they do work in vineyards, dairy and poultry. They do no maintenance work (carpentry, electricity, plumbing), but they do office work (accounting, bookkeeping, secretarial), and they clearly predominate in the kitchen, clothing workshop, laundry, and education.[35]

The point, of course, is not that we couldn't do better. The point is that to a certain extent we are being brainwashed by day-care enthusiasts, and that we have to read reports of successful group care in other societies with the skepticism born of the knowledge that, while group care does confer benefits, it also exacts penalties, and Utopia is as hard to find when you drop your baby off at 8 A.M. as when you don't. Our reading of the situation leads us to believe that group dependence is a real problem in group-reared children; that this same group rearing provides an arid climate for the development of creativity; and that the society as a whole loses a valuable chance to strengthen its humanitarian, caring, and loving role.

NOTES

[1] Bruno Bettelheim, *Children of the Dream* (New York: Macmillan, 1969), p. 3.

[2] George Guthrie and Papita Jacobs, *Child Rearing and Personality Development in the Philippines* (University Park: Pennsylvania State University Press, 1966), p. 98.

[3] Israel, Israel Program for Scientific Translations, Publications Services Division, *Facts About Israel* (Jerusalem: Keter Books, 1969), p. 56.

[4] Susan Jacoby, "Who Raises Russia's Children?" *Saturday Review*, August 21, 1971, p. 41.

[5] Ibid.

[6] Dale Meers and Allen Marans, "Group Care of Infants in Other Countries," in Laura Dittman, ed., *Early Child Care* (New York: Atherton, 1968), p. 274.

[7] Lawrence Fuchs, *Family Matters* (New York: Random House, 1972), p. 190.

[8] Urie Bronfenbrenner, *Two Worlds of Childhood, U.S. and U.S.S.R.* (New York: Russell Sage Foundation, 1970), p. 51.

[9] Ibid., p. 4.

[10] Ruth Sidel, *Women and Child Care in China* (New York: Hill & Wang, 1972), pp. 86-87.

[11] Fuchs, op. cit., p. 209.

[12] Sidel, op. cit., p. 82.

[13] Melvin Spiro, *Kibbutz, Venture in Utopia* (New York: Schocken, 1970), pp. 29-30.

[14] Bettelheim, op. cit., p. 127.

[15] Ibid., p. 213-14.

[16] Margaret Mead, "A Cultural Anthropologist's Approach," in Mary D. Ainsworth, ed., *Deprivation of Maternal Care: A Reassessment of Its Effects* (Geneva: World Health Organization, 1962), p. 57.

[17] Jacob Bronowski, *The Ascent of Man* (Boston: Little, Brown, 1973), p. 24.

[18] Bettelheim, op. cit., p. 119.

[19] Sidel, op. cit., p. 186.

[20] L. I. Novokova, quoted in Bronfenbrenner, op. cit., pp. 87-88.

[21] Bronfenbrenner, op. cit., p. 86.

[22] Bettelheim, op. cit., p. 234.

[23] Leslie Y. Rabkin and Melvin E. Spiro, "Postscript: The Kibbutz in 1970," in Spiro, op. cit., pp. 275-76.

[24] Spiro, op. cit., p. 276.

[25] Ibid., p. 279.

[26] Lionel Tiger and Joseph Shepher, *Women in the Kibbutz* (New York: Harcourt Brace Jovanovich, 1975), p. 6.

[27] Ibid.

[28] Ibid., p. 272.

[29] Ibid., pp. 272-73.

[30] Ibid., p. 273.

[31] Bronfenbrenner, op. cit., p. 88.

[32] Marjorie Boyd, "The Case Against Day Care," *Washington Monthly*, December 1976, p. 27.

[33] Bettelheim, op. cit., p. 111-12.

[34] T. Berry Brazelton, "Working Parents: Fifteen Months," *Redbook*, February 1975, pp. 65-69.

[35] Rabkin and Spiro, op. cit., p. 285-86.

7

THE DOCTORS SPEAK OUT

How *can* we protect our children at the same time that we safeguard the rights of our women? Our research took us to two prominent scholars in the field of child development—two men who believe day care has a place in our society and can work.

THE INTERVIEWS

Jerome Kagan, professor of developmental psychology at Harvard University, was in the middle of a five-year study of the effects of day care on child development. Together with Dr. Richard Kearsley, then principal research associate in pediatrics at Boston's Beth Israel Hospital, Dr. Kagan had established the Tremont Street Infant Center. This center is located in the Castle Square Housing Center in Boston's South End, a racially mixed area that includes many Chinese families. There were 32 children in the Infant Center, aged 3 ½ months to 30 months. A matching control group of 32 children was being raised at home. Most of the caretakers were bilingual neighborhood mothers in their 30s and 40s, chosen for their humane and maternal qualities. The cost to the center was $75 a week per child. The scrutiny was intense, and Dr. Kagan readily admitted that this was a study of the best day care available; one could not generalize from his day-care center to just any day-care center. The interview continued as follows:

Q. Given your present state of knowledge about infants, would you rather see *your* infant (birth to 3 years) raised in a "good" traditional home or a "good" day-care center?
A. That question cannot be answered in any state of knowledge because there is no optimal recipe for development. There is only a best guess, depending upon what profile of intellectual, motivational, and emotional characteristics will make a child best adapted to his society. So that is not a reasonable question.
Q. I had an idea you wouldn't like it.
A. It's not that I'm reluctant or shy. It is impossible to answer. It's not a good question.
Q. Yes, but there are a lot of people who are being faced with this question every day.
A. They should know that that's not a good question.
Q. But then how are they to make their decision?
A. They have to make their decision on *practical* grounds. Do they enjoy their baby? If they enjoy their baby, then they should keep their baby with them. If they enjoy their baby but they must go to work, then they have to find a day-care center.
Q. Do you believe that the biological family should remain the responsible agent for the child?
A. Yes, of course, in our society there *is* no other agent who *can* take responsibility. Whenever you have an important enterprise, be it a university, a factory, or raising a baby, and decisions have to be made, it is very important that someone be in charge for two reasons. One, so

that there is maximum involvement of the person in charge, giving life and integrity to the enterprise, be it parent, plant, or university, because that agent has to feel both the guilt of failure and the joy of success and not scapegoat each. Moreover, unlike factories, children *must* perceive that there is someone who is particularly concerned about them. There has to be an agent. It can't be delegated.

Q. How much does a child have to see his parents to become aware that there is some particular agent who is taking care of him?

A. It's not the time, it's quality.

Q. Dr. Kagan, why is this so? Why is it that it's quality of the time . . .

A. I don't know. Suppose it's like Vitamin A and one needs a minimal amount. Suppose a baby needs a minimal amount of affective and gratifying contact with an adult the first year, and after that you don't need much more. . . . It's not the number of *hours* a baby is mothered!

Q. The one thing that bothers me about the quantity and the quality thing is that I sort of liken it to a marriage when two people, in order really to know each other and really grow together and understand each other have to go through a variety of experiences, lots of love and laughter, but also lots of hostility, lots of anger, lots of sadness, and lots of—the *whole* thing. All right. Is not the same thing applicable to the relationship between a child and a mother? You know, I read some of these things and my hair stands on end. It's almost like a cocktail hour. From six to seven, after the child has come home, then mother and father vigorously play with this child and read him a story, and everything is happy, happy, happy. Well, that's not . . .

A. You don't *know*!

Q. What you're saying is we don't know what *happens* in that house.
A. We don't even know whether you're *right*! Maybe an hour's *enough*!
Q. When a mother comes home at six o'clock, she's in no mood to give an hour's high-quality care to a three-month-old child. She's tired, her husband wants dinner, and before the child falls asleep she doesn't have that *time*! Regardless of whether or not that time would be sufficient.
A. You don't know what a baby *needs*—you're projecting. We're projecting our own needs onto the infant. Suppose all he needs is someone who's familiar to come when he cries, freedom from long periods of pain, and opportunity to move around. Suppose that's all he needs in the first year. Then anybody can give that.
Q. What happens when it's somebody different every time that comes? Bettelheim said it didn't matter [in the kibbutz] because the security was coming from the other kids. But where is this child's security coming from? Or attachment?
A. They're different. They're different. I suspect if it were a different person every time—*every time*—the child would be upset. But there's no place in the world where that happens. There is always a core set of people.
Q. Right. Like at [one center we visited] it's one of six to eight people every day.
A. No problem. Children can adjust to that. I was in [the] Metera in Athens [an institutional home for motherless babies] in which the average infant had six caretakers. There was no problem in the first year of life. No problem.
Q. Because you get used to what you know. Is that it?
A. See, children are made of iron, not Scotch Tape. You say a child can only get attached to one person. Well, that's

like saying a person can only love one other person. And that's nonsense. A child can be attached to several people. He may have one favorite. My view is something like this. As long as the child is free from extreme physical pain and extreme unpredictability—that means he's fed regularly and cleaned moderately regularly, and there is variety in his life and an opportunity to practice his maturing abilities—it may be that is all he needs. And there'll be no crisis. . . . Can I tell you something which surprises me? There's no difference in attachment between the children you saw [at my day-care center] and a child of the same age and social class, working or middle, reared at home.

Q. How can you tell?

A. We've measured separation anxiety, proximity to mother, and playing with mother.

Q. In the North Carolina study they say they can't measure separation anxiety because maybe the child has never made an attachment in the first place.

A. All of our infants are attached. Now you may say to me your measures aren't sensitive enough. It's possible. But with the measures we use, we find they are equally attached.

We reminded Dr. Kagan of his views on attachment expressed in his book *Change and Continuity in Infancy*, in which he said "frequency and quality of interaction with the mother form the basis of an attachment."[1] He found that middle-class children tended to be more attached to their mothers than lower-class children, that stronger attachment meant more frequent interaction with the mother, and that strongly attached children showed "more marked verbal competence, sustained attention and inhibition."

Q. Is it then fair to say that you consider attachment to be an important and necessary part of development?

A. Yes, but I would change some of those ideas. A good scientist has to check his ideas continually and shed bad ones.
Q. How would you change it? Frequency and quality of interaction with a *number of caring adults*?
A. In the first place, I had an old-fashioned conception about attachment when I wrote that section.
Q. And you really consider that's old-fashioned?
A. Very old-fashioned.
Q. Anybody agree with you?
A. Just my staff.
Q. Then, what *are* your current views on attachment?
A. First, I don't know what attachment means.
Q. You won't accept the definition that when an eight- or nine-month-old child gets hysterical when his mother leaves . . .
A. I *know* that's not attachment.
Q. That's fear?
A. That's fear. As a matter of fact, I can show you any day of the week, if you want to come with me, we'll go into an apartment to an eight- or nine-month-old who has never seen you. And we'll stay around for an hour or two. And then we'll leave. In some of the cases the child will cry upon your leaving. Is that child attached to you?
Q. Upon *my* leaving?
A. Upon your leaving. So. Crying at parting is not attachment. Separation anxiety is not a measure of attachment. That doesn't mean there isn't anyone he's attached to.
Q. Is he screaming because he's lost something?
A. No, he's screaming because something happened he doesn't understand. Crying in a baby in that situation is analogous to when you and I become anxious when something unpredictable happens that we don't understand, as, for example, landing gear sounds strange when a 707 is coming in to land. We get a little anxious.

Or we don't hear the landing gear go down. Or we can't see the lights below. We become anxious.

Q. Because the other studies we've seen have just fudged the whole question. The one from North Carolina said "We don't know how to measure attachment because a child who can leave easily may never have been attached or they may be very. . . ."

A. I don't like the word but if you force me to use it I would say . . . Among all the people that the child in the first year is in contact with, a small number, sometimes one, have a special power to placate the baby when he's anxious or upset, and others can't. These people, these very same people, tend to buffer fear, that is to say, the child becomes less afraid when he's with these people than when he's not. I would say those people are the objects of attachment. We all know that some babies become less distressed when they're with a certain person.

Q. I feel that way about myself. . . . I am much more comfortable with certain people . . .

A. But it's different with adults. I would say the concept of attachment should not be generalized after the first year. Otherwise, I'm attached to my pipe because I'm anxious if I give up my pipe, I'm attached to my summer cabin, to my tennis racket, and the concept loses its meaning. Let's use the word "attachment" only for the first year of life and only for this real phenomenon. I think that children are attached to people. I have never met a child who wasn't attached to someone—no matter where it was in the world. Now whether that has anything to do with later trust, I don't know, or whether it has anything to do with later personality. If a black child in Harlem is attached in the first year and then is thrown into the world of the ghetto he's going to end up hating everybody. It is not because he wasn't attached.

Attachment is no protection against being an anxious or hostile adult.

Q. So attachment has nothing to do with Erikson's trust.

A. I think Erikson's wrong in this case.

Q. We wanted to ask you if you'd explain it to us because this is something—what we got out of Erikson is that the child, having his mother constantly with him and knowing that his wants are going to be supplied, gradually internalizes a sense of security that then enables him to stand alone.

A. I know what the catechism sounds like.

Q. All right. Well, I'm repeating it to you so in case I'm wrong you can stop me.

A. No, that's exactly what everyone—what Erikson believes. A majority of people believe that.

Q. Let's go on to something else. Is it then fair to say that you consider attachment to be an important and necessary part of development?

A. Yes. I would say yes to that. I think it's important that a child becomes attached. I don't want a child anxious. If he has an attachment figure, he will be less anxious at that time. It *is* important.

Q. But you feel that a good day-care center allows him to attach plenty?

A. To both their mother and auntie [caretaker]. Our children are attached to both.

Q. Does anyone know now how much time, in hours a day or number of interactions, is necessary to form an attachment?

A. The answer is that no one knows.

We asked about the kibbutz child who saw his parents for two or three hours a day. How did he develop an emotional attachment to parents with such limited contact and interaction?

A. When he's older?
Q. When he's younger, when he's older.
A. Well, when he's older, it's easy. It's symbolic.
Q. I should think it would be harder.
A. John F. Kennedy, Jr., was about two when his father died. If we could bring him here now, we would see an emotional identification with his father. I know children who *never* saw their fathers, who were killed in World War II, and they are identified with them. We're symbolic organisms and after 18 months symbolism becomes important. After that, interaction becomes less relevant and number of hours becomes less important. If I think you love me, you don't have to be with me at all. Consider the love for Jesus. People have never seen Jesus, and a great many people love Jesus and believe he loves them. It's not interaction. It's what you believe! Love is a beautiful tale one weaves out of experience. It makes you feel good to believe that your biological parents valued you. But there's no recipe by which that is done. There's no fixed, absolute pattern of kissing, hugging, and spanking that produces it.
Q. I find that very hard to accept. It seems to me . . . if the children are going to be peripheral and you're not going to interfere in any way, if they're going to be something that happens in odd hours of the day . . .
A. It depends on the child's *interpretation*. . . . It depends upon why he thinks his parents act in a special way.
Q. But why should parents do that unless they thought that what they were doing was more interesting and more exciting and more worthwhile than staying with the child?
A. But they can do *both*! They can say, "I am entitled to my pleasures and I also have a certain responsibility to you." I can imagine parents who could manage both. It's not *impossible*!
Q. But we keep thinking of the number of hours in the day.

A. American presidents and senators do not have much time for their children, but their children feel loved. Ask Tricia Nixon if she believes her father loved her. I'm quite sure she'll say, "He loved me." And you say, "But he was rarely home." She will reply, "I know, but he had important things to do." . . . The point is that as far as her personality is concerned, what is important is that she believes she is loved.

Q. Do you think day care can break the poverty cycle?

A. As intervention? No. The poverty cycle can only be broken by money. . . . How could day care break the poverty cycle?

Q. Not by making the kids a little bit more quick in school because they can. . . ?

A. Day care doesn't do that. It's impossible to break.

Q. When you say money, Dr. Kagan . . .

A. Poverty is caused by money.

Q. Because when you're only concerned about going hungry that's damned well what you're only concerned about.

A. Right.

Q. Will group care raise a different kind of person than family care?

A. Not independent of what the culture values. There is *no* absolute effect of any intervention. That is, there is no absolute effect of group care, of family care, independent of the values of society, the concepts with which the child grows. What is the effect of a temperature of 70 degrees? Isn't that a silly question? Wouldn't you say on *what*? On plants? On animals? On buildings? If I ask you, what's the effect of day care? You should say, *ON WHAT!*

Q. We talk a lot about the other cultures. Can we transplant other cultures' methods?

A. No, because you *can't* remake a method from the culture. Hence you can't expect kibbutz rearing to have the same effect here as there. Israel is fighting Arabs.

We're not fighting Arabs. That's a big difference. Israel is a small country that feels surrounded. You can't generalize a sound procedure from them to us.

Q. No. Maybe we can formulate something you can agree with. Many people say "It's no problem. Put your child in day care." Would you agree that it's not that simple?

A. Because there are a lot of problems. Good day care is very expensive, and good day care isn't that readily available. There is bad day care but no one wants any child in bad day care.

Q. We saw a very interesting group several weeks ago. We saw an 18-month-old baby boy, and we talked to the father of this child and he said, "My child has been raised in day care since he was one month old. Weekends are *hell* for us, because he cannot relate to us on a one-to-one basis. He is such a group-oriented child."

A. I doubt that.

Q. This is just what he said. And, he said, therefore my child is just going to be a different kind of child than children who are reared at home.

A. I would have believed that a year ago. I wrote two long articles on the evils of day care. I was against it.

Q. So, we're not so far *behind* you?

A. I wrote an article for *Psychology Today* and gave speeches against day care. And now I run a day-care center and I changed my mind. All of us have strong prejudices that are religious in intensity but not always based on *fact*. You believe in God or you don't believe in God—and that's it. We go around looking for facts to support our bias and there are no facts. *Something* has to be true and I hope our research uncovers something of truth.

Q. What do you think of separate vacations for mothers and small children under the age of two?

A. You always ask me questions I can't answer! What do you think of three steaks every six months?

Q. I'm asking your opinion.
A. I don't know what it means unless you mention the mother and child relationship, who's taking care of the baby, how the child's doing. I don't *know*! I wouldn't make a blanket statement.
Q. Some psychologists say that until a child is two you should not go away for any length of time, it's too traumatic for them.
A. Fine. I think it gives mothers security. All statements do. That doesn't mean it's true. It gives mothers security to have a statement.
Q. Speaking of mothers—do you see growth and development in parents as a result of nurturing? What *are* the positive effects for parents?
A. The positive effects for parents are if the child turns out in a way that the parent regards as creatively good and productive, then the parent feels like an artist, or as a scientist does after an important new discovery. . . .
Q. Do you think that our contemporary style of living—the isolation, the separation from family, and so on—contributes to the demand for day care?
A. No. No. No. There are at least three bases for valuing your children in the history of society and we have eliminated two of them. The most frequent reason in the history of man is that the child was an economic asset. In most of the world parents need the boy to help plant and the girl to help cook and care for infants. Therefore one takes care of them because they are valuable. That's a fundamental reason for valuing children. But we can't rely on that rationale today in America.

Then there is the matter of future value. Now that comes in two ways: In one case, you're lower middle class and your child is going to Yale or Princeton. You never went to college and your child will enhance your status. This essentially is an investment in the future for the parents. Or you went to college, but you went to a small college and your child is going to go to Harvard.

In a second instance, as in parts of Africa or South America, there's enormous prestige in having babies. I was in Kenya in December. There's nothing more honorific for a woman than to have a baby. The woman gets status as much as you may from owning a Mercedes. We've taken that status from the mother; we do not award status to a woman because she is having her third child.

A final reason rests with the personality of the mother. She may enjoy the creativity of sculpting and shaping a baby. In other times in Western society all three forces were operating to increase the investment of parent in baby. Now we only have one, because the other two have been taken away. Some women don't think they're temperamentally ready to be mothers. They doubt that they will enjoy the experience. I enjoy science, some of my friends don't. I enjoy tennis and hiking, some of my colleagues don't. You enjoy it or you don't enjoy it. My wife had enormous fun raising our daughter—it was lovely to watch. It's wonderful. I wish all mothers were able to take that much pleasure from raising a child. But the press, the mass media, make some women feel guilty about being a mother. That is too bad. It's like the Old Testament story of Esau being talked out of his birthright. It's a sad thing.

All right. Well—if you can persuade mothers to enjoy being mothers again you'll have done a social service. I think it would be great if you could do that.

So, we have Jerome Kagan, and if you found him to be in turn academic, sweeping, precise, contradictory, irascible, resigned, informed, prejudiced, compassionate, amused, and amusing, then you have shared with us an experience. And perhaps together we have deepened our understanding of the issues involved in day care.

Shortly after the interview with Dr. Kagan we visited T. Berry Brazelton, M.D., practicing pediatrician, associate professor of pediatrics at Harvard Medical School, chief of the Child Development Center, and author of two books, *Infants and Mothers* and *Toddlers and Parents: A Declaration of Independence*.

Dr. Brazelton, like Dr. Kagan, accepts day care as a way of raising infants. But Dr. Brazelton comes at the problem from the point of view of the practicing pediatrician, and that makes both his concerns and his way of expressing them different. The pediatrician, to underline the obvious, treats mother-baby *pairs*. Sick or well, the baby is largely dependent on the doctor's ministrations as filtered through the mother's care, and therefore the mother's physical and emotional well-being is crucial to the doctor's ability to treat the baby. So that is a constant in Dr. Brazelton's view of the problem. Moreover, 25 years of dealing with mothers has also undoubtedly had an affect on his manner with female interviewers. Dr. Brazelton is very calm. (An upset mother is not going to do as good a job as a calm mother.) Dr. Brazelton is restrained. Dr. Brazelton is downright laconic. But he is also concerned about his mothers and babies, and he gets in his share of zingers when he thinks they are threatened.

Q. Dr. Brazelton, we're concerned about the growing separation of mothers and infants and the trend toward day care. A lot of people who are pushing day care don't know anything about children. You know, a lot of things that you read . . .
A. A lot of people who are talking about children don't know anything about day care.
Q. Is day care going to make a different kind of person?
A. Probably is. There's certain evidence . . . there are very different kinds of people in Israel in the kibbutzim where the mothers' work plays a major role. No, I'm very confused right now. I'm not at all—I think that

there are some dangers in the kind of book you're talking about which I really think would be *dirty* to get into at this stage of the game because I think our society is in such a state of turmoil right now.

Q. You think it would be *what*?
A. Dirty.
Q. Dirty?
A. Yeah, and I worry about it in *my* book. To put down mothers who either *have* to use day care, *have* to give up their children or make them feel guilty if for their *own* reasons they have to, and I think this is true of a lot of the middle-class women I see, the intellectuals that I see, that whatever their reasons—whatever *we* might think about their reasons, they still are representative of fairly deep-seated needs on their part, and it may be more honest of them to face them and get out and get a job than to stay home and be ambivalent about these kids.

I think that I agree with Margaret Mead who said that we really set up an almost *impossible* situation for young girls to mother their children in this country by setting up these lonely nuclear family situations where —for which girls have not in *any* way been prepared, and they suddenly have a baby and *everything* that they've been prepared for suddenly dissolves around them and they're stuck at home.

Q. But we've met some girls in this situation. And we see that instead of remaining isolated, they sooner or later get together and by sharing . . .
A. They get together. Well, this is what I think, and I think that this is one of the most *positive* forces for our day care, community centers, parent-child centers, and all the rest. And I see them as *terribly* important and whether they're important to children, they *certainly* are to their mothers, and indirectly they become so to the children.

One of the most desolate, needs-supplementing groups I know of are the young, unwed mothers in a center we've been working with who get together in the center, and without it really would be lost, angry, hostile, all sorts of things, and what they do to their children in the process, you know, is—doesn't take much imagination. And in the day-care center they *all* sort of get fed each day. So, I guess what I'm saying is that I'd hate for you to go at this just to reinforce "a lonely mother-infant" situation.

Q. Dr. Brazelton, how does a baby attach to a mother he sees for an hour in the morning and an hour in the afternoon?

A. I really wouldn't have any question about the fact that a baby could. His needs are *so* great, and if *her* needs are great, and if she recognizes them and is able to meet them because of the supplementation they have during the rest of the day, I think she'll do a lot more attaching and giving the baby a chance to attach in an hour in the morning and an hour at night than she ever might over a 12-hour period when she wasn't having her own needs met at all.

Q. Dr. Kagan says he sees no difference in attachment between home-reared babies and center-reared babies, so far. Does that square with your experience, that—and if it does, *why*? I don't understand *why*!

A. I don't like that kind of sweeping statement. Do I agree with it? There are just so many variables in something like that that I wouldn't attempt any way of answering it. I can't honestly say that I *do*. But I don't know enough about it to—that would mean a damn thing.

Q. We saw Dr. Kagan, and we came in with all these quotes and we said to him, "What about all these things you said in your book?" and he said, "I don't believe them any more." We have the same kind of a quote from you. You say in *Infants and Mothers*, "Each extra month of mothering is like money in the bank for both mother and child. . . . The mother loses out on an intimate knowledge of the baby as he grows, and she suffers from ambivalent feelings when she shares children with mother-substitutes."[2] And now you're supporting day care. You guys change grounds on us too fast!

A. I agree with that quote though.

Q. You *do* agree with. . . ?

A. I still do. But I don't think I want to make everybody feel guilty.

Q. No. To get back to attachment—we've read, for example, that one of the unhappy possibilities about family day-care homes, that is, a home where one woman is taking care of a number of children, is that a baby is liable to make his strong attachment to the family-care mother rather than to his own mother, and that it is very painful to a mother to see her child prefer someone else. So, many people prefer group day care because there isn't going to be this strong attachment. Do you think . . .

A. I wouldn't say that so much as I'd turn it another way. I'd say we ought to be educating these home day-care operators to *not* be looking at just the baby, to be looking at the whole mother-infant relationship as their goal, and if they were not setting themselves in *competition* with the mother—unconsciously—which I think is awfully easy to do around a baby because everybody feels competitive about taking care of a baby—if they could be somehow motivated and trained to see this young girl as *just* as needy as the baby, and just as dependent and just as helpless as the baby, and could then see their goal as cementing these two by helping the mother free herself for a while and giving her something that she lacked . . .

Q. Is this competition for the baby less at a center?

A. Let me tell you what we saw at [one] day-care center. Here we have girls that are mostly unwed, certainly feel unloved and unwanted, bringing their babies in the morning and the day-care operators, who come from the same group of people as the mothers do, will *snatch* the baby away, give it a bath right in front of the mother, feed it, and then they say, "Now you can go." Well, what they're saying implicitly is, "You don't know how to take care of your baby so *we'll* get the baby in shape and then you can go." Well, of course the mother runs. Of *course* she snatches the baby [back in the evening] and runs. But I don't think it needs to be that way.

Q. Dr. Kagan said that perhaps a minimum amount of affective and gratifying contact with an adult is all an infant needs.

A. I don't think I'd say that a *minimum* amount of affective and gratifying contact would be the way I'd put it at all. It would be the opposite of the way I'd put it. I'd say that the *kind* of affective and gratifying contact the baby needs is *so* specialized and has to be *so* individualized to meet the child's needs that if a mother can do this for a few periods during the day, *that* may keep them cemented and keep things going even though the rest of the day they haven't the opportunity to be together.

I think we ought to be trying to *cement* families, not tear them apart, and I think this is what appeals to me about [certain] day-care centers—and the kinds of day-care centers we ought to be thinking about as alternative models. . . . We ought to be setting up different alternatives for people but *always* with the major goal of keeping families together and keeping children and their mothers interacting with each other in an optimal way, not in quantity but in quality.

Q. How can you strengthen a family by taking the children away? That sounds to us like the kinds of things that are occasionally put forth as strengthening marriage. You know, prostitution, adultery, and now divorce is considered as one of the things that really saves marriage. If people marry sequentially, then the institution survives.

A. You see, you go at it with an entirely different point of view from mine. Just the way you say, "Taking the child away from the family" implies that this is a goal, "to take the child away." *My* goal is to supplement the family with choices and with models for supplementation for both the mother and the child and the father, to make it work for them and to keep the family together and to keep the mother caring about the child rather than throw it out the window! . . . Once a woman has *made* a decision to have a baby, then I think *all* of our goals ought to be, including day care and whatever else, and not just one model, ought to be to try to make it as exciting an interaction and as rewarding a one as we can make it. And I guess what I'm really worried about would be that you take day care as a sort of whipping post and make enough mothers feel that, "Gosh, I've done the worst thing possible for my child."

Q. Why do you emphasize quality of time and discount quantity of time? Because I figure if someone wants to spend time with me, it's because they like me. And if they don't bother to call me for four months, I begin to question, you know, that they don't think so much of me. So why do babies do different? If the mother chooses to have her baby someplace else for most of her week, why doesn't the baby get the feeling that the mother doesn't feel that strongly about it?

A. Well, I don't think they're as fixed in some of their mechanisms as we may be.

Q. But the thing about quality is, you see, from all the literature we've read, *tons*, and the interviews we've done, when mom gets home with pop, between six and seven, and she wants at that point to provide this quality care, what about this baby? Maybe this is not the baby's time to be responsive.

A. Well, I think we ought to see that it is. I think the center ought to keep the baby and give it a long nap and have it ready for her when she comes, and we ought to put enough value on that for mothers so that *they* are ready when the time comes, and fathers and mothers who are working ought to make it a *priority* to have a time with their baby when it's appropriate for the baby.

In my practice, when I see a mother who is working, I tell her to tell her sitter or her day-care operator to give the baby a good two-to-three-hour nap and then the child will stay up to 9 o'clock at night so they have the time together.

If you can do this, and we do it all the time, with kids whose fathers are doctors and interns and never see them, the mothers set it up so they get up when the father gets home at eight or nine and they all have a family time. . . . But there's no reason to be so rigid and so fixed in our ideas about what can and can't be done, if you have priorities . . . and you value the quality of family interaction.

The way we come to judge centers now, in our study last year, the most important thing was to see if really they fitted into the *rhythms* of the children, and whether they respected the kind of need to let down and build up, let down and build up, and this is one of the things that I think goes into the quality of the mother-child interaction and whether it can be done in a short time or not. If a mother can be sensitive to a child's needs even for a very brief . . .

Q. But we still don't understand this. It's not a question of a mother being sensitive. It's that a mother has between 6:30 and 7:30, or between 6:30 and 9:30. There it is. That's the time she has when she gets home from work and before bedtime and it seems very hard because you don't know when kids are going to come up with something that's really bothering them, and you can't say to them at 6:30, "Now, I want to hear what's on your mind." How can you give an hour's quality interaction to a six-month-old? You'd go bananas! You have quality interactions in two-minute bits with a six-month-old all through the day, not between 6:30 and 7:30.

A. You've got a rigid model. A six-month-old would lap it up! So I don't agree with you. . . . I think you may be looking with blinders on, and excluding an awful lot of people that can't *afford* the ideal. And so you may not only be losing out on helping people that really could use it more than the ones that fit into this model, but you may be turning off a lot of people, turning them off about themselves and doing some damage that way . . .

Q. What do you think of Dr. Blaine's suggestion that school should be open 11 months a year, 6 days a week, 8 A.M. to 6 P.M., and children should be in school from age 3 months to 18 years?

A. That would be just the opposite of what I'd be trying to aim at. I think we ought to be trying to cement families, not tear them apart, and [that is what I look for] in the kinds of day-care centers we ought to be thinking about as alternative models . . . *always* with the major goal of keeping families together and keeping children and their mothers interacting with each other in an optimal way, not in quantity but in quality.

Q. Are pediatricians being trained to deal with the needs of young working mothers and infants?

A. Absolutely not. No. Pediatricians are not being trained for—we're just starting to now.

Q. You're going to train them for day care?

A. We're going to train them to think about infants and chil-

dren and parents. Well, gee, I wish you good luck on your venture.
Q. We'll try to be more broad-minded.
A. Yeah, do.

THE AUTHORS REPLY

A number of major issues raised in the preceding interviews call for more careful examination from us than was possible at the time. Is this a dirty book? What *about* attachment and separation anxiety? Is the final word truly to be that quality is more important than quantity? Can the natural rhythms of both mother and child be synchronized so that they are ready for quality interaction at the same time? And finally, what is the likelihood of our being able to set up large numbers of centers that provide good growing environments for children from one month to four years?

First, what about Dr. Brazelton's charge that this may be a dirty book? Is it dirty to question malnutrition because a lot of parents can't afford to feed their children properly? Is it dirty to question the carnage caused by automobiles because so many of us have no alternative but to use cars? Is it dirty to question the pollution caused by many industries because workers must work to support their families? Is it to the greater good of all of us to let these conditions go unchecked because guilt is such a burden?

Nonsense. Such an attitude would be ridiculous and irresponsible. And it is equally ridiculous and irresponsible not to question day care simply because society has arranged things in such a way that some people have no choice but to use it.

The point is that our responsibility is different from Dr. Brazelton's. His job is to protect mothers and babies in the world in which he finds them. Our job is to say, "Is this the best world we can set up for mothers and babies? If it is, fine. If it isn't, let's change things." So no, Dr. Brazelton, we must respectfully disagree. This is not a dirty book.

The quality-versus-quantity issue has become an argument conducted with great heat and no light on both sides, as might have been expected when complex human problems become reduced to three words. The necessity to take sides seduces even normally rational people into totally untenable positions, an indictment that falls equally on all of us. For example, time and again we have found ourselves opting for quantity over quality. But we don't *believe* that! Never would we prefer a very young child to have 24-hour-a-day contact, 365 days a year, with any mother, no matter how loving, saintly, and skillful. What we mean, of course, but usually forget to say in the heat of opposing the quality people, is that we want enough quantity to allow for *numerous* high-quality interactions, and that's a very different thing.

On the other hand, those who opt for quality certainly don't mean five minutes worth of quality interaction every two weeks, or ten minutes every day. They know that there has to be some quantity mixed in there somewhere. But the people who take comfort from experts who tell them that quality is more important than quantity sometimes arrive at strange interpretations, as witness a young woman we talked to recently. She holds a doctorate in psychology, is at her desk from 7 A.M. to 5:30 P.M. every day, and told us with touching sincerity that she was sure she could fit a baby into that schedule. "I'd find a good day-care center," she said earnestly, "and when I would be with my baby, it would be very high-quality time, because I think quality is more important than quantity. We could," she continued, visibly searching for a really high-quality thing she and this future baby could do together, "we could," she concluded triumphantly, "search for pine cones at dusk!" As a quality activity for a baby this left something to be desired, we thought, but as a conversation-stopper it was a blockbuster.

So quality versus quantity is an issue we wish would go away, and then all of us could sound as intelligent as Dr. John Bowlby, who wrote to us, "I think that the issue of quality of time spent with an infant being more important than quantity of time is rather a red herring, *because both are important. Without sufficient time for relaxed enjoyment, the quality is bound to suffer* [our emphasis]."3

Closely allied to this nonissue of quality versus quantity is Dr. Brazelton's emphasis on setting things up so that when working mother and baby are together they are physically and emotionally prepared to give to and take from each other all the emotional sustenance that he believes is so important to them both. We thought at the time, and still do, that it is an ideal devoutly to be wished. But there are internal contradictions in Dr. Brazelton's own work that make us wonder if it is an attainable ideal.

There are two points to consider. First, Dr. Brazelton told us that it is important to see if a center really fits into the rhythms of the children, and if it respects the normal need of children to let down and build up, let down and build up. But he also wants the center to nap a very young child for a long time in the afternoon so that the child will be ready to spend some time with his parents in the evening, rested, content, and ready for real emotional, physical, and intellectual contact.

We see some problems here. To enforce a long afternoon nap is essentially manipulative and has nothing to do with respect for a child's natural rhythms. We recall, for example, sitting quietly on the floor, backs against the wall, beside a lovely 18-month-old girl who had been put down on her mat for a two-hour rest period. She was good as gold, that baby. She looked at pictures in a book, played with her fingers, turned side to side and back to front, and obediently put her head back down every time she raised it and the day carer spotted her—

for two hours! And this is one of the finest centers in the Boston area. Sure, most of the other children needed the nap time, and a few hardy souls rebelled sufficiently that they had to be taken from the room. But this was a *good* baby, and so she suffered.

We also worry about a working mother's natural rhythms. Most working women don't have a chance to set up their day so that they are rested and content and able to give the best of themselves to their children at five-thirty in the evening. Dr. Brazelton told us that in his practice he sees many young mothers with intern and doctor husbands who arrange their babies' schedules so that, when the father comes home at 9 P.M., they can all, mother, father, and baby, have a family time together. We have no argument with the fact that with a little pushing and pulling an at-home mother could have her child rested, alert, and ready to interact with his intern father who arrives home at 9 P.M. after 36 hours on call. But we have a lot of doubt about whether a bright, alert, ready-to-go baby is going to look better to that tired father than a soft bed in a quiet room.

The second point that bothers us is that, while Dr. Brazelton insisted in the interview that mothers can work and babies can be cared for elsewhere, and both can thrive, his book, *Toddlers and Parents: A Declaration of Independence*, is replete with problems that arise when mothers and infants are apart. Granted that the doctor uses the device of presenting problems so that he can then offer solutions. Still, it seems clear that the problems he mentions are built-in and the solutions are hard to find.

For instance, we mentioned earlier the story of the 15-month-old girl who, together with several other children, was cared for all day in the home of a calm, motherly woman. As Dr. Brazelton presents the case, when the mother picks up the child at the end of the day the mother is ready for some loving. But the baby girl is ready for a tantrum. Says Dr. Brazelton:

This is a typical response in this age group due to the combination of fatigue, the pent-up excitement of getting home to mother, the steam which she'd stored up all day, plus the opportunity and safety her own surroundings provided to let herself go.[4]

Dr. Brazelton points out that the need among toddlers to work out the issues of independence, ambivalence, and negativism is so great that though the need can be postponed all day long, the feelings will eventually burst out. He worries that "Too calm and pacific an atmosphere may not offer as many opportunities for learning about oneself as a child this age might have at home."[5] He would prefer to have the baby cared for by someone whose personality would somehow allow the baby to act out her negative feelings during the day instead of saving them all up for her parents.

Well, of course it would be better. But after you've found someone to care for your child whom you can afford, who is reasonably convenient to get to, who has room for your child, who seems warm and loving, whose house is clean and safe, who is responsible and creates an atmosphere in which the children seem secure and busy and happy—after you've found this marvelous woman, isn't it expecting a lot to demand that she also somehow—and she may not *know* how—allow, indeed encourage the baby to act out his or her negative feelings there rather than at home with you in the evening?

On second thought, would it really be better? After all, learning to handle one's own anger and frustration constructively, finding that balance between the two destructive alternatives of turning it all inward and turning it all outward, is a pretty momentous thing. Giving a child freedom to feel but setting necessary limits as to the ways he can express these feelings is important! While handling tantrums certainly doesn't rate high in anyone's personal hierarchy, deep close relationships are built on the full range of emotions, not just the sunny side we try to turn to strangers, and the emotions that erupt around the age of two may never again surface as easily to enable a kind of open resolution.

On balance, of course, Dr. Brazelton is perfectly right. When a mother works all day and comes home tired, but with a day's worth of love saved up to expend on her child, it is hard and undoubtedly counterproductive to have the child meet the proferred love with a day's worth of stored-up anger and frustration. Still, unless we are all of the picking-up-pine-cones-at-dusk school of thought, we have to recognize that working mother and day-care baby are missing out on valuable chances to know and understand each other.

The issue of attachment in day care caused a lot of confusion in the interviews. Dr. Kagan doesn't know what attachment is but he does know that all his day-care children *are* whatever it is. Dr. Brazelton thinks that day-care babies *could* attach and certainly seems to feel strongly that they *should*, only he prefers them to *cement* to their mothers rather than to *attach*, which to an untutored mind might seem the same.

A recent study at Harvard University by three Ph.Ds, one of whom is also an M.D., illustrated the work currently being done on attachment. If a mother takes a baby into a strange place, settles him down with some toys, then ostentatiously waves good-bye and walks out, leaving the baby alone, the baby will cry. He will cry whether he has been reared at home by his mother or in a day-care center by one particular caretaker. And he will start to cry sooner when he's older (nine-and-a-half months) than when he's younger and it takes a while for him to realize what's happened.

This is the study that led Dr. Kagan to say that crying at separation is a measure of cognitive ability rather than attachment. Well, it certainly is interesting to have some graphs to look at, which the study has, and to know the following:

Analysis of variance for groups (day-care and home-reared) and sex with age as a repeated measure revealed that age was the only significant result (F = 44.22; $df = 5/164$; $p < .001$). Large decreases in latency to cry occurred from 7 1/2 to 9 1/2 months (+ = 4.62; df = 38; p < .001) and again from 11 1/2 to 13 1/2 months (+ = 5.39; df = 33; p < .001).[6]

We are going to do our own checking on this some day. It will be a simple investigation. We'll line up ten mothers and grandmothers and ask them what will happen when you dump a baby in a strange room and walk out on him, leaving him alone, and if they tell us that the 3 1/2-month-old may not notice right away but the one-year-old will holler, well then, we'll know Kagan et al. really have something.

We have not gone through the above exercise to prove either Dr. Kagan's stupidity or our own. Our serious intent, aside from having a little fun at our own expense, is to indicate what tiny, discrete pieces of information on mothers and babies are being conscientiously studied and quantified by diligent researchers, and how far their results still are from being able to say anything definitive. Beyond that, our hope is that young mothers, realizing this, will find the confidence to say, "This can't be good for my baby. Look how miserable it makes him!" and have some faith that someday someone will produce statistics that prove beyond a shadow of a doubt that what they knew was right all along *was* right all along.

So the issue of attachment was left pretty much up in the air in the two interviews, with both doctors agreeing that a child should attach (or cement) and that a child can and will attach, but with uncertainty on Kagan's part as to how attachment is measured or defined, and with a stringent set of requirements on Brazelton's part as to the behavior of the mother and the caretaker to insure that "cementing" between mother and child does take place.

In contrast, John Bowlby is very clear about the issue, and his views must be considered in rebuttal. In one of his papers he talks about the concept of a secure base:

> Evidence is accumulating that human beings of all ages are happiest and able to deploy their talents to best advantage when

they are confident that, standing behind them, there are one or more trusted persons who will come to their aid should difficulties arise. The person trusted, also known as an attachment figure, can be considered as providing his (or her) companion with a secure base from which to operate.[7]

Bowlby goes on to point out that the need of an attachment figure, a secure base, continues through life, although not with the urgency found in the earliest years. Moreover, the need probably differs both between sexes and at different times in life.

There are two variables involved—the partial or complete presence or absence of someone willing and able to act as a secure base, and the ability of the individual to recognize such a person:

> Throughout life the two sets of variables interact in complex and circular ways. In one direction, the kinds of experience a person has, especially during childhood, greatly influence both whether he expects later to find a secure, personal base, or not, and also the degree of competence he has to initiate and maintain a mutually rewarding relationship when opportunity offers. In the reverse direction the nature of the expectations a person has and the degree of competence he brings play a large part in determining both the kinds of person with whom he associates and how they then treat him. Because of these interactions, whatever pattern is first established tends to persist. This is a main reason why the pattern of family relationships a person experiences during childhood is of such crucial importance for the development of his personality.[8]

All this does not mean that Bowlby is suggesting that we raise dependent people. Rather, his healthy individuals have the ability to move back and forth between two positions—to provide a secure base for someone else when necessary and to make use of a secure base for themselves when they need one. (This view of the healthy personality is also advanced by

Abraham Maslow.) And of course the beginning of all of this is the infant who is cared for *principally* by one mother figure. (The Harvard Pre-School Project, for example, suggests that a mother be available to her baby for at least half his waking hours.)

Bowlby continues, "Evidence suggests that infants always become attached to one preferred figure with two or three others with whom they are happy provided nothing has gone wrong, e.g., they are hurt, frightened or unwell. On those occasions, they are usually not happy except with their preferred figure."[9] Based on his views and experience, Bowlby believes that a comparison between children in day-care centers and those at home would show that the day-care children cried more, played less, and engaged more in comfort habits such as thumbsucking and rocking.

Finally, we have to deal with the fact that Drs. Kagan and Brazelton were talking about "best" day care. What are our chances for finding such a center for our children?

The center set up and observed by Dr. Kagan was located in a large (40' by 50') carpeted room with floor-to-ceiling windows looking onto a courtyard. Infants (3 1/3 to 14 months) were separated from toddlers (14 to 30 months) by multilevel movable platforms that encouraged freedom of movement within a safely sheltered area. Adjacent to the main room were a sleeping room and a room for sand and water play. The center, you will remember, was staffed by mature mothers from the area, all of whom were chosen for their ability to relate to children with warmth and enthusiasm, and all of whom were familiar and dependably there.

The cost of this day care was $75 a week in 1973. (In 1976 the cost jumped to $85 a week.) That's $3,750 a year per child for a 50-week year. The director of the center, Alma McKinnon, was a highly trained, knowledgeable, and concerned woman. The director and the caretakers were all conscious of the fact that they and the children under their care were constantly being studied and tested in a five-year effort that was going to make a significant impact on the future of day care.

When you put all this together—adequately paid, rigorously selected, well-trained, highly motivated adults, a one to three adult-child ratio, a carefully designed environment, and constant professional supervision—you get the best. And someone who studies this best can look and report, "This works! This really works!" And maybe it does. The only thing is, Dr. Kagan, most of us don't have access to such a center, and if we did, most of us couldn't afford it.

On second thought, we'd like our center to include some of the philosophy expressed by Dr. Brazelton and his associate Dr. Edward Tronic. We would like to know that the staff thought of our family as a unit and kept uppermost in their minds the goal of cementing our children to us, even in our day-long absence. We wouldn't have had the children, after all, if family hadn't been of importance. So although we don't know how it's done, we want the staff to remember us and our problems and our rhythms. Somehow, without doing violence to our children, we want the staff to turn them back to us in the evening happier to see us than they were all day with them, yet not distressed by being with their second-best preferred people for nine hours; rested and alert enough so we can enjoy them, and still not so thoroughly emotionally catharticized that we don't have a chance to get emotionally involved with them; and in short, prepared to cram a full day's living into the few short hours before we all collapse.

It may be possible to set up some few centers here and there that meet the standards for good substitute care. We do not see the possibility that day care on a large scale could measure up to the standards set by Dr. Kagan under optimal conditions or the human requirements hoped for by Dr. Brazelton, and so we take issue with the implication that since they did it, therefore it can be done.

We offer the view of Dr. Mary Elizabeth Keister, director

of the Demonstration Project: Group Care of Infants, at the University of North Carolina at Greensboro:

> Shall we serve infants in group day care? We wish we knew! We wish we could give an unequivocal answer, but we believe it must remain open to question. At times we even wish our own findings were not so encouraging. We find it disturbing to hear the casual comment, "It's O.K., you know. Down there in Greensboro they've shown it's O.K., the babies aren't harmed." And we expect that to the visitor to our Nursery it all looks deceptively simple, really quite easy. But we should emphasize that it is *not* easy, this warm, affectionate, individualized care. Those beneficent intimacies of home life, so important, are impossible to guarantee in any and every setting. Yes, it can be done. This we have shown. Can anyone do it? We hope so, but we doubt it. Not that we are the only ones with the requisite know-how. Rather, we have hardly defined for ourselves yet what it is that we must provide. We cannot at this point state with certainty what is a necessary minimum, what is sufficient, what is optimal. So much remains to be learned, to be demonstrated, before there is a model or models for many to follow. In the meantime, babies are vulnerable, toddlers at the mercy of our groping efforts to learn. We would urge: let us move into this field cautiously, carefully, putting the babies' interests ahead of new projects, of mothers' demands, of the excitement of another pioneering effort.[10]

NOTES

[1] Jerome Kagan, *Change and Continuity in Infancy* (New York: Wiley, 1971), p. 167.

[2] T. Berry Brazelton, *Infants and Mothers* (New York: Dell, 1969), p. 280.

[3] John Bowlby, personal correspondence, June 25, 1973.

[4]T. Berry Brazelton, *Toddlers and Parents: A Declaration of Independence* (New York: Delacorte, 1974), p. 41.

[5]Ibid., p. 37.

[6]Richard B. Kearsley et al., "Separation Protest in Day Care and Home-Reared Infants" in *Pediatrics*, (vol. 55, No. 2, February 1975, p. 171-75).

[7]John Bowlby, "Self-Reliance and Some Conditions That Promote It," in *Support, Innovation and Autonomy* (London: Tavistock, 1972), p. 1.

[8]Ibid.

[9]John Bowlby, personal correspondence, June 25, 1973.

[10]Mary E. Keister, *A Demonstration Project Report, Group Care of Infants and Toddlers* (Greensboro: University of North Carolina, 1970), p. 63.

8

CHOOSING

Jean Matson, 22, has a high school education, a two-room apartment, an 11-month-old baby, a husband who ran off two weeks ago, $25 in cash, and a determination to earn her own way. Jean needs a job fast—and she needs to find someone to take care of her baby while she's working.

Fran Bennett, 28, is an assistant admissions officer at a small city college and the wife of an executive in a chain of discount stores. Fran is seven months pregnant and she's shopping for baby care in advance of the time, five months hence, when she plans to return to work.

Roz Livoli, 46, is in a community action group concerned with the development of children under the age of six. What programs should her group support?

Women like Jean are in a bind. They're going to take the first kind of child care they can find. Later, perhaps, they will be able to look around. Women like Fran have their choice. Should they hire women to come in? Ask their mothers or mothers-in-law if they'd like to start raising a baby again in their 50s? Look for a family day-care home or an infant day-care center? And Roz and her fellow activists are listening to day-care advocates, family home-care advocates, advocates for guaranteed income, and those who believe a woman's place is in the home and that she should be supported. The one thing that Roz and her committee are sure of is that they must see to it that whatever care is available for a child, it will foster and not hinder that child's development.

It is the purpose of this chapter to throw more light on the pros and cons of the various alternatives for child care presented in chapter 2. This, we hope, will help parents make wiser choices.

GUIDELINES

First, no one answer is best. Any kind of alternative care is just as good—and just as bad—as the person who is doing the caring. As we consider the alternatives we will point out the good and the bad in each.

Second, we have come away from our investigation convinced that if *one* single, mostly present, warm, loving, dependable, mother-substitute figure is not absolutely necessary, a whole battalion of rotating mother-substitute figures is absolutely undesirable. For under-threes, the fewer adults who give primary care the better.

Third, we have come to understand that any care giver can create a gulf between a child and his parents—or can actually, even in the parents' absence, strengthen the child's growing conviction that he belongs to a family unit that is paramount in his life.

And last, we believe that in a free society there must be choices, a range of options that will give each child a place where he can thrive and be secure in his parents' absence, and where his parents will be comfortable about leaving him.

Given these guidelines, we will look at care by a woman who comes to one's home, care by a relative, care in a family day-care home, and care in a group day-care center.

THE CAREGIVER WHO COMES TO YOUR HOME

When you are looking for someone to come into your home, you start with references. Everyone must know *someone* who can attest to her reliability, sobriety, honesty, and even temperament. Written references are a start, but a telephone conversation will get you farther, faster. If the references all check out, then you and your baby should interview the woman. Past experience with children is a definite plus. Any mother will tell you that she was much more relaxed raising her second than she was with her first, and someone who is experienced will be a less nervous caretaker.

But what you're really looking for is a match. Is she crazy-clean while you are neat but dirty? How does she feel about pets, walks, TV, naps, diapers, toilet training? Is she a polish-the-plate kind of person while you are one to put the plate down and then take it away and trust in Providence and your child that he will get enough to eat? How does she hold your baby? Does she look comfortable? Does the baby look comfortable? How does she come on to your touch-me-not eight- or nine-month-old? If you have a crawler, is she as alert to the fact that he's chewing on the lamp cord as you are? (If neither of you notices it, that's a whole different kind of problem!)

When you are sure in your own mind that this is the woman for you and your baby, then interview several more applicants. Practice makes perfect, and at each interview you notice a little more, pick up a few more clues. You may very well go back to your first woman, but you'll be a lot surer if you've spoken to several.

The advantages of this kind of care are many, and one of the most significant is the fact that you can handpick the person who will care for your child. Then, too, on a purely practical level, you don't have to dress the baby and take it out of the house on cold, dark mornings, and if the baby is sick your helper will probably still come and you won't have to miss work. Most important, of course, your baby will have one person other than his parents who understands and reinforces his early attempts at communication, one person whose ways your baby will soon be able to fit into the growing order of his world.

Dr. Humberto Nagera, professor of psychiatry and chief of the Youth Services of the Department of Psychiatry at the University of Michigan, points out that a child's brain grows to three-fourths of its adult size in its first two years, and the stimulation that the child receives is crucial to his brain's development to its full potential.[1]

By stimulation Nagera does not mean a cacophony of undecipherable sounds and sights. He talks about very new babies. They have, he says, short periods of alertness surrounded by long periods of somnolence. This is not quite the same as saying the baby sleeps a lot. Anyone who has cared for an infant can remember times when they checked the baby and found it wide awake, eyes open, but not yet crying. And most of us, particularly if the child is ours and if we are alone with him, are so delighted—"charmed," Nagera says—by this unexpected alertness and the prospect of a little human company that we fall all over ourselves talking and chirping to this wide-eyed waiting bundle. "Well, hello!" we will say, "were you just waiting for me to come in? Finally got bored with all that sleeping? I don't blame you. How are you doing? Dry? That'll be the day, won't it? There. How's *that* feel? Good? What say we go into the other room for a while?" And so on. "This type of interaction," says Nagera, "has a chain effect: such states of alertness tend to arise more frequently when the child is responded to. Thus, the mother's response leads to increased alertness and to the wish for more contact."[2]

Nagera worries that, in a group, the caretaker may not notice the baby until it is in distress and hollering, and a vital chance for interaction will have been lost. By extension, we would guess that Dr. Nagera would see the chance for more interaction from a woman who comes into your home than he would see in a group-care situation.

Of course, there are disadvantages to a come-in woman, too. A baby-sitter is only human, and if she gets sick you're out of luck, and also out of work, until she's on her feet again and back in your house. One helpful suggestion from a veteran of these particular wars is to try to get a backup caretaker who will be on hand in an emergency before the emergency arises—a friend of yours, or perhaps a friend of your caretaking woman.

When your woman is on the job, no one is supervising her. And she is liable to all the problems of isolation and loneliness that face mothers marooned in their own homes with infants. Here a lot depends on your home. If you are in an apartment in an inner-city area, it may not be a particularly safe place for a woman and baby to go for a stroll. If you are in a neighborhood where there are no other children, the problem will obviously be more severe than if you are in a safe neighborhood in a warm climate with other mothers and babies around. Are you within walking distance of a store or two, so that your baby-sitter can vary her day—and that of your baby—with a walk and visit with a neighbor or storekeeper?

While the opportunity for a little sociability is always important for the woman who is caring for your baby, it will become increasingly important for your baby as he nears 18 months. Then you will have to balance his continuing need for a secure, known, and loved day carer with the beginnings of his need to be at least occasionally around other toddlers and other children of varied ages.

At this point many mothers feel that it is time to move their child to a small group setting. Frankly, we're stumped on this one. In general, we feel that the more constancy and the more predictability there is for under-threes, the more secure and adaptable these children will be as adults. So perhaps you feel that you yourself can begin to introduce your child to other children on weekends. Church nurseries on Sunday morning, for example, are a classic first step into a group setting, as is the simple experience of a Sunday afternoon visit with relatives or friends who also have a small child. These slow and easy introductions to others may be sufficient to allow your now-toddler to continue spending his days with his preferred day carer.

CARE BY RELATIVES

Care by grandmothers, aunts, or other relatives, which is the kind of alternative care most used in this country, has many of the same pluses and minuses as care by a woman who comes into your home, with two exceptions. You don't have to advertise and interview, and you probably will have to take your baby to their house. Additionally, unless your mother and sister are different from our mothers and sisters, you will find that relatives will do things their own way without taking much from you by way of instruction. But on the other hand, your mother or sister may well think much as you do in terms of raising children and will not need much direction, even if they are disposed to take it.

Grandmothers are often great for infants. By the time the infant becomes a toddler there may be two problems. Does the grandmother have enough physical get-up-and-go to chase a toddler all day long and keep her temper? And will the grandmother have access to other small children when it is time to think about socialization? Sisters and sisters-in-law who are home probably have one or two or more children of their own, so you don't have to worry about socialization. But you do have to give thought to the one-to-one reinforcement. Will your sister have the emotional surplus to be as delighted as you are with your baby's small triumphs?

These are all very individual problems, and every mother-father-baby-caretaker quartet will bring a different mix to any situation. We can only alert you to broad kinds of considerations. The exact measurements will have to come from you.

FAMILY DAY CARE

In chapter 2 we described in some detail family day-care homes, and in particular a family day-care home program designed to eliminate the problems of this kind of care and emphasize its positive aspects. We happen to be partisans of good family day care. There are those, and we will quote them, who disagree. But first, here is the best that a well-supervised program can offer your child.

We begin with the belief that if a child needs certain conditions to grow and thrive physically, emotionally, and intellectually at home, and he can't be at home, then the best way to proceed is to duplicate those same conditions as far as possible in his home-away-from-home. A day-care home will be more like your home than a day-care group center. By day-care home we mean, as you will remember, a private home where your child or children plus one or two others are taken care of by the woman—or man—who lives in the home and probably has one or two young children of his or her own.

When well done, this can be a much warmer, more stimulating, less threatening experience for a very young child than the best centers—and it may be your only alternative because infants and toddlers are often not accepted by centers. If you do find a center that accepts infants and toddlers, you have to ask yourself some hard questions about their philosophy, method of operation, adult-child ratio, and cost structure that allow that center to accept infants when most cannot. It may be that the occasional center that takes infants is better run than the majority of centers that don't, but satisfy yourself on these points first.

A good day-care home can offer all the individualized attention, security, close relationship with a single mother substitute, and intellectual stimulation that a day-care center offers. It often offers more. Chances are that a child will be in a group with an age range somewhere between one month and five years. In a group-care center he is likely to be in his own age group. There are advantages to a mixed-age group, the kind of advantages that used to be present in large families. The littlest ones have the example of a somewhat older child that they can try to copy—a sitter will watch a crawler, a crawler sees a toddler, a child who can build a stack of blocks can try to imitate an older child who has a tower as tall as he is. On the other hand, an older child gets a sense of his own growing capabilities compared to younger children and a chance to begin to learn responsibility toward those more helpless than himself.

Family day care offers a home environment with which many parents feel more comfortable. But there are additional distinct advantages to such a home environment. Because we all are so familiar with homes and many of us are unfamiliar with centers, we tend to overlook the enormous variety of things that happen in a home that aren't likely to happen in a center. Beds are made, floors are swept, bathrooms are cleaned, laundry is done, meals are cooked, tables are set, dishes are washed, errands are run. The phone rings and must be answered, or the day-care mother makes a call out. Someone comes to the door—the paper boy, mailman, delivery boy, repairman. A neighbor comes in to borrow a stick of margarine or have a cup of coffee. A baby gets bathed, changed, and fed, plants are watered, the spaghetti sauce goes on to simmer on a back burner, the laundry is folded and put away.

Talk about learning concepts and language development and motor stimulation! Then think about the single experience of four children aged one to five in the bedroom helping to make the bed and straighten the room. Don't think about the day-care mother *trying* to make the bed and straighten the room—she asked for the job, she's getting paid for doing it, and she's probably enjoying it as much as the children are. Some of us are like that!

So think about the children. They are *on top of* or *underneath* the bed. The bed is *big* or *small*. It is *soft*. The floor is *hard*. The pillows are *softer*. The chair is *clean*. The floor is *dirty*. *First*, the *mattress pad*. *Then,* the *sheet*. *Pull* the sheet *tight*. *Smooth* out the *wrinkles*. *Tuck* it *under* the mattress. *Then* the *second* sheet, and *one* or *two* or *three* blankets. Put the *red* blanket on first, then the *blue plaid* blanket. Where is the baby? *Behind* the chair? What is this bump in the bed? Oh my goodness, it's the *baby*!

What's going on here? Spatial concepts, motor development, language development, ordering (first, second, third), object constancy (that's when someone realizes that even if the baby is out of sight under the covers, he's still there), following directions, and the pleasure of the group effort, capped off with the pleasure of completing a necessary task. There's a *lot* going on here and we haven't even moved out of the bedroom to the rest of the house or the yard or the local supermarket.

So for all these reasons of cost, convenience, homeyness, and the availability of a flood of learning concepts many parents choose family day-care homes as their preferred alternative. A good family day-care home offers a richness and diversity of experience that is hard to match in group-care centers. Some of the best group centers approach it, but even then they are dealing with make-believe—a make-believe playhouse, a make-believe kitchen—and it just isn't the same. Three or four children can learn more from making a playhouse out of upside-down chairs, blankets, pillows, and blocks that can be arranged differently every day than they can out of the most elaborate preconstructed playhouse.

ANOTHER VIEW

The other side of the picture is set forth in a 1972 report by two educators at the University of North Carolina at Greensboro—Minta M. Saunders, Ph.D., who undertook a study of family day-care homes for United Day Care Services, and Mary Elizabeth Keister, Ph.D., who directed a demonstration group-care center for infants. Their findings on family day care were extremely discouraging.[3]

Before we tell you of these findings, there are several points of which you should be aware. The family day-care mothers were part of a program and not individual women operating on their own. The size of the study's sample was very small—51 children in all, ranging from 1 month to 18 months of age, of whom only 12 children remained in the program for the two years of the study. So the tests, designed to measure mental, motor, physical, and social development, were given to only 12 children.

These children were cared for by 15 day-care home mothers who remained with the program and 25 who dropped out during the two-year period. These mothers, in the words of the study, were recruited from "low-income, low-educational-level groups." The agency was not successful in recruiting middle-class mothers to offer family day-care services.[4] Women who were interested were "rather carefully screened," helped with certification and administrative problems, and given "some 20-30 hours of training in child care [and] child development." Equipment was supplied, money was loaned for construction of fences and minor renovations, and "supervisory staff and some on-going training" were provided.

The program was self-supporting—there was no government subsidization. United Day Care Services, a private organization, paid the day-care home mothers $12 per week per child, plus reimbursement for expenses incurred. With a maximum of five children allowed, the most a day-care mother could earn, if she had no children of her own to fill up some of the five places, was $60 a week. The findings noted:

> In a group of 12 infants entering family day care before one year of age and followed over a period of two years, one-third of the children showed losses in mental development quotients, 42 percent in motor development quotients and half of the babies in the group scored losses on social quotients.[5]

There was a lot of moving around. One-fifth of the children remained less than a month in family day care, three-fifths less than eight months. One child was in six different family day-care homes in 18 months. Ten others had two to three different day homes.

However, in direct contradiction to commonly held "plus" beliefs about family day-care homes, these homes were not neighborhood based, at least for middle-class mothers. Brothers and sisters were rarely accommodated in the same home. If, for example, a family day-care mother had one infant of her own, she was allowed, under federal regulations, to take only one other infant. So if she had only four children in care and one was a three-year-old, the remaining place couldn't be given to that three-year-old's infant brother or sister. Confusingly, though, day-care mothers tended to be older women without preschoolers of their own. Their mean age was 47. In less than half of the homes were there men in the household.

The project directors were understandably disheartened by their study, which seemed to indicate that children did not thrive physically, mentally, or emotionally in family day care, and had very little stability and predictability in the series of changing arrangements to which they were subjected. Meanwhile the agency, which was providing a continuing program that supervised the homes, was finding its supervisory ability stretched beyond the breaking point to produce even such poor results as were obtained.

With all due respect for Dr. Saunders and for Dr. Keister,

whose views we quoted in chapter 7 and whose research day-care center does seem to be a model of its kind, it is still necessary to make several observations that researchers surely take into account:

1. The sample of 12 children is, as we have said, very small and not representative of children nationwide.
2. The 12 children were not matched to any control group. In other words, we don't know how children who seemed to start out with the same scores and who had the same family backgrounds in terms of parents' intelligence, education, emotional and social makeup, income, and family structure would have scored if left at home with their mothers or if placed in excellent group-care programs.
3. The day-care mothers, coming as they did from "low-income, low-educational-level groups," might well, had they infants and toddlers of their own, have benefited from the kinds of intervention or supportive program we discussed earlier. "Some 20-30 hours" of training in child care and development is one five-day week of half days, and this may not have been enough to move middle-aged women out of lifelong habits and beliefs.
4. We don't know the meaning of "rather carefully screened" and "supervisory staff and some on-going training."
5. We do know that $12 a week per child, or $60 a week for five children, is a level of earnings that even in 1972 in North Carolina must have been about as low as earnings could get.
6. Finally, tests of emotional, mental, social, and physical abilities on infants from 1 month to 18 months are perhaps of some value. But for every Ph.D. who makes up such tests and believes in them, there's another Ph.D. willing to lay down his life that the tests aren't

worth the paper the directions are written on. There used to be nothing certain in life but death and taxes, and now medical men are in violent disagreement about what constitutes death. Testing, at this writing, is in a state of such confusion that all tests are subject to a lot of doubt, and at the very least to a lot of expertise in evaluating their meaning.

All this being said, the North Carolina results still underline the fact that one must be very cautious about selecting a family day-care home.

A Checklist for Choosing a Family Day-Care Home

A checklist that one might keep in mind when answering the ads that offer "warm, loving care to your child in my home" would include both concrete fact and gut feeling.

In the realm of the concrete: In states that offer licenses for family day-care homes, is your prospective day carer licensed? While we all know that a child can be cared for more lovingly in the right hovel than in the wrong mansion, certification usually assures you that the day-care mother has been checked for T.B. and has a home that is clean and free of lead paint, contains a sufficient number of fire exits, a fenced yard, or whatever else goes into licensing in your particular locality.

Day-care homes may not be licensed. Then you will check the above points yourself and add to them. Is the home close to where you live or close to where you work, depending on your preference? Is the woman not so young as to be inexperienced and not so old as to be unable to get through the day with reasonable energy? (This is not a matter of chronological age.) Is the house neat and clean, but not so neat and clean that it is clearly the day-care mother's prime concern? (You're not looking for a housekeeper.) Will it be well heated in winter, well ventilated in summer? Does it have a fenced yard for safe outdoor play?

Are the meals well balanced? Will your child have a crib or a place to nap? Will there be a place where he can be quiet and alone and still safe? Will there be a place for your child to keep his own things—washcloth, towel, blanket, toys?

In the realm of gut feeling: Does the day-care woman like children? Do they like her? Does she show any sign of a sense of humor? Are you going to be happy leaving your child with her every day?

Then there are business matters. What hours will you leave your child in her care? Is the day-care mother perfectly clear about who will bring your child to her in the morning and, even more important, who is authorized to pick your child up at night? How much will you pay and when? Do you pay for weekdays when your child does not come? For your vacation days when you keep him home?

Does the day-care mother know where to reach you during the working day? Does she ask? Does she know how to get help in case of a medical emergency? It's best to write all this out and make duplicate copies, one for you and one for the day-care mother, so you both know what you have agreed on.

Last but not least, is she understanding of the fact that you want to introduce your child to her and her home gradually, leaving him for only short periods of time at first until he begins to get the idea that he is not being abandoned forever but simply visiting until you come to get him again?

These suggestions are meant to be read in conjunction with the sections on how to choose a woman who comes into your home and how to choose a day-care center. The locales may change, but the children's basic needs remain the same.

DAY-CARE CENTERS

Finally, for parents who must leave their infants and toddlers to work outside the home, there is the possibility of having their children cared for in a group day-care center. Group centers have distinct advantages and distinct problems. Centers, given that fewer centers care for larger numbers of children than any other form of other-than-mother care, are more susceptible to government regulation. They must meet certain standards in physical environment, staffing, and health and nutrition, and while this regulation doesn't insure the best care, it is a protection against the worst abuses.

Center staffs have a higher degree of professionalism than other kinds of care. Directors usually have college degrees in early childhood education and good centers make sure that their staff members receive continuing education to upgrade their knowledge and abilities. In turn, exposure to a good staff is at least reassuring to a parent, and at most it offers a positive learning experience that shows young parents that there are different ways of handling problems and of enriching a baby's life.

There is constant supervision. No one is going to take a two-hour nap while your child is left to his own devices. No one is going to forget herself and strike your child in anger or annoyance when there are other adults present. And no one working under the eye of a good director is going to demand much more than your child can produce or expect much less than he is capable of doing.

Caretakers are not isolated in discrete dwellings all day, and so do not suffer all of isolation's attendant problems. Many centers have men on staff. Given that a large proportion of children in full day care have no fathers or grandfathers present in the home, male day carers may provide virtually their only contacts with men. Such contact is equally important for two-parent families, because children don't see enough of their fathers.

Centers are dependable—they are always open and there is always someone to care for your child. If it is not your child's preferred caretaker, who may be out sick or on a day off, it is probably someone who has been around enough so that she isn't a complete stranger to your child and vice versa.

Centers also provide a continuity of place and of routine. If caretakers are multiple or change from time to time, children can, in most cases, stay in a particular center from infancy (or whatever is the admission age) until they are ready to go to public school and derive a sense of security from the familiarity of place and routine. A good center will probably have a sick bay to care for mildly ill children, and the center will also have access to related medical-psychological services. If it has financial problems, a center usually can get some kind of government aid. That there are too few centers, too little funding, and too many parents and babies in need is one of the pressing problems of our time.

Finally, some centers have active parent organizations that give parents a chance to meet and make friends. They also have jobs available, and many teachers in day-care centers started out as day-care mothers.

Then there are the disadvantages—and looming above all others is the loss of a one-to-one relationship for your infant and toddler during those years when such a relationship is most important. A center is, after all, an institution, as are public schools, hospitals, and nursing homes. As such, the administration has to work very hard to guard against institutionalization of care. Six-month-old children nap at *this* precise time, middle-group fourth-graders use *this* text and workbook, unrestricted hospital diets offer *these* two choices, aged who are not ambulatory eat from trays *in their rooms*—the whole "institutional" approach that, not necessarily from meanness but rather in the interests of economy and efficiency, treats people as members of a class rather than as individuals who may need something very different.

One university day-care center, in the spirit of Henry Ford of Model T fame, assembly-lined their babies, who went from receiving station to bathing station to dressing and diapering station to eating station to play station to nap station. Each station was manned by a different adult who presumably became very efficient and skilled as the wet or hungry or sleepy babies passed through his or her hands—a concept that, to our minds, rivals Frankenstein's monster for macabre fascination.

In the best infant care-group centers, one adult has primary care for three babies at each shift. Whether your baby will get the precise amount of care it needs when it needs it to insure optimum development will be a function of the caretaker and the amount of energy, love, delight, and sensitivity she possesses, *and* the demands on her attention of the other two infants in her care.

Of course, while a children-to-caretaker 3-1 ratio is prevalent in the best and most expensive centers, the ratio is more likely 4-1 or 5-1, and there are more likely to be a number of adults, rather than a particular adult, sharing in the care of one infant. We visited one research center in an educational setting in which any one of eight to nine different adults—teachers, volunteers, students, teachers' aides, visiting parents—went to any child who needed attention. This seems to make it extraordinarily difficult for an infant to build up a workable decoder that will help him make sense of his world. And, as Dr. Nagera points out, while we can eventually ascertain whether or not this infant attains a level of development that we choose to call "normal," there is no way that we can know whether or not he develops as fully as he might have had he spent his early years under different conditions.

There are other disadvantages to center care beyond lack of individual attention and multiple care givers. All babies do not do equally well in large group settings. Babies can be as different as adults. There will be aggressive, extroverted individuals who make their own way regardless, and more retiring individuals who are more comfortable in smaller groups, with fewer distractions and less clamor.

At the same time that it is a distinct plus, there is a distinct minus to the professionalism of day-care center teachers. Parents who would assert themselves with a relative or with another woman whose situation and background are much like their own may feel a lack of confidence when facing professionals. Sensitive professionals can handle this problem and build the parent's self-confidence. Insensitive professionals can mishandle the parents and build the problem to the point at which it becomes a real stumbling block. Even two graduate degrees do not a warm and loving person make, and parents should not be too humble.

Expense is another disadvantage of group centers. With salaries taking the lion's share of costs and day-care givers moving toward unionization and dollar recognition of their education, training, and responsibility, it seems clear that the $80 per week cost that the best centers budgeted in 1977 for tuition—and that very few parents can meet without substantial subsidies coming eventually from tax money—is bound to rise. Day-care centers provide the most expensive form of other-than-mother care and it is not likely that this situation will change.

We have been discussing the disadvantages of good centers. There are bad centers. They meet government regulations, but barely. They have the required ratio of adults to children, but often not all day. We know of a center in which the day carer, a student of ours, was the only adult on hand at 7:30 A.M. to receive the earlycomers and by 9 A.M., when the full staff arrived, she had as many as 30 children all to herself. In a northern winter that's 30 snowsuits, 60 boots, 60 mittens, 30 dripping noses, a dozen or so wet diapers, and one very tired, irritated caretaker—and she, you will remember, was a student!

The bad centers serve breakfast, lunch, and two snacks. They meet regulations, but the staff "brown-bags it" rather than eat the center food. They have almost no contact with parents. Parents drop off and pick up, and often the adult they see at those times will not be or has not been with their child all day.

Children in these centers seem subject to interminable cases of sniffles and diaper rash. They arrive sleepy and leave tired and cranky—or they leave overnapped and ready to go right through the night. The category of wrongs goes on and on. Not many centers manage to be so bad as to make *all* the mistakes. But they can make a lot of them.

HOW TO CHOOSE A CENTER

How do you identify good group care? And if you have enrolled your children at a particular center, with no other practical choice available, how do you and the other parents identify the areas where you should put on pressure to change things for the better? You can, you know. There are good and bad centers that care for the children of people who have money to burn. There are good and bad centers in which the children are subsidized by welfare funds. The best center we saw was almost completely welfare-subsidized. And it was a beauty—clean, attractive, safe, well run, with a good staff, lots of parent involvement, and abundant staff concern for the children.

What do you look for and what do you try to avoid? First, let us consider examples of things you are going to encounter that should start the red lights flashing and the alarm bells ringing.

If the day-care center you are thinking of advertises that it is situated in a roomy, colonial mansion on six acres of rolling wooded grounds, or in a lovely old townhouse on one of the best streets in the neighborhood, *watch out*. The administrators are thinking of what is appealing to you as an adult and not about what your baby needs—a warm, affectionate, steady, mother substitute on whom he can depend to care for him when you're not with him.

If the center emphasizes as most important "the finest in cognitively oriented play equipment," *be careful*. They may be trying to snow you with jargon. The most important "equipment" is an excellent teaching staff completely dedicated to the children. "I do not believe that there are more than a very small number of commercial toys [for young children] that are worth buying,"[6] says Harvard professor Burton White, who in 1976 finished a study on how to raise competent children. "I advise parents to be extremely suspicious of the so-called 'educational toys.' "[7]

If center people talk about helping your child become "self-actualized," *hold on a minute*. Ask them what they mean. If they mean that they are going to provide enough highly skilled staff so that someone can really get to know your child, understand what he likes, what he wants to do, and what his interests are, and that adults will help him to pursue those interests, fine. If you don't understand their explanation, maybe the center isn't for you and your child.

If the center that's after your child advertises "early formal reading and computation skills" or "group recitations" or "programmed group activities" or "graduation exercises," be wary. These administrators obviously aren't informed about the needs of very young children:

> To pre-empt early years with tasks for which the child lacks neurological, physiological and emotional readiness may create hybrid successes that have little real meaning to the child as he acquires them, and *cheat* him of the excitement experienced when the time is ripe—excitement that provides drive for further learning. *Rote* learning does not arouse curiosity and *memorization* does not lead to understanding.[8]

If your center tells you it's in business to free you to be a productive wage earner, *bring them right back to how they are going to care for your child*. You know what they're freeing you to do, but *their* objectives should be child related.

If the ratio of children to adult is higher than one to one for under six weeks, or three to one for children up to one year old, or four to one beyond that, *stop and think*. Many states permit a 10-1 ratio. But then, many states permit a lot of things of which we don't approve:

> [With too many children] the caretaker has little opportunity to become sensitized to the individual characteristics and vulnerabilities of a given child. . . . With the dispersion of mothering function among several caretakers, the likelihood of their developing feelings of attachment to an individualized child is diminished. Sensitive, individualized adaptation of the caretakers' behavior to a child and associated feelings of personal emotional involvement are among the major deficiencies of group care situations for young children.[9]

Finally, if the director of the center makes you feel uncomfortable, incompetent, unlearned, and ignorant, *grab your baby and run*. If she or he is insensitive to you, you can bet she or he is going to be insensitive to your child and hire a whole bunch of caretakers who aren't sensitive either. Trust your instincts on this one.

What *do* you look for in a good day-care center? Near the top of the list is health and safety. Group centers must meet a higher standard in this regard than any of us may choose to meet in our own homes. With many infants and children gathered together, the possibility of contagion is greater and the potential for accidents is higher than in the home. Supercleanliness is required in cribs and kitchen and exacting safety standards must be met in securing high chairs, strollers, and crib rails. Babies must never be left alone sleeping in cribs or in other areas when awake. Babies must be held for bottle feeding by staff who wash their hands as regularly as does a doctor who is seeing a number of patients. Look for an outdoor area for fresh air and sunshine. You should also look for a sick bay that can provide the care and comfort a baby would have at home. Minor illness can be treated at some centers. Find out about this provision and what their procedure is in case of an emergency illness or accident.

Look for a center whose director and staff understand that it is not easy for parents and their babies to separate. The transition from home to center has many bumpy periods for many reasons. Your baby's caretaker should understand your baby's preferences before initial separation. This is very important. Preferred foods, sleeping habits, where he likes to go on awakening, how he likes to be held—these are some of the personal items to be discussed. Your center should encourage you to bring your baby's favorite blanket or cuddly toy. These favorites can comfort a baby who is having anxiety about his strange environment.

If you agree that a good center should be as much like a good home as possible, look for indications that your baby is going to be with someone who knows him very well. Look for a teacher who thinks your baby is very special. Look for someone who is really turned on when your baby smiles, gurgles, or coos, and communicates her delight in his progress. You want that someone to do a lot of touching—holding, rocking, and cuddling. You want your baby to be with someone who understands him; someone who has eyes in the back of her head and a third ear that picks up cues from a baby who is just learning to communicate; someone who knows what makes him comfortable and what soothes his distress and what tickles his fancy. You want someone who talks to him when she's feeding him and talks to him when she's diapering him, and endlessly retrieves toys and plays peek-a-boo and pat-a-cake and where's-the-baby, and enjoys it. You want someone who will give your baby room to grow and provide periods alone, and will not smother him, at the same time that she remains alert that it's not more room or more time alone than he can handle.

Look for a care giver who is always a half step ahead of your baby—who understands the baby's development so she can interpret his signals and provide appropriate opportunities for growth. She should be able to recognize that he's ready to reach for objects, that he'll enjoy repetitive play with her, that he likes to hold a spoon for banging even if he's not ready to feed himself.

You want this someone to see him securely through those periods when he begins to notice other children, when he starts to play beside them but not yet with them, when he first begins to interact actively with them. You want him to have some things that are his and a place to keep them that is his own so that he can learn the difference between what is his and what is to be shared with others. You want him to have the freedom, as he grows older, to work out differences and difficulties by himself, under the watchful eye but not under the thumb of his care giver.

You want your child to be with care givers who recognize that he screams because something is bothering him, that he's fussy because he's tired or teething, that he's negative because he's two years old, not because he's a rotten child. And you want him to be in a place where his special someone can try to find out what's bothering him, or nap him if he's tired, or put him in a less stressful situation.

You want him to live through a day that is more predictable than unpredictable, more affirmative than negative. He needs someone who offers a suggestion for something that he can do rather than a scolding for something he shouldn't do, and offers him realistic, honest choices. You want your child to be free to express his feelings and be helped to understand them and deal with them constructively. You want your child to be with someone who is clean, smells good, dresses neatly, and is strong and vital enough to do all the heavy physical work that the tiniest babies cause to be done.

Finally, you want your child and his caretaker to understand that he belongs to *your* family, and that, in Dr. Berry

Brazelton's words, the "cementing" of your relationship is of primary importance to all of you. To that end, you prefer a care giver who communicates clearly and eagerly with you, who learns what your particular situation at home involves and adjusts her care of the child accordingly, and who does her best to ease his separation from you in the morning and to accustom him to look forward to your return in the evening. The key here is to look for a center that has the role of *supplementing* and not replacing parental care.

In summary, you want your child, in your absence, to be well cared for physically, nurtured emotionally, stimulated intellectually, comfortable in your leaving, and delighted in your return.

Select for your consideration three or four day-care centers that are reasonably close either to home or to your place of employment. In-house centers that are located where you work, usually in factories, hospitals, or large companies that employ numbers of young women, are particularly good for mothers with infants. The baby travels to and from work with you, you can nurse him or visit him at lunch hour and coffee breaks and be readily available in any emergency, and your hours apart are substantially reduced. On the other hand, for older toddlers of three and four, neighborhood centers offer your child the opportunity to meet children with whom he will enter public school, and that gives him a nice continuity of friends. In either case transportation must be figured in. Do you drive to work? Do you take public transportation? Will the center call for your child or bring him home?

There are a number of ways to find three or four likely centers. We recommend that you evaluate reports from friends very carefully. If a friend tells you a day-care center is awful, that's a real red light. But if she says it's terrific, that's only a yellow light—proceed with caution. You probably wouldn't have picked your best friend's husband to marry. It's not likely that you raise your child as she does, and you are the only one to decide which center will care for your child.

We are very wary of run-for-profit centers. The profit motive is powerful, your baby is still very powerless, and the conflict is uneven. That doesn't mean that a particular run-for-profit center is *necessarily* bad. We're just flashing another yellow caution light.

There are several sources of information about day-care centers. Your local chapter of the National Association for the Education of Young Children is a good place to seek recommendations. So is the social service department of your local hospital, a teaching college or university that has a child-study program, your church or synagogue, or a local family service organization.

When you have three or four likely prospects, call the director of each center and speak to her or him. If you already have a good deal of information about the center from your original source, you may simply want to make an appointment for a visit. If not, you will want to know how much it will cost. (If you can't afford it, you don't want to waste your time.) Then you want to know the hours—will the center be available when you need it? Ask about the director's background and training —education, degrees, where taken, experience, where, and in what capacities. "Can you tell me a little about your professional background?" ought to get you more information than you need, because someone who is well trained is usually proud of it. Besides, you want to know if this director is a warm, responsive person, right?

Then ask about the ratio of teachers to children in your child's age group, and what the arrangements are if your child is sick or gets sick during the day. Is there an infirmary or sick bay? Is a nurse in attendance and a doctor on call?

That's about all you can accomplish with the phone call except that, all else being satisfactory, you will make an appointment to visit the center. If possible, go alone on your first visit; then make a return visit with your child. Visit several centers and you will acquire a feel for the best center for your child when you have this basis for comparison.

Plan your visit for the morning. If you come after lunch you will spend two hours watching little children sleeping and care givers relaxing or cleaning house. Take a notebook along in which you have listed the major things you want to notice and the questions you know you have for the director. Then make notes during your visit. The visit will be more productive if you think of it as a four-part job. First you will want to give some time to soaking up the environment. Then focus on one particular child and what he or she does or doesn't do in a half-hour period. Then focus on one particular care giver for the same amount of time. Finally, speak to the director.

Here are some other things we look for when we visit a day-care center: a pleasant, well-lit, airy, comfortable, and colorful room or rooms; areas for books, music, block building, push and pull toys; a sand table and a water table, well equipped for building and measuring and pouring into and out of, and bathing dolls and washing toys; a housekeeping corner; a painting and coloring area, with easels and fingerpaints, crayons and watercolors.

We look at the kind and the conditions and the availability of the materials that a child can go to. Are the puzzles complete? Are there more playthings made out of wood, which is a solid, tactilely pleasing material, than are made out of plastic? Are the trucks, trains, cars, tracks, dolls handy to the blocks so that a care giver can encourage a child to build a garage for his trucks, a bridge over the train tracks, a house for the dolls, a dog house for the puppy? Is everything clean and attractive to handle? Is there a place for everything, but freedom to take what is needed?

Is the room filled with children's pictures? Have they been made by the child and not from a pattern in a teacher-directed activity? Are there areas for large-muscle play and for quiet resting times?

We look at the children. We look for involvement, concentration, joy. We watch out for aimlessness, the wandering of a child who has nothing to do, and we make a distinction between that and the child who is actively engaged in observing or thinking or just plain resting.

We look for small-group play with a teacher or care giver who is providing material—extensions—to develop further play that the children have initiated. We watch the way the teacher handles aggression. Does she set limits that don't embarrass the child in front of his friends, and does she direct him into other, positive kinds of activity?

Is there opportunity for a child to become immersed in a favorite activity? Can someone who wants to spend hours at the water table, or who is really into building a city, have the time to do what he wants?

Can the boys play with the dolls and the girls build the bridges? Do the staff members like one another? Are they cooperative and helpful to each other as well as to the children?

We watch for language development. Is a child really given the time to tell a teacher an interminable story? Does the teacher listen?

At music time, is there opportunity for creative movement? Is a child encouraged to explore his body and the space around him? Or is music a directed, orchestrated activity, using toy instruments and precise ballet steps?

We watch the food that is served. Is lunch attractively presented and nutritious? Is the snack food nutritious, too—apple slices, orange segments, carrot sticks, raisins—or is it junk food? Are children encouraged to feed themselves with cut-up finger foods when they are ready, or does the care giver continue to spoon-feed them because it's quicker and neater?

Is there an adult-sized rocking chair in the room? Is it used?

How about toileting? We look for children who are encouraged to go to toilet when they need to and staff who are alert to the signs of individual need rather than prescribed times for toileting.

We check the outdoor play area. Is there one? Is there a place for running, climbing, hiding? Does it look safe? Does the staff keep it so by maintaining a watchful eye, or by being overprotective?

When you speak to the director, bring your notebook and ask questions. Take your time—your decision for selecting the home away from home will be based on all the factors discussed in this chapter, and on many of your own. You might ask, for example:

1. Is there one person who will be responsible for my child?
2. What happens if my child is very anxious in the transition period from home to center?
3. Does the staff remain fairly constant?
4. Do parents participate in planning and decision making?
5. Are parents free to visit at any time, or only by appointment? (If only by appointment, does the reason for this restriction sound reasonable to you?)
6. Are community people, particularly grandparents or people of that age, encouraged to take part in center activities?

In summary, *you* are the best judge of what is right for your child and your family. Trust your own good judgment and instincts.

THE ROLE OF GOVERNMENT AND INDUSTRY

For those of our readers who have the financial ability to pay for other-than-mother care and who are interested in guidelines that will help them decide for one alternative over another, one day-care center over another, perhaps we have done our job. But for many of our readers we may merely have succeeded in filling a window of Tiffany's with a choice of attractive baubles that can be looked at but not touched. We appear to have raised more questions than we have answered.

For many mothers who want to be with their children during their first three years, or who choose quality day care, the problem is *money*. Where is the money going to come from that subsidizes without taking away self-respect? For the mother who prizes her freedom to work outside the home, who will influence industry to extend paid maternity leaves, sponsor in-plant day-care centers, and create shared- and part-time jobs that will permit this mother to keep her work options open while raising her child in the critical early months and years? And for mothers who can't find high-quality day-care available, who will pay for the construction and upkeep of the additional facilities needed?

Only government and industry have the money to restructure our country's child-care system so that all parents can keep both family life and working life in a healthy, harmonious balance. But much more than money is needed. The plethora of family aid programs created by government in our country—62 separate aid programs in all—points to a many-headed bureaucracy that requires drastic overhaul to help stop the continuing decay of family life in the United States, decay exemplified by Senator Abraham Ribicoff's statement that "millions of children are falling through cracks in the bureaucracy."[10]

Here we look at some encouraging steps that have been taken, problems created by these steps, and recommendations for future actions that are necessary if parents are going to have *real* choices in the ways they want to raise their children.

As Americans become increasingly discouraged with the results of large, institutionalized solutions to societal problems, they are returning to long-held beliefs about the importance of the family unit as the basic building block of a society. President Jimmy Carter has said, "There can be no more urgent priority . . . than to see that every action our government makes is designed to honor and support the American family."[11] Unfortunately, our experience in the past has been that the majority of well-intentioned financial support programs that have developed in this country have turned out to be inefficient, demeaning, and destructive of family life.

In December 1974 a House committee under Martha Griffiths reported that a man who earned $2 an hour and who had a wife and two children could increase the income of his family by an average of $2,158 a year by deserting them. In 1976 a woman and her three children on welfare in Detroit received the equivalent in relief, food, and average medical benefits of $7,340 gross earnings. That's tough competition for a lower-bracket working man. As a result of facts like these, the proportion of families without a father has risen 50 percent since 1959. In half the states in the country we have made it more advantageous for men to run off than to stay.

To achieve this cataclysmic family destruction we have created 62 separate aid programs. We had a $6 billion food-stamp program in 1974 that may have risen to $10 billion in 1976. We have housing allowances, transportation stamps, clothing vouchers, fuel coupons, aid to families with dependent children. These jigsaw puzzle pieces of aid have been created by 21 committees of Congress, 50 state legislatures, and 1,500 county welfare departments. Our aid program, taken as a whole, is, as the saying goes, "no way to run a railroad." It certainly is no way to help families who need help.

Many people believe that one solution is for society to pay parents for raising their children, just as society pays workers for building buildings or roads or for maintaining natural resources. Vice president Walter Mondale put it concisely and dramatically: "Children are 40 percent of our population and 100 percent of our future."[12] Welfare is simply not the answer:

> Welfare makes you feel like you're nothing. Like you're laying back and not doing anything and it's falling in your lap. . . . But you must understand, mothers, too, work. My house is

clean . . . I'm home and I'm working. I am a working mother. . . . It's living off welfare and feeling that you're taking something for nothing the way people have said. . . . You feel degraded. . . . The other day I was at the hospital and I went to pay my bill. This nurse came and gave me the green card. Green card is for welfare. She went right in front of me and gave it to the cashier. She said "I wish I could stay home and let the money fall in my lap." I felt rotten. I was just burning inside.[13]

Instead of this kind of punishing, paternalistic system, many people feel that the money should be paid directly to the parent or parents, in the conviction that most people, if treated as responsible adults, will behave in an adult, responsible manner. Over the last five years knowledgeable people from all walks of life have made the same suggestion, and we have chosen to cite a sampling—an anthropologist, a judge, a politician, a journalist, and an economist—all of whom have looked at the scene of the 1970s and come to the same conclusion.

In 1970 anthropologist Margaret Mead called for some form of annual income—or negative income tax—so that individuals and families could make their own choices of residence and exercise control over the rearing of their young children.[14]

In 1972 Dr. Mary Rowe, Cambridge economist, wife, and mother of three, called for a change in the legal, social, and financial status of homemakers. We should, said Dr. Rowe, consider a public-service employment plan such as Canada's, in which the government pays a minimum wage to those who are engaged in socially constructive projects, and among these projects we should include homemaking. Further, says Dr. Rowe, spouses should be legally entitled to 50 percent of each other's income (as is already done in community property states.) Dr. Rowe talks carefully about homemakers and spouses because she includes within the category of homemaker househusbands as well as housewives, and all those who work at home caring for the sick, the elderly, and the homeless.[15]

In 1973 David L. Bazelon, chief judge of the United States

Court of Appeals for the District of Columbia Circuit and a member of the Joint Commission on the Mental Health of Children and the Advisory Committee on Child Development of the National Academy of Science, called for income distribution:

> [We must take] a step toward *preventing* trouble rather than waiting for it and hoping to cure it. That step is to guarantee to every family an income sufficient to enable parents to provide the kind of home environment they want for their children. Of course we cannot be sure that more money given directly to the family will enhance the children's development, but I think it is our best—if not our only—hope.
>
> The only thing that my expert colleagues know for sure is that the family is the most effective child-developing agent around when it wants to be and *can* be. Out of the plethora of studies of day care and early intervention one thing stands out. A child needs a family—that is where his roots and his education are at.[16]

Judge Bazelon believes that income distribution should be as automatic, as acceptable, and as nonpejorative as Social Security is today, and that the income must be sufficient to allow families to make choices for their children free of government intervention or agency oversight.

In 1975 Richard Strout, columnist for the *Christian Science Monitor* and author of *TRB COMMENTS* in *The New Republic*, wrote on income distribution:

> What should be done? Sooner or later everybody in the country, rich or poor alike, will file income taxes, and those below the poverty line will get a moderate direct cash grant from the government related to income, while the low and moderate-income workers will get tax relief. Why not cash on a uniform basis instead of food stamps and payments that drive husbands from home? *Conservative economist Milton Friedman says it would be cheaper and many in Congress agree* [our emphasis].[17]

In 1976 Sargent Shriver, former director of the Office of Economic Opportunity, urged consideration of a change in Social Security rules so that mothers who stay home would not lose credits toward later benefits. One possibility, he suggested, would be building up a special homemakers' benefit fund out of which Social Security benefits could be paid, not only for periods of paid work outside the home but for periods of unpaid work at home in holding the family together and raising children.[18]

The rationale behind this thinking—the reason people think that basic family support and support for mothers at home is economical—is the idea that up-front money will replace the enormous sums of money currently being spent with very mixed results for remedial, custodial, supportive, medical, and psychological care. Most families, relieved of the heaviest financial pressures and treated with dignity, will respond by rising to meet their responsibilities. In so doing their behavior will provide us with a healthier, more independent, and more contributing citizenry.

Of course, another of our dearly held beliefs is that you can't make a problem go away by throwing money at it. And certainly some of our parents and children will need more help than a somewhat fatter wallet can provide. So a flexible approach by government will also include more funding for the kinds of intervention programs that we have described, such as BEEP and the Parent-Child Centers. Vice president Mondale said in 1970:

> I wonder whether many preschoolers, especially the very young, would not be better served by programs lasting several hours rather than all day, or by programs that send tutors into their homes to work with them and their mothers.[19]

Home-based programs are now recognized as more effective and *cheaper*. An early feminist cry was that no society could afford the waste involved in a set-up in which individual mothers, each in her own home, duplicated the efforts of other mothers, and therefore, in the name of efficiency, child care must be centralized. It is becoming apparent that centralized care is much more expensive than home care. More and more people such as Walter Mondale are beginning to agree with Professor Earl S. Schaefer of the University of North Carolina when he urges that teachers work once a week with parents of young children in the home rather than bringing the child into a preschool situation. He believes this approach is more effective and less costly.[20] When Jerome Kagan puts the cost of a good center at $85 per child per 1976 week, we can appreciate Schaefer's point.

Another governmental effort that would give more options to those who want to raise their own children are laws that insure adequate housing in communities of peoples' own choosing. Antisnob zoning laws demanding that every community provide a certain percentage of low- and moderate-income housing must be supported, with full recognition of the extremely difficult problems of enforcement. Even in liberal states where such laws have been on the books for years, little or no progress has been made.

But a mix of housing in terms of cost will offer an alternative to the enforced ghettoization of many families into huge pockets of inner-city poverty and despair. It will also mean that low-income young marrieds, as well as low-income retirees, will be able to live in the communities in which they were raised or spent their productive years. In many cases this will make available the physical support and presence of extended families that is so lacking in many areas today.

Government, industry, and business can join in encouraging part-time, shared-time, and flex-time work. Government could lead the way. If the millions of federal, state, and local employees are offered these work alternatives, it will be a long step forward in prodding the private sector to offer such alternatives as well.

The Swedish Experience

We have a lot to learn from the Swedish approach to family life and day care. If we keep in mind that Sweden has not been able to do much of what it wants to do, and that we will be able to do even less than it has done, the Swedish experience can be helpful.

On the plus side, they begin with a firm governmental policy to support families and children and an understanding that children's welfare cannot be separated from the welfare of the family. Since 1948 the Swedish government has provided an allowance to the family on the birth of each child. It is now the equivalent of $414 per baby. Housing allowances give large families with low incomes the opportunity to live in modern housing in an attractive environment. Mothers or fathers are allotted seven-month leaves from their jobs to care for new babies. A government insurance plan reimburses parents at more than 90 percent of the earned income thus lost. Even a parent who has not held a paying job previously gets a guaranteed $5.75 a day for 210 days.

Current proposals call for a reduction in the nine-hour day spent by many children in day or family nurseries. Sweden is making an all-out attempt to reduce the work day to six hours in order to give parents and children more time together. All of this is the result of the expressed philosophy that "It is absurd to build a society on the two-income breadwinning principle unless that society does something in return to give parents reasonable opportunities to combine work with family life."[21]

The day nurseries operate under a tripartite regulation of state, county, and municipal boards, with the municipalities having the major role in operation and finance. Governmental strictures require that most facilities be roomy, airy, well designed, and well equipped, and that the ratios of adult to child are those that we have described earlier as being reasonable.

But goals have not been met. Day care is not universal—in 1974 only 14 percent of all preschool children were in day nurseries and family day-care homes; admissions are limited—priority is given to children from single-parent families, children with medical problems and handicaps, children from families having social problems, children from non-Swedish-speaking homes, children from low-income homes, and children whose parents both work or are in school; day-care centers do not meet established standards—in 1973, 97 percent of the centers fell short; centers are understaffed—ratios of six to nine children per adult were common and in 10 percent of the centers reached 10-13 children per adult; and even in the best centers parents find the environment sterile and cold. Nor can every parent like a system that sends a different woman every time to care for a sick child at home while his parents go off to work.

That our problems will be more difficult to solve than Sweden's is almost insured by the fact that their population is 8 million, as against our 220 million, and that their tiny, socialistic country is homogeneous in makeup as compared to our heterogeneous complexity. We would have to build day-care facilities for an additional 2,500,000 children in the next two years in order to meet the Swedish goal of enough centers to care for the children of working mothers by 1980!

Nevertheless, the concern of the Swedish people for families and children as reflected in official government policy is a model we would do well to follow. And there are straws in the wind to indicate that we are beginning to move in the right direction.

Legislation: The Plus and Minus

While we are still far from six-hour work days and seven-month maternity leaves, our government *has* been moving toward legislation that eases the burdens of working parents faced with child-care problems. The Tax Reform Act of 1976 is a case in point. It replaced an itemized deduction for child-care expenses with a tax credit. The deductions had been of no help to most low- and moderate-income families, which did not have enough deductible expenses to bother with itemizing. But under the tax credit, most working families paying for the care of children under 15 will be able to realize tax savings. For example, a working family spending $60 a week ($3,120 per year) on day-care fees for two children will earn a tax credit of $624.

An amendment offered by Senator Edward M. Kennedy provided that if the amount of the credit exceeded the taxes owed, the balance would have been refunded to the taxpayer. This amendment, unfortunately deleted, would have benefited low-income families.

There is still another helpful provision in the 1976 tax bill. Payments to relatives for child care may now be included as eligible expenses against which the amount of tax credit is figured. Formerly, families received tax advantages only if their children were cared for by strangers. Now even relatives who are members of the household, so long as they are not dependents, can be paid for child care, and the parents can deduct these payments as long as the relative reports them in his or her own income-tax return.

In another move that gives more alternatives to working mothers, the maximum for deductible expenses, which used to be greater for care of a child within the home, has now been equalized with the expenses for care outside the home.

Federal money for child day care comes from what is known as Title XX money. Title XX is an amendment to Social Security legislation and provides 75 percent federal money for almost any social service states want to plan, with the other 25 percent coming from the state or through the state from local public or private sources. "Five states have already defined eligibility in a way which makes possible universally accessible services. Under this plan, the poor are subsidized, the wealthy pay for their own services, and the working families not able to afford full costs pay a sliding fee based on their income."[22] When there is no sliding fee, there are problems.

In Massachusetts, for example, "Catch 22" works this way. People earning up to 68 percent of the state's median income of $14,393 for a family of four are eligible for free child care. The minute their income rises above that $9,800, which is 68 percent of the median, they must pay the full cost of child care—which of course they can't afford, whether it is the $85 for a fine private center, or the $45 for a publicly supported center, or the $30 or $40 for a family day-care home.

So if the husband earns less than $9,800, which is substantially less than what the Bureau of Labor Statistics regards as the cost of living for a low-middle-income family, and therefore his wife wants to go to work, they will find that the minute their combined income rises above $9,800 they have to pay for the full cost of a day-care center. This, together with the wife's lunches, clothes, and carfare, make her work virtually useless as a way of improving their economic lot. The new tax credit in the 1976 bill may be of some help but not enough to make a significant difference.

People manage to thread their way through these problems, but at great cost:

> Yeah, my husband and I, we both work. My mother takes care of the baby. See, she works at night in a nursing home. So she can take care of the baby days. Sleep? Oh, she takes naps here and there. She's used to it, I guess.

Many professionals who have seen innumerable families tossed from despair to hope and back again are bitter about the effect Title XX can have when states do not make wise use of it. Efforts to eliminate widespread injustices are badly needed, and the most obvious corrective measure is a sliding scale of fees for child care so that parents are not faced with the current either-or situation.

There are other instances of well-meaning legislation wreaking havoc on those who are not able to buy their way out of the system. The child who had to be taken out of a day-care home where he was happy and loved because the home was not certified to care for infants is one example of the way things shouldn't be. And more problems are caused every time a state tightens up its regulations and improves, for example, the adult-child ratio. The children whose care is paid for by the state get better care, but more people who could otherwise afford day care find themselves priced out of the market.

A number of ideas are currently receiving attention. The institution of a voucher payment system that will offer greater flexibility and more free choice for parents is one possibility. Central clearing houses from which parents could receive all information about child care without having to tackle the state bureaucracy would certainly help. Business and industry can be offered tax credits for establishing on-site centers. There should be more thought about moving the centers closer to where the children and parents are located.

A new resource for day-care provision is becoming increasingly available—local public schools. With today's low birthrate, more and more communities are finding themselves with empty classrooms and ready-made organizations—the PTAs—that can influence communities to open a whole range of opportunities for nuclear mothers and children. Local elementary schools often, although certainly not always, are within walking distance of one's home, and already meet safety, health, and zoning regulations, making them perfect places for drop-in centers, YMCA-type programs, full day-care centers, and afterschool centers for older children. And there is a nice continuity of place for the toddler who grows up to be a kindergartener in a building with which he is already familiar, and for his mother, who may already have one or two children in the schools in the regular grades.

Think what a difference a local school making full use of its space could mean to a mother like Margaret, a woman in her early 30s who is on welfare but struggling to get off:

> Hey, I wanta tell you I am just *tired*. I got one child, she's seven years old, she goes to school *way* on the other side of town, and I have to walk her to the bus stop every morning. Then my three-year-old, I bring him here to the center, as soon as the bus leaves. Then I still got the baby, he's eleven months old, and they don't have no room for him here yet. So I bring him to the baby-sitter. *Then* I got to go to school. I'm going to be a medical technician, but first I got to finish high school. And I'm tellin' you, I am *tired*, and I haven't even begun to study yet!

While some people worry about "getting their heads together," there are some mothers with more pressing, practical problems who would settle for getting their families together in one place. For them, an extension of the neighborhood school program downward in age to encompass our very youngest and lengthwise in hours to provide afterschool day care would answer a lot of problems.

Parents of young children today face many pressures and have found many alternatives from which to choose as they look for ways of caring for their children. These solutions have come from people with a great deal of ingenuity and independence.

But all their ingenuity and independence cannot be enough. We are an interdependent society: *their* children represent the future for *all* of us, and so we, in our hearts, minds, offices, and legislative bodies, are going to have to do our share to see that parents can make truly free choices between good alternatives, and are free to parent their children as they wish—not as they must.

NOTES

[1] Humberto Nagera, "Day Care Centers: Red Light, Green Light or Amber Light" (undated paper, Department of Psychiatry, University of Michigan, Ann Arbor), p. 6.

[2] Ibid., p. 15.

[3] Minta A. Saunders and Mary E. Keister, *Family Day Care: Some Observations* (Greensboro: University of North Carolina Press, 1972).

[4] Ibid., p. 31.

[5] Ibid., p. 30.

[6] Burton L. White, *The First Three Years of Life* (Englewood Cliffs, N.J.: Prentice-Hall, 1975), p. 194.

[7] Ibid., p. 74.

[8] Helen Beck, "Pressure in the Nursery," *Children Today*, September-October 1972, p. 21.

[9] Leon J. Yarrow, "Conceptualizing the Early Environment," in Laura Dittman, ed., *Early Child Care* (Chicago: Aldine, 1968), p. 22.

[10] U.S., Congress, Senate, *Congressional Record*, 91st Cong., 2d sess., Abraham Ribicoff, "Justice for Children," December 9, 1970.

[11] James P. Gannon, "1976: The Year of the Family," *Wall Street Journal*, September 15, 1976, p. 26.

[12] Walter Mondale, speech to 1976 graduating class of Wheelock College, Boston, Mass., May 22, 1976.

[13] Studs Terkel, *Working* (New York: Pantheon, 1972, 1974), pp. 303-4.

[14] Margaret Mead, *Manpower Magazine*, June 1970.

[15] Mary Rowe, "Up With Homemaking," *McCalls*, August 1972, p. 37.

[16] David L. Bazelon, "Juvenile Justice: Love-Hate Story," *Boston Globe*, May 6, 1973, p. A-3.

[17] Richard Strout, "TRB Comments," *The New Republic*, October 4, 1975, p. 2.

[18] R. Sargent Shriver, "Shriver Urges Aid for Families," *Boston Globe*, January 14, 1976, p. 14.

[19] U.S., Congress, Senate, *Congressional Record*, 91st Cong., 2d sess. Walter Mondale, "Justice for Children." December 9, 1970.

[20] Earl S. Schaefer, "Grades Start at Home", *Boston Globe*, Parade Magazine, March 11, 1973, p. 22.

[21] Camilla Odnoff, "Equality Is for Children, Too", *Current Sweden*, December 1975, p. 2.

[22] Massachusetts Children's Lobby, "Title XX and Child Day Care," *Minor Affairs*, vol. 2, No. 5, December 1976, p. 1.

9

EPILOGUE

We have seen the way external pressures are infiltrating the integrity of the family unit. We have seen the ways parents are responding to these pressures by seeking alternative ways of sharing the care and in some instances the rearing of their children. We have consulted our social scientists for their advice and come away confused. We have looked for clues in the behavior of animal families and in the child-rearing practices of other nations and we have caught a glimmer of promise here and there. We have given our advice on how to evaluate alternative methods of care. And even though we have written a book, we realize that we are really just starting on our inquiry for answers to the basic questions that caused us, the authors, to write this book. These questions represent a dilemma for society as a whole, a dilemma that requires continuing, exhaustive exploration to understand and control what appear to be two irresistible forces bent on collision: our desire to protect and nurture our children and the multimotivated drive of women for their working rights.

We recognize large areas of agreement as to goals. We all want healthy, happy, creative, loving, adventurous, optimistic children with the ability to make commitments, take responsibility, live independently when that is desirable, depend on others when that is necessary, and make use of the full range of their natural abilities.

We all want mothers who have the chance to express themselves completely—biologically, emotionally, intellectually, maternally, sexually, vocationally.

And if we had our druthers, we'd all like to see our children born into secure, loving, competent families that, if they don't have everything they want, have enough of what they need to be able to give the best of themselves to that most important enterprise—the raising of their children.

So that is the basic strength of our situation—we know what we want. All that remains is for us to get it. You, the reader, will come away from this book with your own conclusions as to how our society will get what it wants. Here are ours.

We see infants and toddlers as having certain nonnegotiable needs. These include the need for one loving, trustworthy relationship with a primary caretaker. Our children also need the feeling of safety and security in their daily life that derives from a stable, predictable rhythm of activities and relationships. And our children need surroundings that stimulate and stretch their minds and bodies, rewarding them with the joy of living and the freedom to explore opportunities for being all that they can be.

We have come to believe that these needs may be met in many different day-care situations, and that with a great deal of selectivity and considerable expense children in full-time, other-than-mother care may be as competent, responsible, bright, and healthy as children raised at home.

But we believe in preserving the integrity of the family unit, and we wonder whether diluting the intensity of parent-child interaction in the very early years will weaken the strength of families in the future, and thereby weaken our society. In infancy, in adolescence, in sickness, in old age, at any time, we all need warm, supportive care, or at least the certainty that we know where to get it. This perception has traditionally come from the family, whose stored-up love stands ready to see us through difficult times many years later.

On the other hand, we do not believe it reasonable or desirable to expect that mothers will ever return full time to the home. They are going to continue to be income-minded, career-minded, and future-minded.

For all these reasons, when mothers must work we support part-time work—or part-time schooling—during a child's early years. This gives children more time to establish their roots in the family, more time to draw on the family's nurturing power. And it insures reasonably well-rested parents who have something to give their children besides end-of-day leftovers of goodwill and energy.

Half-time work or schooling allows parents to have the best of both worlds. Their career goals will remain in view and they will have the strength to give their best to the children and to receive the joy and satisfaction in the parental perception of a job well done.

For those parents who are so minded and who will be away from their young children for either full- or part-time days, we would like to see alternative child care made available, affordable, and acceptable in terms of quality. We think it is a mistake in a free society for government to take any single position on this matter other than making it possible for parents to have choices. Government edicts that deny support to group-care centers in the belief that mothers will be forced to do what government thinks they should are equally as bad as government edicts that throw the full weight of federal financial support to group day-care centers, or to family day-care homes, or to *any* single solution.

With our present lack of knowledge, we cannot commit ourselves totally to only one system, and there is no need for us to take the risk of all or nothing guessing. There is too much at stake. All children are our children.

REFERENCES

Ainsworth, Mary D. "Review of Findings." In *Deprivation of Maternal Care: A Reassessment of its Effects*. Geneva: World Health Organization, 1962.

Ainsworth, Mary D. *Infancy in Uganda*. Baltimore, Md.: Johns Hopkins University Press, 1967.

Ambrose, Anthony. *Stimulation in Early Infancy*. New York: Academic Press, 1969.

Arnold, Arnold. *Teaching Your Child to Learn*. Englewood Cliffs, N.J.: Prentice-Hall, 1971.

Beadle, Muriel, *A Child's Mind*. Garden City, N.Y.: Doubleday, 1970.

Beck, Helen. "Pressure in the Nursery." *Children Today*, September-October, 1972, p. 21.

Bergstrom, J., and Gold, J. *Sweden's Day Nurseries: Focus on Programs for Infants and Toddlers*. Washington, D.C.: Day Care and Child Development Council of America, 1974.

Bettelheim, Bruno. *Children of the Dream*. New York: Macmillan, 1969.

Binstock, Jeanne, "Motherhood: An Occupation Facing Decline." *The Futurist*, June 1973, pp. 99-102.

Blaine, Gordon B. *Are Parents Bad for Children?* New York: Coward, McCann and Geoghegan, 1973.

Bonham, Marilyn. *Laughter and Tears of Children*. New York: Macmillan, 1968.

Bowlby, John. *Attachment and Loss*, vol. 1. New York: Basic Books, 1969.

Bowlby, John. "Self-Reliance and Some Conditions That Promote It." In *Support, Innovation and Autonomy*. London: Tavistock, 1972.

Boyd, Marjorie. "The Case Against Day Care." *Washington Monthly*. December 1976, pp. 22-31.

Brazelton, T. Berry. *Infants and Mothers*. New York: Dell, 1969.

Brazelton, T. Berry. *Toddlers and Parents: A Declaration of Independence*. New York: Delacorte, 1974.

Brody, Sylvia. *Patterns of Mothering*. New York: International Universities Press, 1956.

Bronfenbrenner, Urie. "Early Deprivation in Mammals: A Cross-Species Analysis." In *Early Experience and Behavior*, edited by Grant Newton and Seymour Levine. Springfield, Ill.: Charles C. Thomas, 1968.

Bronfenbrenner, Urie. *Two Worlds of Childhood, U.S. and U.S.S.R.* New York: Russell Sage Foundation, 1970.

Bronowski, Jacob. *The Ascent of Man*. Boston: Little, Brown, 1973.

Bruner, Jerome. *Processes of Cognitive Growth*. Heinz Werner Lecture Series, vol. 3. Worcester, Mass.: Clark University Press, 1968.

Cotton, Dorothy. *The Case for the Working Mother*. New York: Stein and Day, 1965.

Coles, Robert. *Erik H. Erikson, The Growth of His Work*. Boston: Little, Brown, 1970.

Current Sweden, June, July, October 1976. Stockholm: The Swedish Institute.

Decter, Midge. *The New Chastity and Other Arguments Against Women's Liberation*. New York: Coward, McCann and Geoghegan, 1972.

Dittman, Laura, ed. *Early Child Care*. Chicago: Aldine, 1968.

Durant, Will. *The Age of Faith*. New York: Simon and Schuster, 1950.

Durant, Will. *Caesar and Christ*. New York: Simon and Schuster, 1944.

Durant, Will. *The Life of Greece*. New York: Simon and Schuster, 1939.

Erikson, Erik H. *Childhood and Society*. New York: W. W. Norton, 1950.

Escalona, Sibylle K. *The Roots of Individuality*. Chicago: Aldine, 1968.
Evans, Belle, and Saia, George. *Day Care for Infants*. Boston: Beacon, 1974.
Featherstone, Joseph. "Kentucky Fried Children." *The New Republic*, September 12, 1970, pp. 12-16.
Fein, Greta G., and Clarke-Stewart, Alison. *Day Care in Context*. New York: Wiley, 1973.
Foss, B. M., ed. *Determinants of Infant Behavior I*. New York: Wiley, 1959.
Friedan, Betty. *The Feminine Mystique*. New York: Dell, 1963.
Fuchs, Lawrence. *Family Matters*. New York: Random House, 1972.
Gaylin, Willard. "Skinner Redux." *Harper's*, October 1973, pp. 48-56.
Geiger, Kent H. *The Family in Soviet Russia*. Cambridge, Mass.: Harvard University Press, 1968.
Gerzon, Mark. *A Childhood for Every Child*. New York: Outerbridge & Lazard, 1973.
Gewirtz, Jacob L., ed. *Attachment and Dependency*. Washington, D.C.: V. H. Winston, 1972.
Greer, Germaine. *The Female Eunuch*. New York: McGraw-Hill, 1971.
Groch, Judith. *The Right to Create*. Boston: Little, Brown, 1969.
Guthrie, George, and Jacobs, Papita. *Child Rearing and Personality Development in the Philippines*. University Park: Pennsylvania State University Press, 1966.
Harlow, Harry F. "The Nature of Love." *American Psychologist*, 13, 1958, pp. 673-85.
Harlow, Harry F. *Learning to Love*. San Francisco: Albion, 1973.
Harlow, Harry F., and Zimmerman, R. R. "Development of Affectional Responses in Infant Monkeys." In *Determinants of Infant Behavior II*, edited by B. M. Foss. New York: Wiley, 1961.
Heinicke, Christoph, and Westheimer, Ilse. *Brief Separations*. New York: International Universities Press, 1965.
Hellmuth, Jerome, ed. *The Exceptional Infant*, vol. 2. New York: Brunner Mazel, 1967.

Helmstrom, Linda. *The Two-Career Family*. Cambridge, Mass.: Shenkman, 1972.

Jacoby, Susan. "Who Raises Russia's Children?" *Saturday Review*, August 21, 1971, pp. 40-53.

Janeway, Elizabeth. *Man's World, Woman's Place*. New York: Morrow, 1971.

Janor, Arthur. *The Feeling Child*. New York: Simon and Schuster, 1973.

Kagan, Jerome. *Change and Continuity in Infancy*. New York: Wiley, 1971.

Komisar, Lucy. *The New Feminism*. New York: Franklin Watts, 1971.

Lerner, Max. *America as a Civilization*. New York: Simon and Schuster, 1957.

Levine, James A. *Who Will Raise the Children? New Options for Fathers (and Mothers)*. Philadelphia: Lippincott, 1976.

Life Nature Library. *The Primates*. New York: Time, Inc., 1965.

Lifton, Robert. *The Woman in America*. Boston: Houghton Mifflin, 1965.

Maier, Henry. *Three Theories of Child Development*. New York: Harper & Row, 1965.

Maslow, Abraham. *Toward a Psychology of Being*. Princeton, N.J.: D. Van Nostrand, 1962.

McCandless, Boyd R. *Children, Behavior and Development*. New York: Holt Rinehart, 1967.

Mead, Margaret. "What Is Happening to the American Family?" *Journal of Social Casework*, November 1947, pp. 323-30.

Mead, Margaret, and Wolfenstein, Martha. *Childhood in Contemporary Culture*. Chicago: University of Chicago Press, 1955.

Mead, Margaret. "The Life Cycle. Its Variations: The Division of Roles." *Daedalus*, Summer, 1967, pp. 871-75.

Medinnus, Gene, ed. *Readings in the Psychology of Parent-Child Relations*. New York: Wiley, 1967.

Millett, Kate. *Sexual Politics*. Garden City, N.Y.: Doubleday, 1970.

Moore, Raymond, and Moore, Dennis. "The Dangers of Early Schooling." *Harper's*, July 1972, pp. 58-62.

Montagu, Ashley. *Touching: the Human Significance of the Skin*. New York and London: Columbia University Press, 1971.

Mussan, Paul H.; Conger, John J.; and Kagan, Jerome. *Child De-*

velopment and Personality. New York: Harper & Row, 1956.
Nagera, Humberto. *Early Childhood Disturbances, the Infantile Neurosis and the Adulthood Disturbances*. London: International Universities Press, 1966.
Newton, Grant, and Levine, Seymour, eds. *Early Experience and Behavior*. Springfield, Ill.: Charles C. Thomas, 1968.
Peck, Ellen. *The Baby Trap*. New York: Pinnacle Books, 1972.
Piaget, Jean. *The Origins of Intelligence in Children*. New York: W. W. Norton, 1952.
Piaget, Jean. *Plays, Dreams and Imitations in Childhood*. New York: W. W. Norton, 1951.
Queen, Stuart A., and Habenstein, Robert W. *The Family in Various Cultures*. 4th ed. Philadelphia: Lippincott, 1974.
Rabkin, Leslie Y., and Spiro, Melvin E. *The Kibbutz in 1970*. New York: Schocken, 1970.
Rebelsky, Freda, and Dorman, Lynn. *Child Development and Behavior*. New York: Knopf, 1970.
Rheingold, Harriet F., ed. *Maternal Behavior in Mammals*. New York: Wiley, 1963.
Salk, Lee. *Preparing for Parenthood*. New York: David McKay Company, Inc., 1974.
Saunders, Minta A., and Keister, Mary E. *Family Day Care*. Greensboro: University of North Carolina Press, 1972.
Seidman, Jerome. *The Child*. New York: Holt, Rinehart, 1966.
Shannon, William V. "A Radical, Direct, Simple, Utopian Alternative to Day Care Centers." *New York Times Magazine*, April 30, 1972, p. 13.
Sidel, Ruth. *Women and Child Care in China*. New York: Hill & Wang, 1972.
Slater, Philip E. *The Pursuit of Loneliness: American Culture at the Breaking Point*. Boston: Beacon, 1970.
Slater, Philip E. *The Glory of Hera: Greek Mythology and the Greek Family*. Boston: Beacon Press, 1968.
Smith, Mary. *Kids*. Boston: Houghton Mifflin, 1972.
Spiro, Melvin. *Kibbutz, Venture in Utopia*. New York: Schocken, 1970.
Spitz, Renee. *First Year of Life*. New York: International Universities Press, 1965.

Spitz, Renee. *No and Yes*. New York: International Universities Press, 1957.
Sullerat, Evelyne. *Women, Society and Change*. New York: McGraw-Hill, 1971.
Talmon, Yanina. *Family and Community in the Kibbutz*. Cambridge, Mass.: Harvard University Press, 1972.
Terkel, Studs. *Working*. New York: Pantheon Books, 1973, 1974.
Thorsell, Siv. "For Children's Minds—Not Just to Mind the Children." *Before School Starts*. Stockholm: The Swedish Institute, 1969, pp. 1-15.
Tiger, Lionel, and Shepher, Joseph. *Women in the Kibbutz*. New York: Harcourt Brace Jovanovich, 1975.
Toffler, Alvin. *Future Shock*. New York: Random House, 1970.
Watson, John B., *Psychological Care of Infants and Children*. New York: W. W. Norton & Co. Inc., 1928.
Weaver, Kitty D. *Lenin's Grandchildren: Pre-School Education in the Soviet Union*. New York: Simon and Schuster, 1971.
White, Burton L. *Human Infants: Experience and Psychological Development*. Englewood Cliffs, N.J.: Prentice-Hall, 1971.
White, Burton L. *The First Three Years of Life*. Englewood Cliffs, N.J.: Prentice-Hall, 1975.
Yang, C. K. *Chinese Communist Society: The Family and the Village*. Cambridge, Mass.: M.I.T. Press, 1959.
Yarrow, Marion R.; Burton, John D.; and Campbell, Roger V. *Child Rearing*. San Francisco: Jossey-Bass, 1968.

DAY CARE REFERENCES

A Study In Child Care: prepared by Abt Associates, Cambridge, Mass. 02138 for The Office of Economic Opportunity, Office of Program Development, 1200 19th St., N.W., Washington, D.C. 20506. Vol. II—B System Case Studies. *This work gives detailed descriptions of the following regional day-care centers.*

Berkeley Children's Centers
2031 Sixth Street
Berkeley, California 94701

Child Development Day Care Centers
427 West Fourth Street
Charlotte, North Carolina 27705

Family Day Care Career Program
349 Broadway
New York, New York 10013

Kentucky Child Welfare Research Foundation, Inc.
314 West Main Street
Frankfurt, Kentucky 40601

Neighborhood Centers Day Care Association
9 Chelsea Place
Houston, Texas 77006

Springfield Day Nursery
103 Williams Street
Springfield, Massachusetts 01101

DAY CARE AGENCIES AND INFORMATION CENTERS

Association for Childhood International
3615 Wisconsin Avenue N.W.
Washington, D.C. 20016

Black Child Development Institute
1028 Connecticut Avenue N.W.
Washington, D.C. 20036

Child Development Associate Consortium
7315 Wisconsin Avenue
Washington, D.C. 20014

Child Study Association of America
School of Social Work
New York University
New York, N.Y. 12206

Child Welfare League of America, Inc.
67 Irving Place
New York, N.Y. 10003

Day Care and Child Development Council of
America, Inc.
1012 Fourteenth Street N.W.
Washington, D.C. 20005

Department of Labor
Women's Bureau
Constitution Avenue and Fourteenth Street N.W.
Washington, D.C. 20210

National Association for the Education of Young
Children
1834 Connecticut Avenue N.W.
Washington, D.C. 20009

Office of Child Development
U.S. Dept. of Health, Education and Welfare
Washington, D.C. 20201

INDEX

Ainsworth, Mary D., 125
Anderson, John, 31
Animal research: contact comfort, 95, 99–100; critical periods, 95, 98–99; deprivation studies, 95–97; general discussion, 93–107; love systems in primates, 105–07
Annual incomes, 12
Attachment, 120–27; amount of interaction necessary for, 122; Brazelton's view, 177–78, 188; first, 124; Ganda study, 125; Harvard study on separation protest, 188–89; Kagan's view, 165–69, 188; as a need, 123; second, 124; separation protest as a measure of, 125–26; signs of, 121; third, 124

Babysitter: home child care, 65–66, 197
Bazelon, David, 225–26
Bettelheim, Bruno, 141, 144–45, 148–49, 158, 165
Binstock, Jeanne, 15
Biological ladder, 94–95
Blaine, Graham, 24, 182
Bombeck, Erma, 29
Bowlby, John, 98–99, 105, 106, 185, 189–91
Braithwaite-Burke, Yvonne, 45
Brazelton, T. Berry, 8, 121, 158–59, 175–89, 191, 192, 217–18
Bronfenbrenner, Urie, 151
Brookline Early Education Project (BEEP), 49–51, 227

Budget for Stride Rite Corporation Children's Center (table), 81
Bureau of Labor Statistics, 59, 232
Business and industry, role of, 18–19, 56–57, 61, 63–64, 222–28, 233
Business-based centers, 78–83

Caretaker's home, 67. *See also* Family day-care programs
Carson, Rachel, 107
Carter, Jimmy, 223–24
Castle Square Day-Care Center, 75–77
Change and Continuity in Infancy (Kagan), 166
Child-care alternatives, 3–4; babysitters, 66–67; community-based support programs, 43–54; cooperatives, 46; day-care centers, 74–92; family day-care homes, 68–72; fathers, 58–61; grandmothers or other family members, 67. See also *chapter 8*
Child experts, 3, 5, 35. See also *chapter 7*
Child-care problems, historical view of, 1–2
Child-free marriage, 39–41
Children of Crisis (Coles), 118
China, 4, 129, 131–35, 137–39, 142, 143, 149–50, 159
Coles, Robert, 118
Communes, 54, 145
Community-based support programs, 43–54, 233
Community cooperatives, 46

247

Creativity in group-reared children, 147–51
Cue cards for day-care workers, 115

Day care: concern about in other countries, 157–58; definition, 7
Day-care centers: advantages and disadvantages of, 209–13; community-sponsored, 82–83; cooperative, 83–85; definition of, 7; for federal employees, 90–92; government-supported programs, 75–77; hospital employees center, 89–90; how to choose, 213–22; industry-sponsored, 78–83; private, run-for-profit, 85–87, 219; university-sponsored, 87–88; YWCA, 88–89
Day-care teachers, 35
Dependency, 23–25
Dickens, Charles, 1
Durant, Will, 1

Economic hardship, 2, 3, 10, 11–14, 171, 232
Education, influence of, 2, 16–18, 57
Erikson, Erik, 117–18, 149, 169

Family day-care programs: advantages, 201–03; attachment to day-care mother, 178; how to choose, 207–08; negative view, 204–07; training of caretakers, 68–72
Family planning, 39–41
Father, 58–61
Featherstone, Joseph, 85
Federal Employees' Centers, 90–91
Female Eunuch, The (Greer), 32
Feminine Mystique, The (Friedan), 32
Feminists, 2, 25, 31–35, 111
First Three Years of Life, The (White), 55
Flex-time, 63, 228
Foster grandparents, 76
Freud, Anna, 6
Friedan, Betty, 32–33, 111
Fuchs, Lawrence, 22, 124
Full-time father care, 58–60
Full-time mothering, 43–54
Future Shock (Toffler), 19, 24

Ganda Study (Ainsworth), 121, 125
Gaylin, Willard, 32
Generation gap, 10
Government: role of, 222–28; legislation by, 230–33
Greer, Germaine, 34, 111
Griffiths, Martha, 224
Group dependency in group-reared children, 140–47, 172
Guidelines for day-care choices, 196–222

Hardwick, Elizabeth, 23
Harlow, Harry, 7, 102–07, 135
Harvard Pre-School Study, 55, 191
Hewlett-Packard, 64
High/Scope Educational Research Foundation, 49
Homemaker Child-Care Training Program, 65–66
Honeywell, Inc., 61–62
Househusband, 59–61
Hutterites: on group dependency, 145

Independence, American attitudes toward, 22–23
Industry-based centers, 78–82
Infant learning and responses, 109–11, 181
Infant needs. See *chapter 5*
Infants and Mothers (Brazelton), 175, 177
Intimacy in group-reared children, 153–55, 158
Isolation, 18–22, 173
Israel. *See* Kibbutzim

Job opportunities, 2, 61–64
Job sharing, 63–64, 228

Kagan, Jerome, 3, 8, 125, 162–74, 179, 188–89, 191–92, 228
Kearsley, Richard, 162
Keister, Mary Elizabeth, 192–93, 204, 205, 206
Kennedy, Edward M., 231
Kibbutzim, 4, 131–35, 139–44, 148–50, 153–59, 165, 169, 171–72, 175
KLH Child Development Center, 82–83
Komisar, Lucy, 25, 111

Learning to Love (Harlow), 105–07
Levine, James, 59, 60
Liberation of women, 2, 25, 31–35, 111
Life expectancy, 14–15
Living and Learning Centers, 85–87
Love systems in primates, 105–07

McGovern, Mrs. George, 45
Marans, Allen, 135
Martha movement, 45
Maslow, Abraham, 118–19, 157, 191
Mead, Margaret, 24, 27, 145, 176, 225
Meers, Dale, 135
Metapelet, 132
Middlesex County Hospital Child-Care Program, 89–90
Millet, Kate, 33
MIT Child-Care Center, 87–88
Mondale, Walter, 224, 228
Montagu, Ashley, 100
Monthly Labor Review, 12
Mother: attachment to baby, *see* Attachment; definition, 6; devaluation of, 26–30; full-time, 43–54; importance of, see *chapter 5*; pressures on, see *chapter 1*
Multiple mothering, 132–33

Nagera, Humberto, 148, 198
National Association for the Education of Young Children, 219
Newtime, Inc., 61
New Ways to Work (Palo Alto), 64
Norway, 62
Novikova, L. I., 150
Nursery school, 127

Oliver Twist (Dickens), 1
Other societies. *See* China; Kibbutzim; Sweden; U.S.S.R.
Oxford Street Day-Care Cooperative, 83–85

Parent-Child Centers: Brazelton reference to, 176; in Dorchester, Massachusetts, 51–54; Mondale reference to, 227
Parent cooperative centers, 83–85
Parenthood, responsibilities of, 30–31, 170
Part-time work programs, 61–62, 228

Peck, Ellen, 24
Pines, Lois, 63
Play groups, 45–46
Pressures, 2, 3, 10, 14–15, 35; of education, 16–18, 57; of isolation, 18–22. *See also* Economic hardship; Feminists
Primate research: cloth-and-wire surrogate mothers, 102–05; Harlow experiments, 102–07; love systems, 105–07; social groups, 101–02
Private, run-for-profit centers, 85–87

Quality versus quantity, 164–65, 179–80, 184–85

Rabkin, Leslie Y., 154–55
Radl, Shirley, 24
Rebelsky, Freda, 17
Reciprocal learning and interaction, 113–17, 169, 198
Ribicoff, Abraham, 223
Rowe, Mary, 40, 225

Sabra, 153
Salk, Lee, 40, 99
Saunders, Minta M., 204
Schaefer, Earl S., 228
Separation anxiety. *See* Separation protest
Separation protest, 125–27, 166–68, 188–89
Sexual Politics (Millet), 32, 33
Shared parenting, 58–60
Shared-time work, 63–64, 228
Shepher, Joseph, 155–57
Shriver, Sargent, 227
Sidel, Ruth, 137, 138
Silent Spring (Carson), 107
Single parent families, 10–11, 14
Single women, 38–39
Slater, Philip, 21, 28, 29
Small families, 41–43
Societies, differences between day-care goals of, 131–32, 170–71
Society's responsibility for child care, 6, 222–28, 230–34
Spiro, Melvin E., 154–55, 158
Stride Rite Corporation Children's Center, 78–82
Strout, Richard, 226

Support programs for full-time mothering: Brookline Early Education Project (BEEP), 49–51; community cooperatives, 46; High/Scope Educational Research Foundation, 49; Martha movement, 45; parent-child centers, 51–54; play groups, 45–46; YWCA, 47
Sweden, 62, 63, 229–30
Symbiosis, 33, 110–12
Symbolism, 170

Talbot, Nathan B., 25–26
Tax Reform Act of 1976, 231–32
Tiger, Lionel, 155–57
Title XX funds, 71, 231–32
Toddlers and Parents: A Declaration of Independence (Brazelton), 175
Toffler, Alan, 19, 24
Touching (Montagu), 100
Transient families, 18–19
Tremont Street Infant Center, 162, 191–92

Tronic, Edward, 192
Trust, 117–20, 169
Tunney, John, 61

University of North Carolina Demonstration Nursery Center, 114, 193
U.S.S.R., 4, 129, 131–39, 140, 142, 150–51, 157, 159

Washington Opportunities for Women, 61
Watson, John B., 24
Weikart, David, 49
White, Burton, 55, 58, 214
Women in the Kibbutz (Tiger and Shepher), 155–57
Women's Educational and Industrial Union of Boston, 64, 69–72
Working women, numbers of, 11

Yarrow, Leon, 100
YWCA-YMCA, 47, 88–89, 233